EFFICACY, AGENCY, AND SELF-ESTEEM

THE PLENUM SERIES IN SOCIAL/CLINICAL PSYCHOLOGY

Series Editor: **C. R. Snyder**

University of Kansas
Lawrence, Kansas

Current Volumes in this Series:

AGGRESSIVE BEHAVIOR
Current Perspectives
Edited by L. Rowell Huesmann

DESIRE FOR CONTROL
Personality, Social, and Clinical Perspectives
Jerry M. Burger

THE ECOLOGY OF AGGRESSION
Arnold P. Goldstein

EFFICACY, AGENCY, AND SELF-ESTEEM
Edited by Michael H. Kernis

HUMAN LEARNED HELPLESSNESS
A Coping Perspective
Mario Mikulincer

PATHOLOGICAL SELF-CRITICISM
Assessment and Treatment
Raymond M. Bergner

PROCRASTINATION AND TASK AVOIDANCE
Theory, Research, and Treatment
Joseph R. Ferrari, Judith L. Johnson, and William G. McCown

SELF-EFFICACY, ADAPTATION, AND ADJUSTMENT
Theory, Research, and Application
Edited by James E. Maddux

SELF-ESTEEM
The Puzzle of Low Self-Regard
Edited by Roy F. Baumeister

THE SELF-KNOWER
A Hero under Control
Robert A. Wicklund and Martina Eckert

A Continuation Order Plan is available for this series. A continuation order will bring delivery of each new volume immediately upon publication. Volumes are billed only upon actual shipment. For further information please contact the publisher.

EFFICACY, AGENCY, AND SELF-ESTEEM

EDITED BY

MICHAEL H. KERNIS
University of Georgia
Athens, Georgia

PLENUM PRESS • NEW YORK AND LONDON

Library of Congress Cataloging-in-Publication Data

On file

ISBN 0-306-44934-X

©1995 Plenum Press, New York
A Division of Plenum Publishing Corporation
233 Spring Street, New York, N.Y. 10013

10 9 8 7 6 5 4 3 2 1

CONTRIBUTORS

STEVEN R. H. BEACH, Department of Psychology and Institute for Behavioral Research, University of Georgia, Athens, Georgia 30602

JERRY M. BURGER, Department of Psychology, Santa Clara University, Santa Clara, California 95053

NANCY CANTOR, Department of Psychology, Princeton University, Princeton, New Jersey 08544

CHI-YUE CHIU, Department of Psychology, Hong Kong University, Hong Kong

EDWARD L. DECI, Department of Psychology, University of Rochester, Rochester, New York 14627

DEBORAH L. DOWNS, Department of Psychology, Ohio State University, Columbus, Ohio 43210

CAROL S. DWECK, Department of Psychology, Columbia University, New York, New York 10027

SEYMOUR EPSTEIN, Department of Psychology, University of Massachusetts at Amherst, Amherst, Massachusetts 01003

JEFF GREENBERG, Department of Psychology, University of Arizona, Tucson, Arizona 85721

KEEGAN D. GREENIER, Department of Psychology, University of Georgia, Athens, Georgia 30602

ROBERT E. HARLOW, Department of Psychology, Princeton University, Princeton, New Jersey 08544

YING-YI HONG, Division of Social Science, Hong Kong University of Science and Technology, Hong Kong

MICHAEL H. KERNIS, Department of Psychology and Institute for Behavioral Research, University of Georgia, Athens, Georgia 30602

MARK R. LEARY, Department of Psychology, Wake Forest University, Winston-Salem, North Carolina 27109

BETH MORLING, Department of Psychology, University of Massachusetts at Amherst, Amherst, Massachusetts 01003

TOM PYSZCZYNSKI, Department of Psychology, University of Colorado–Colorado Springs, Colorado Springs, Colorado 80933

RICHARD M. RYAN, Department of Psychology, University of Rochester, Rochester, New York 14627

CAROLIN J. SHOWERS, Department of Psychology, University of Wisconsin–Madison, Madison, Wisconsin 53706

SHELDON SOLOMON, Department of Psychology, Skidmore College, Saratoga Springs, New York 12866

ABRAHAM TESSER, Department of Psychology and Institute for Behavioral Research, University of Georgia, Athens, Georgia 30602

STEFANIE B. WASCHULL, Athens Area Technical Institute, Athens, Georgia 30601

PREFACE

Efficacy, agency, and self-esteem: Each of these constructs has had a long and somewhat checkered history in the behavioral sciences. Numerous factors could be cited as reasons for the waxing and waning of interest in such motivational and self-related constructs. However, it is not my purpose here, nor is it the purpose of this edited volume, to dwell on these reasons, for interest in these constructs is currently extremely high. At the same time, although efficacy, agency, and self-esteem clearly have implications for one another, these implications are often left unstated. Therefore, it is my hope that this book will foster increased cross-fertilization of ideas and research agendas among people who are concerned about these constructs and their implications for psychological well-being. We live in a time in which it is easy to become traumatized and to lose faith in our capacity to live full and rewarding lives. It is exceedingly important, therefore, that we seek to better understand how people can develop and utilize their capabilities to the fullest and in the process, one hopes, achieve favorable and secure feelings of self-worth.

The overriding goal behind this volume is to bring together scholars whose work either challenges existing notions in the self-esteem literature or has considerable implications for self-esteem that have yet to be fully explored. It began with a conference of the same title at the University of Georgia sponsored by the university's Institute for Behavioral Research, Abraham Tesser, Director. The speakers at this conference, organized by myself, were Nancy Cantor, Edward Deci, and Carol Dweck. Each speaker was asked to talk about her or his research, especially as it related to self-esteem processes. The level of excitement generated by their presentations made it clear that the time was right for a book with the same agenda.

I then sought out other prominent investigators and asked them to also contribute chapters that were to focus on the implications of their work for our understanding of self-esteem. Much to my delight, I had no difficulty recruiting people. Moreover, their enthusiam for the task was readily apparent to me as I read with great interest each arriving chapter. New insights abound in each and every one of their contributions. Taken as a group, they show quite clearly that the domain of inquiry pertaining to self-esteem-related issues can be (and should be) considerably broader than what is often seen in the literature. My hope is that investigators as well as practioners who are concerned with the roles of efficacy, agency, and self-esteem in mental health and psychological functioning will find much of interest in these chapters for many years to come.

I want to thank Rick Snyder, the Series Editor, and Eliot Werner, Executive Editor for the Medical and Social Sciences at Plenum, for their much-appreciated guidance and encouragement. It has been a distinct pleasure to work with them. Thanks are also due to the conference participants, Abraham Tesser, members of the Attitudes and Opinion Research Group in the Institute for Behavioral Research, and the graduate students in the Social Psychology Program at the University of Georgia for their roles in ensuring that the conference was a success. Finally, I would like to give very special thanks to my wife Vicki for her help, support, and love throughout all phases of this project and beyond. Neither this book nor I would be the same without her.

CONTENTS

Introduction   1

Michael H. Kernis

Intrapersonal Dynamics.   1
Interpersonal/Contextual Concerns   3
Conclusion   5

PART I. INTRAPERSONAL DYNAMICS

Chapter 1

Is the Self Motivated To Do More Than Enhance
and/or Verify Itself?.   9

Seymour Epstein and Beth Morling

Introduction   9
Cognitive–Experiential Self-Theory.   10
   Two Systems for Processing Information   10
   The Four Basic Needs and the Corresponding Beliefs   12
CEST in Relation to Psychodynamics.   13
Self-Verification or Self-Enhancement?.   14
A Study To Test for Compromise Formation   16
   Enhancement and Verification Results.   16
   Relationship Results.   18

Implications of Two Levels of Processing for the Measurement of
    Self-Esteem 19
Application of the Model to Adaptive and Maladaptive
    Behavior... 21
  Balancing the Four Basic Needs in Normal and Abnormal
    Adjustment 22
  Self-Enhancing Illusions 23
  The Reasons People Maintain Negative Self-Views 23
An Example of Successful Adjustment 25
Summary 26
References 26

Chapter 2

Human Autonomy: The Basis for True Self-Esteem........... 31

Edward L. Deci and Richard M. Ryan

Introduction.. 31
A Differentiated View of Self 34
The Regulation of Behavior.................................. 36
Intrinsic and Extrinsic Motivation 37
Extrinsic Motivation: A Differentiated View 38
Aspirations, Autonomy, and Well-Being 40
Self-Determination and the Social Context.................... 42
Conclusions... 45
References 46

Chapter 3

Not All High (or Low) Self-Esteem People Are the Same: Theory and Research on Stability of Self-Esteem 51

Keegan D. Greenier, Michael H. Kernis, and Stefanie B. Waschull

Introduction.. 51
Defining Self-Esteem Instability 52

Assessing Self-Esteem Instability............................. 53
Why Do People Vary in the Extent to Which Their Self-Esteem Is ·
   Unstable? 54
   Contemporaneous Factors................................ 54
   Early Childhood Experiences............................. 57
The Essence of High Self-Esteem........................... 58
   Self-Enhancement 60
   What about Self-Protection?............................. 61
The Essence of Low Self-Esteem 64
Summary and Conclusions.................................. 67
References.. 68

Chapter 4

Toward a Dual-Motive Depth Psychology of Self
and Social Behavior.................................... 73

Jeff Greenberg, Tom Pyszczynski, and Sheldon Solomon

Introduction 73
Terror Management Theory 74
   Research on the Psychological Function of Cultural
      Worldviews 76
   Research on the Functions of Self-Esteem................. 79
   Self-Esteem and Defensiveness 80
   Summary 81
Beyond Terror: A Growth-Oriented Enrichment Motive
   System... 82
Toward a Dual-Motive Depth Psychology 84
   Unique Aspects of the Enrichment System................. 85
   Expansive and Defensive Conceptions of the Self.......... 86
   Why So Defensive—Is it Society or Reality?............... 88
   Freedom or Balance? 88
   Relationship between Defensive and Enrichment Motives 89
   Variables That Influence the Dominance of Defensive vs.
      Enrichment Concerns................................ 91
Conclusion: The Dynamic Dialectical Balance between Defense
   and Enrichment...................................... 94
References.. 96

Chapter 5

The Evaluative Organization of Self-Knowledge: Origins,
Process, and Implications for Self-Esteem 101

Carolin Showers

Introduction... 101
Formal Model and Initial Evidence 104
   Evaluatively Integrative Thinking 106
   Compartmentalized Category Structure 108
A Process Model of Evaluative Organization 110
   Stability and Certainty 113
Origins of Evaluative Organization 114
   Cognitive Origins... 115
   Affective Origins 115
   Motivational Origins.. 116
Conclusions.. 117
References 118

PART II. INTERPERSONAL/CONTEXTUAL CONCERNS

Chapter 6

Interpersonal Functions of the Self-Esteem Motive: The
Self-Esteem System as a Sociometer 123

Mark R. Leary and Deborah L. Downs

Introduction... 123
Definitional Issues 124
Explanations of Self-Esteem Motivation 125
   Self-Esteem Promotes Positive Affect 125
   Self-Esteem Promotes Goal Achievement....................... 126
   Self-Esteem Is Associated with Dominance 127
Self-Esteem and Social Exclusion 128
   The Function of Self-Esteem 128
   The Self-Esteem Motive 129
Evidence for the Sociometer Hypothesis 130
   Esteem-Deflating Events Are Those That Undermine Inclusion ... 130

Social Exclusion Lowers State Self-Esteem 131
Low Trait Self-Esteem Is Associated with Perceived Exclusion 132
Threats to Self-Esteem Motivate Approval-Seeking 132
Inclusion Facilitation or Exclusion Avoidance? 133
Self-Esteem and Affect.. 134
Self-Esteem Motives of Low and High Self-Esteem People.......... 135
Domains of Self-Esteem.. 137
When the Sociometer Malfunctions 138
Conclusions 139
References.. 140

Chapter 7

Self-Esteem and the Extended Self-Evaluation Maintenance
Model: The Self in Social Context 145

Steven R. H. Beach and Abraham Tesser

Introduction 145
The Self-Evaluation Maintenance Model.......................... 147
The Original SEM Model 147
The Extended SEM Model 148
Combining the Original and the Extended SEM Models.......... 149
Strategies for Staying Close 151
Extending the SEM Model to Close Relationships: Empirical
Support.. 151
Affective Outcroppings 151
Shared Activities and the Extended SEM Model................. 154
Distribution of Power and the Extended SEM Model 155
Communication following SEM Challenge...................... 156
Jealousy and Envy 157
Implications for Self-Esteem................................... 158
Pressure to Change Self-Definition........................... 158
Narrowing or Deleting Areas from One's Self-Definition 159
Allowing the Self To Be Outperformed by the Partner 160
Adding Areas to One's Self-Definition......................... 161
Indirect Pressure on Self-Esteem from SEM Processes in Close
Relationships 162
Effects of Relationship Dissolution 162
Help-Giving... 163

Are Some People More Extreme in the Maneuvers They Use To
    Protect Self-Evaluation? 164
The Self in Evolutionary Context: Future Issues and Directions..... 165
Summary 167
References 168

Chapter 8

Overcoming a Lack of Self-Assurance in an Achievement
Domain: Creating Agency in Daily Life 171

Robert E. Harlow and Nancy Cantor

Introduction. 171
Self-Doubt and Life-Task Pursuit 172
Academic Self-Doubts and Task Appraisals 175
Reassurance Seeking: A Strategic Response to Self-Doubt 176
Benefits of Strategic Reassurance-Seeking 180
Overcoming Obstacles and Paying a Cost 182
Fanning Self-Doubts or Building Self-Confidence?. 183
Keeping Costs Down. 185
Life Transitions and Self-Concept Revision 187
Self-Doubts and the Dynamics of Self-Esteem. 189
References 191

Chapter 9

Implicit Theories of Intelligence: Reconsidering the Role of
Confidence in Achievement Motivation 197

Ying-yi Hong, Chi-yue Chiu, and Carol S. Dweck

Introduction. 197
Implicit Theories and Their Assessment. 198
Assessment of Self-Confidence in Intelligence. 200
The Role of Implicit Theory in Negative Self-Inferences about
    Intelligence 201
Mastery-Oriented vs. Helpless Coping 204
Does Confidence Help? 206

Implicit Theories and the Maintenance of Self-Confidence 208
   Standards 208
   Achievement Goals. 209
Vulnerability of the Self System and a Possible Alternative
   Intervention 210
Concluding Remarks 212
References. 213

Chapter 10

Need for Control and Self-Esteem: Two Routes to a High
Desire for Control

Need for Control and Self-Esteem: Two Routes to a High
Desire for Control 217

Jerry M. Burger

Introduction 217
Desire for Control and Self-Esteem. 219
   Correlations with Measures of Self-Esteem. 219
   Correlations with Measures Related to Self-Esteem 220
Two Routes to a High Desire for Control 222
   The High Self-Esteem Route. 222
   The Low Self-Esteem Route 226
Conclusions 230
References. 231

PART III. CONCLUSION

Chapter 11

Efficacy, Agency, and Self-Esteem: Emerging Themes and
Future Directions

Efficacy, Agency, and Self-Esteem: Emerging Themes and
Future Directions. 237

Michael H. Kernis

Introduction 237
Embedding the Construct of Self-Esteem within Broad Theoretical
   Frameworks 238
Self-Esteem Is Multifaceted. 242
Self-Esteem in Context: Self-Evaluation Maintenance and State
   Self-Esteem. 244

Cognitive Factors 248
Control, Self-Determination, and Self-Esteem 249
Evolutionary Considerations 251
Summary 252
References 252

Index 255

EFFICACY, AGENCY, AND SELF-ESTEEM

INTRODUCTION

Michael H. Kernis

In this introductory chapter, I will briefly describe each chapter in this volume. These brief descriptions cannot possibly do justice to the richness of the theoretical frameworks and empirical evidence contained therein, but will give the reader some insight into the questions and issues that are addressed. The chapters are divided into Parts I and II on the basis of their relative emphasis on intrapersonal dynamics or interpersonal/contextual concerns. However, this division is necessarily somewhat arbitrary, given that each chapter addresses to some extent both intrapersonal and interpersonal/contextual processes.

INTRAPERSONAL DYNAMICS

In Chapter 1, Epstein and Morling address a number of important self-esteem issues from the perspective of Cognitive–Experiential Self-Theory (CEST). They begin by presenting the essential features of CEST that are most relevant to self-esteem issues. For example, according to CEST, people respond to the world through two separate but interacting systems: a rational, conscious, logic-driven system and an experiential, preconscious, affect-driven system. CEST also assumes that the motive of self-enhancement is only one of four basic motives that are equally im-

Michael H. Kernis • Department of Psychology and Institute for Behavioral Research, University of Georgia, Athens, Georgia 30602.

Efficacy, Agency, and Self-Esteem, edited by Michael H. Kernis. Plenum Press, New York, 1995.

portant and that serve as checks and balances on one another. Epstein and Morling present research that shows that compromises among these motives account very well for how high and low self-esteem individuals respond to favorable and unfavorable feedback. Following this presentation, they discuss some implications of distinguishing between the rational and experiential systems for the conceptualization and measurement of self-esteem. They conclude by applying CEST to issues related to psychological adjustment.

In Chapter 2, Deci and Ryan introduce and elaborate upon a critical distinction between what they call "contingent" and "true" self-esteem. Contingent self-esteem involves feelings of self-worth that are dependent on matching standards of excellence or expectations (i.e., ego-involvement). Moreover, it is thought to be associated with various narcissistic and defensive processes that reveal less than optimal psychological well-being. In contrast, true self-esteem is more solidly based and stable, and it reflects positive mental health. Deci and Ryan then discuss how this distinction fits into their well-known theory of self-determination, and they describe in detail various self-regulatory processes that are thought to promote either contingent or true self-esteem. Deci and Ryan also discuss how these various self-regulatory processes are related to mental health, and they describe the social conditions that are thought to promote self-determination and the development of true self-esteem.

In Chapter 3, Greenier, Kernis, and Waschull present research and theory on the joint roles of stability and level of self-esteem in psychological functioning. They begin by focusing on the reasons people vary in the extent to which their self-esteem is unstable. Two factors are discussed: the extent to which people are ego-involved in everyday activities and how well-developed (vs. impoverished) their self-concepts are. They then discuss potential early childhood experiences that may promote unstable self-esteem. Following this, Greenier and colleagues focus on the roles of unstable self-esteem among high and low self-esteem individuals. As they note, there is considerable disagreement over the extent to which high self-esteem is associated with self-protective and self-enhancement strategies, as well as the extent to which low self-esteem is related to maladjustment. Greenier and colleagues then discuss research and theory that suggest that these controversies may be resolvable through a consideration of stability of self-esteem.

Greenberg, Pyszczynski, and Solomon present in Chapter 4 an extensive expansion of their Terror Management Theory that focuses on the roles of growth and enrichment concerns in human motivation and behavior. As originally formulated, Terror Management Theory focused exclusively on defensive motivation that serves to minimize anxiety that ultimately stems from humans' awareness of their own mortality. Although they hold to the view that defensive motivation is ultimately more fundamental than growth-oriented motivation, Greenberg and colleagues acknowledge that a full understanding of the human condition necessitates consideration of growth-oriented motives. Implications of this "dual-motive" conceptualization are subsequently dealt with at length, yielding numerous valuable insights relevant to self-processes in general and to self-esteem in particular. The result is a provocative framework for understanding the interplay of defensive and growth-oriented concerns.

In Chapter 5, the last in Part I, Showers argues that above and beyond the content of self-beliefs, the manner in which these beliefs are organized has substantial implications for reactions to evaluative events and for global feelings of self-worth. Three types of evaluative organization of self-knowledge are delineated: positive-compartmentalized (PC), negative-compartmentalized (NC), and evaluatively integrated (EI). PC and NC organization involve sets of self-beliefs of which all or most are, respectively, positive or negative, and are important and frequently activated. EI organization involves sets of self-beliefs that contain a mixture of positive and negative information. A model of the implications of each type of evaluative organization is presented along with the results of several supportive studies. In addition, the ways in which each type of organization may relate to stability and certainty of self-esteem are discussed. Finally, Showers offers some interesting speculations pertaining to the origins of each of these different types of evaluative organization.

INTERPERSONAL/CONTEXTUAL CONCERNS

In Chapter 6, Leary and Downs open Part II by presenting a novel conceptualization of self-esteem that emphasizes its role in the maintenance of interpersonal relationships. They begin the chapter by critically reviewing existing perspectives on why people are motivated to maintain and enhance their self-esteem. They then offer their own evolutionarily based perspective: People engage in behaviors that maintain their self-esteem because such behaviors minimize the potential for social exclusion. Leary and Downs propose that state self-esteem acts as a "sociometer," the functions of which are to monitor the social environment for exclusionary cues and, when such cues are detected, to alert the individual by triggering negative affect. They then present the results of several studies that support this view. They conclude by considering how the self-esteem motive may differ for low and high self-esteem individuals and the implications of a malfunctioning sociometer.

Beach and Tesser focus in Chapter 7 on the implications that self-evaluation maintenance (SEM) processes have for close relationships and global self-esteem. They begin by describing the original SEM model, which emphasizes two antagonistic processes that are crucial to the maintenance of positive self-evaluations: reflection and comparison. They then describe the extended SEM model, which holds that partners in close relationships will react to each other's outcomes as well as directly to their own. Beach and Tesser then describe a number of studies that provide support for the extended SEM model, and they discuss some intriguing implications that the model has for the way in which self-esteem is potentially affected within the context of close relationships. They follow this discussion with a discussion of whether some people take more extreme measures to protect their self-evaluations than do others. Beach and Tesser conclude the chapter with some interesting and provocative speculations about the self in an evolutionary perspective.

In Chapter 8, Harlow and Cantor present a rich analysis of how people deal with self-doubt in an academic domain and the implications that one such strategy has for creating agency in everyday life. Specifically, Harlow and Cantor present a study that focuses on people who are highly influenced by academic outcomes and who believe that positive outcomes are difficult to achieve. These individuals strategically seek reassurance from others in otherwise social situations, promoting perseverance in their pursuit of academic achievements. Costs associated with the use of this strategy are discussed, as well as ways to minimize them. As in several other chapters in this volume, the construct of "ego involvement" is given considerable attention. Harlow and Cantor also discuss some implications that their goal-oriented approach to personality has for our understanding of self-esteem processes. One such implication is that self-esteem research and theory would benefit from using a more contextualized approach that incorporates people's everyday experiences across time, contexts, and tasks.

Hong, Chiu, and Dweck consider in Chapter 9 the role of self-confidence in achievement contexts from the perspective of people's implicit theories of intelligence. Two implicit theories and their assessment are first described: an entity theory, which involves the belief that intelligence is a fixed entity that is not subject to change, and an incremental theory, which involves the belief that intelligence is malleable and increasable through effort. Hong and colleagues present evidence indicating that (1) overall, confidence is a less important factor than implicit theories of intelligence for predicting responses in achievement situations, and (2) the role of confidence differs as a function of one's implicit theory. In addition, Hong, and colleagues show that confidence is more important when the focus is on recent performance and/or the performance context remains relatively stable and devoid of setbacks. When setbacks are likely or the performance context becomes considerably more challenging, self-confidence is less important. They conclude the chapter with a discussion of how implicit theories of intelligence may relate to level and stability of self-esteem.

In Chapter 10, the last in Part II, Burger discusses the relationship between individual differences in desire for control and global self-esteem. Two central questions are addressed: (1) How do individual differences in desire for control relate to individual differences in global self-esteem? (2) What are some of the developmental antecedents of desire for control? Burger's answer to the first question is that although desire for control and self-esteem are positively correlated, the magnitude of this correlation suggests that there may be also be a link between low self-esteem and high desire for control. After elaborating on why and under what circumstances either high or low self-esteem may be associated with high desire for control, Burger discusses some potential developmental antecedents that may promote each of these associations. An important aspect of Burger's analysis is that it suggests that high desire for control may manifest itself differently depending on whether it is based on high or low self-esteem (and its associated antecedents).

As these descriptions suggest, the chapters are quite diverse in their content and they cover a substantial amount of terrain. I hope that in reading them, investigators and practioners will find much that is new and of value.

CONCLUSION

In Chapter 11, I discuss some common issues and themes that emerged in Chapters 1 through 10 and their implications for future inquiries into the role of self-esteem in mental health and psychological functioning.

PART I

INTRAPERSONAL DYNAMICS

CHAPTER 1

IS THE SELF MOTIVATED TO DO MORE THAN ENHANCE AND/OR VERIFY ITSELF?

SEYMOUR EPSTEIN AND BETH MORLING

INTRODUCTION

In this chapter, we hope to demonstrate the value of examining self-esteem from a broad theoretical perspective. We begin with a summary of the most relevant aspects of a global theory of personality, cognitive–experiential self-theory (CEST). According to this theory, there are four basic needs of the self, two of which are self-enhancement and self-verification. The theory further assumes that behavior reflects a compromise among the four needs, and that information is encoded in two different systems of information processing, rational and experiential. It follows from this latter assumption that there is not one, but two self-conceptualizations, one in each system. We illustrate in an experiment the importance of considering needs other than enhancement and verification, of considering compromise formations among needs, and of investigating the effects of two modes of information processing. Finally, we demonstrate how our model can clarify the role of self-esteem in various problems associated with normal and abnormal adjustment.

SEYMOUR EPSTEIN AND BETH MORLING • Department of Psychology, University of Massachusetts at Amherst, Amherst, Massachusetts 01003.

Efficacy, Agency, and Self-Esteem, edited by Michael H. Kernis. Plenum Press, New York, 1995.

COGNITIVE–EXPERIENTIAL SELF-THEORY

CEST is a global theory of personality that emphasizes the self-concept and devotes considerable attention to self-esteem. Before we apply it to self-esteem issues, we think it will be helpful to provide some general background regarding CEST. Although the arguments in this chapter derive from one particular theory, they are widely applicable to other theoretical perspectives in social, personality, and clinical psychology. It is beyond the scope of this chapter to provide a thorough review of CEST. For present purposes, a review that emphasizes CEST's most relevant aspects with respect to self-esteem should suffice. More thorough reviews of the theory can be found in other publications (e.g., Epstein, 1980, 1990,1991).

According to CEST, people's personalities are best understood in terms of their implicit theories of reality, which consist of self-theories, world-theories, and connecting propositions. Like scientific theories, people's self-theories and world-theories include hierarchically organized implicit beliefs that become increasingly differentiated and integrated through the constant process of assimilation and accommodation. The hierarchical structure permits stability at the upper levels of the hierarchy and simultaneously allows for flexibility at the lower levels. Thus, psychological growth normally proceeds gradually, without serious disruption of the self-concept (with the exception of significant life transitions or the occurrence of traumatic events).

Two Systems for Processing Information

A fundamental assumption of CEST is that people respond to the world on two levels, rational and experiential. These are not simply different ways of reacting within a single system, but are conceived as two separate systems for adapting to reality. The rational system, which has a relatively brief evolutionary history, operates primarily at the conscious level according to people's understanding of conventional rules of logic and evidence and represents information in the form of words and numbers. It requires deliberative, intentional effort and is well suited for abstract analysis and delayed action. The experiential system has a much longer evolutionary history and exists in subhuman as well as in human animals, although it is much more highly developed in humans. It operates in an automatic, holistic, concretive, and associationistic manner, represents information in the form of concrete exemplars, and generalizes through the use of prototypes, metaphors, scripts, and narratives. Unlike the rational system, it is intimately associated with the experience of emotions, is primarily responsive to immediate consequences, and, relatedly, is adapted for immediate action. Table 1 provides a comparison of the distinguishing features of the two systems.

Although the systems are independent, they interact with each other, and behavior is almost always influenced by both systems. The two systems are normally so well synchronized that people experience a single, seamless system. However, the seams become visible in situations in which the systems conflict with each other. A common example is a conflict between the heart and the mind, as when people desire to do something that their reason counsels against. In such cases, people make two different judgments of what is a desirable action: one that is an outcome of automatic assessments of the immediate pleasure to be gained or distress to be avoided, and the other that follows from a more deliberative evaluation of long-term consequences.

The experiential system is motivated by affect. It automatically fosters behavior that is anticipated to promote positive affect and avoid negative affect. In contrast, the rational system is more duty- and less passion-driven. This is not to deny that intellectual activities can be pursued with

TABLE 1. Summary of Major Characteristics of the Two Levels of Processing Proposed by Cognitive–Experiential Self Theory

Parameter	Mental system	
	Rational	Experiential
Evolutionary history	Recent	Ancient
Unit of knowledge	Conscious beliefs; verbal rules of inference and evidence; abstract representations	Preconscious schemas; heuristic rules of operation; concrete representations, e.g., images, episodes, scripts, narratives
Source of knowledge	Communication of ways to reason; logical inference from experience	Direct learning from experience
Sources of motivation	Social prescription; conscious inferences about consequences	Affect
How system guides	Conscious, intentional thought	Automatic associations to emotionally significant past experience; habit
Time frame	Considers long-term consequences	Emphasizes short-term consequences
Means of generalization	Abstract rules of categorization	Representation of generalities in concrete form, e.g., prototypes, metaphors

passion, but to suggest that when they are, the passion is derived from the experiential system.

THE FOUR BASIC NEEDS AND THE CORRESPONDING BELIEFS

According to CEST, establishing and maintaining a favorable sense of self (i.e., self-enhancement) is neither the most nor the least important of human motives. (We alternately refer to basic motives as needs in order to emphasize their fundamental importance.) Three other needs that are no less important than self-enhancement are the need to maximize pleasure and minimize pain, the need to develop and maintain a coherent, accurate model of the world, and the need to maintain relatedness with others.

It is noteworthy that each of the four basic needs is considered to be the single most important need in one or more major theories of personality. The need for maximizing pleasure and minimizing pain is assumed to be the most fundamental in classic psychoanalysis, which refers to it as "the pleasure principle." It is accorded equal importance by learning theorists, who incorporate it in their principle of reinforcement. The need to maintain a stable, coherent conceptual system is assumed to be the most fundamental motive by phenomenological psychologists such as Rogers (1951, 1959) and is accorded a central role by Erikson (1959, 1963). Self-esteem enhancement is considered a prepotent motive by Allport (1961), Kohut (1971), and Adler (Adler, 1954; Ansbacher & Ansbacher, 1956). The need for relatedness is developed as a fundamental motive in human behavior by Sullivan (1953), Bowlby (1969, 1988), Fairbairn (1954), and other object-relations theorists. [For elaboration of these positions, particularly with respect to their relation to the four basic needs, see Epstein (1992).] Which of these theorists is right? According to CEST, they are all right, but they are also all wrong for not recognizing the importance of the other needs.

Behavior is considered to be a compromise among the four needs; relatedly, the four serve as checks and balances on each other. For example, although the need for self-esteem could motivate people to seek self-enhancing compliments from others, the need to maintain favorable relationships exerts pressure against such norm-violating behavior. Likewise, the need for an accurate, coherent world model exerts pressure against accepting unrealistic feedback. We discuss the relationships among the four needs in more depth later in this chapter.

As the four basic needs motivate people to attend to and process need-relevant information, people develop networks of four basic beliefs (alternatively called "implicit schemata") that are associated with the four basic needs. Included are the degree to which the world is viewed as benevolent vs. malevolent (associated with the need for a favorable plea-sure–pain balance), the degree to which the world is viewed as meaning-ful, predictable, just, and controllable vs. meaningless, arbitrary, unjust, and uncontrollable (associated with the need for an accurate, coherent model of reality), the degree to which other people are viewed as trust-worthy and supportive vs. unreliable or threatening (associated with the need for relationship), and the degree to which the self is viewed as worthy vs. unworthy (associated with the need for self-enhancement). These be-liefs occupy such a fundamental position in the hierarchy of the self-system that a significant change in any of them would resonate through the entire personality. A sudden, drastic invalidation of any basic need would seriously threaten the stability of the personality, as in posttraumatic stress disorder (e.g., Epstein, 1991; Janoff-Bulman, 1992; McCann & Pearlman, 1990), or actually destabilize it, as in acute schizophrenic disorganization (Epstein, 1979).

Because the experiential system is primarily a nonverbal, emotional, imagistic system, people's standings on the four basic implicit beliefs cannot necessarily be accessed by direct verbal report, rather, the implicit beliefs must be inferred from behavior or from knowledge of the relations between emotions and schemata. It follows that people's experiential sense of self-esteem may not be accurately reflected in their verbal responses to questionnaires. Indeed, because there are two conceptual systems, there are two evaluations of the self. The rational system contains the person's conscious, verbal appraisal of self-worth, and the experiential system con-tains the person's schematic appraisals and consequent feelings about the self. The two appraisals may or may not coincide. People who report high explicit self-esteem at the verbal level may demonstrate low implicit self-esteem in their emotional and behavioral reactions. Such people, who report verbally that they have high self-esteem but display low self-esteem behaviorally, are sometimes described as being high in defensive self-esteem. We will further explore defensive self-esteem and the problems of measuring implicit (nonverbal) self-esteem later in this chapter.

CEST IN RELATION TO PSYCHODYNAMICS

In the preceding discussion we assumed that self-enhancement is one of four basic motives that preconsciously interact with each other and foster behavioral compromises. This view is psychodynamic because it proposes that behavior results from the interactions of implicit strivings and that compromises among the strivings are often reached outside a person's awareness (Westen, 1990).

When psychodynamic processes are interpreted as affectively driven, preconscious cognitive strategies, they are able to retain the positive aspects of the concept without being encumbered by the excess baggage of other, questionable psychodynamic formulations such as energy investments (cathexis) and transformations. The nature of the self-concept as proposed by CEST is consistent with such a reformulation and with other cognitive research and theoretical constructs, such as schemata (see reviews in Fiske & Taylor, 1991; Taylor & Crocker, 1981), the accessibility of mental structures (e.g., Bargh, 1989; Fazio, 1990; Uleman, 1989), working models (e.g., Bowlby 1969; Carnelley, Pietromonaco, & Jaffe, 1994; Markus & Wurf, 1987); and heuristics (e.g., Chaiken, 1980, 1987; Kahneman, & Tversky, 1984; Petty & Cacioppo, 1986). Recent research has also explored the automatic nature of much information processing, supporting the preconscious processing proposed in psychodynamic formulations (e.g., Bargh, 1989, 1990; Bowers & Meichenbaum, 1984; Gilbert, Pelham, & Krull, 1988; Greenwald & Pratkanis, 1984; Kihlstrom, 1987; Nisbett & Wilson, 1977; Straumann & Higgins, 1987). Such research has demonstrated that much human information processing occurs without conscious awareness. Because it draws from both a psychodynamic context and a modern cognitive framework, CEST has the potential to provide a broadly integrative framework.

SELF-VERIFICATION OR SELF-ENHANCEMENT?

Following traditional personality theories, recent popular lines of research in psychology typically assign one need a dominant role. A case in point, particularly relevant to a discussion of self-esteem, is the self-verification vs. self-enhancement debate in social psychology. Briefly, some psychologists (e.g., Aronson, 1968; Festinger, 1957) claim that people strive to self-verify primarily in an effort to gain prediction and control. Others (e.g., Shrauger, 1975; Steele, 1988; Tesser, 1988) claim that people desire primarily to enhance the self and, accordingly, seek feedback from others that serves this goal. Each of these lines of research recognizes that the other motive exists, but subordinates it to the presumably more fundamental motive it emphasizes.

In his own theorizing, Swann (1990) takes an important step forward, because he provides a way of integrating both approaches. Having acknowledged support for both positions, Swann investigates the conditions in which each motive tends to prevail. People's choices of enhancing or verifying interaction partners, Swann writes, entail different cognitive pro-

cesses. Self-enhancement is a more automatic, less cognitively effortful process, whereas self-verification takes more cognitive effort but prevails when people are motivated to be careful (Swann, 1990; Swann, Hixon, Stein-Seroussi, & Gilbert, 1990). The research of Swann and his colleagues indicates that in many important situations, people with low self-esteem choose interaction partners who give them negative feedback, because such feedback verifies their self-views (e.g., Swann & Read, 1981; Swann, Griffin, Predmore, & Gaines, 1987; Swann, Pelham, & Krull, 1989).

From the perspective of CEST, Swann's integration can be extended by adding the need for relatedness. Interestingly, Swann appears to implicitly recognize this, as his major dependent variable requires subjects to indicate their preference for various interaction partners. But Swann views these relationship choices only in terms of how they fulfill desires for self-confirming or self-enhancing feedback. In contrast, from the vantage point of CEST, we suggest that one reason people seek verifying feedback from partners is that if people are evaluated too highly, they might feel they could disappoint the partner later by not living up to expectations, and therefore suffer rejection. Similarly, feedback that is too *un*favorable relative to a subject's self-concept paints a gloomy picture about the future of the relationship. In sum, evaluative feedback, while it can fulfill enhancement and verification needs, also provides important information about the anticipated course of relationships. Furthermore, whereas Swann suggests that people use relationships to satisfy self-verification and self-esteem strivings, we see no need completely to subsume people's striving for relatedness under their strivings for self-esteem and self-confirmation. People do not enter into relationships simply to confirm or enhance their self-images; rather, relationships are an important source of satisfaction in their own right.

CEST also has another contribution to make to extending Swann's research. Swann's discussion implies that the two needs operate on an all-or-nothing basis, as though one need or the other must categorically win out. External factors such as conditions that influence cognitive effort, source credibility, and issue importance determine which path (enhancement or verification) will be followed (Swann, 1990), but there is no compromise. In contrast, according to CEST, rather than choosing to fulfill one need to the total exclusion of others, behavior is often a compromise among needs. For example, given the simultaneous operation of a need to enhance and a need to verify, people's desire for self-enhancing information should normally be constrained by the need for verification and vice versa (Losco & Epstein, 1978). The result should be a modest desire for self-enhancement in most people under most circumstances.

A STUDY TO TEST FOR COMPROMISE FORMATION

We conducted a study to test our view that people's behavior frequently represents a compromise among needs. The study investigated how the needs for self-verification, self-enhancement, and relationship can influence people's attraction to romantic partners. In our study, 281 subjects read vignettes about how five potential partners evaluated them after a meeting at a party. The assessments were presented to the subjects relative to how they viewed themselves. One of the potential partners was said to have assessed them "pretty much as you would describe yourself." This partner corresponds to a self-verifying partner. Four other partners were described as viewing them slightly more favorably, much more favorably, slightly less favorably, and much more unfavorably than the subjects viewed themselves. These four partners corresponded to two levels of positive and negative feedback. Our experiment thus gave subjects the opportunity to demonstrate their level of attraction to partners who provided them with five levels of favorability of feedback. It is important to keep in mind that the relative-feedback design of our study meant that the feedback from the partners was calibrated to the subjects' own self-views.

After reading about each of the potential dating partner's descriptions of them, subjects rated, in turn: their spontaneous, immediate attraction to the partner; their more delayed, considered reaction to the partner, their desire to spend time with the partner on a short- and a long-term basis; and their expectation about the likelihood of being rejected by the partner if they were to develop a long-term relationship. Our subjects also completed items from five scales of the O'Brien and Epstein (1988) Multimodal Self-esteem Inventory, namely Global Self-esteem, Likability, Competence, Identity Integration, and Defensiveness.

ENHANCEMENT AND VERIFICATION RESULTS

Based on the finding reported by Swann (1990) that people's immediate or rushed reaction is to self-enhance, we predicted that people's "gut" feeling of attraction (which corresponds to an automatic response) would increase as the partner's evaluation of the subject increased. This is indeed, what our data show (see Fig. 1). As the hypothetical partners described our subjects more favorably, our subjects' immediate level of attraction rose linearly (a linear contrast on the means was significant).

But Swann and CEST have different predictions for people's more careful, reasoned judgment of attraction (which corresponds to a cogni-

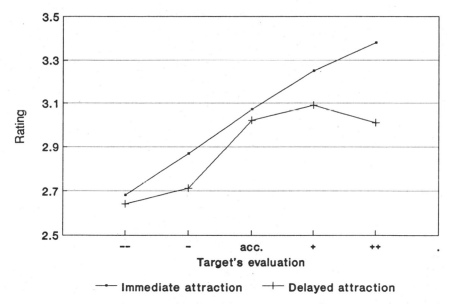

FIGURE 1. Immediate and delayed attraction to potential dating partners as a function of favorability of feedback. Key: (−−) partner describes subject slightly less favorably than subject views self; (−) partner describes subject slightly less favorably; (acc) accurate description, i.e., partner describes subject as subject views self; (+) partner describes subject slightly more favorably than subject views self; (++) partner describes subject much more favorably.

tively effortful response). Swann would predict that delayed attraction would be highest for the self-verifying partner, the one who evaluated the subjects as they evaluated themselves. CEST, on the other hand, predicts that because people compromise between the need for self-enhancement and the need for self-verification, their delayed attraction should be greater for the person who described them somewhat, but not extremely, more favorably than they view themselves. Since other-judgments were presented relative to the subjects' own self-image, we expected few if any differences between low, medium, and high self-esteem subjects. Namely, we anticipated that everyone would prefer feedback that was slightly more favorable than his or her own self-assessment.

Our results for people's deliberative evaluations of their partners supported the compromise hypothesis (see Fig. 1). Reports of their more reasoned, considered level of attraction to the partners showed a peak at the partner who viewed them slightly better than they viewed themselves. A planned contrast performed on the order of the three means that constitute the peak (i.e., the means corresponding to the accurate assessment, the slightly more favorable assessment, and the extremely more favorable assessment) indicated that the curve was significantly inverted-V-shaped.

Thus, our finding that the immediate reactions reflect the self-enhancement motive replicates the findings by Swann and his associates (Swann, 1990; Swann, et al., 1990). But our subjects' delayed preference for the slightly enhancing partner (indicating a compromise between two needs) does not replicate this previous research. In terms of CEST, the results suggest that the experiential system, a rapid, nonreflective system, was responsible for the enhancement effect, whereas the rational system was responsible for the compromise. Although our experiment indicated that the experiential system was responsible for enhancement but not verification, we suspect that in other circumstances, the experiential system would also be motivated to self-verify. In particular, the experiential system's need for confirmation is likely to express itself in situations in which invalidation of personal beliefs is destabilizing and therefore highly emotionally distressing.

In summary, our results support Swann's and CEST's position on enhancement being dominant in immediate reactions, at least under the conditions investigated, and verification being dominant in delayed reactions. The results differ with respect to compromise formation, where the findings are consistent with CEST's position, but not with Swann's position.

RELATIONSHIP RESULTS

Our results also indicate that the implications of partners' evaluations of the quality and outcome of relationships are an important parameter that influences people's reactions to self-evaluative feedback. For instance, we found that expectations about relationships are related to self-esteem. Low self-esteem subjects were most likely to think the hypothetical partners would reject them in the future. Medium self-esteem subjects were slightly less likely, and high self-esteem subjects were considerably less likely, to expect rejection. These results indicate that people's self-evaluations are not independent of their anticipated relationships with others.

Parenthetically, our data also indicate that how the partner's evaluations make the subjects *feel* does not necessarily correspond to how *attracted* subjects are to the potential partners. Subjects' ratings of how the evaluations made them feel about themselves were consistently higher than their ratings of attraction (even, importantly, their immediate attraction). The difference between feelings and attraction becomes especially pronounced as evaluations become more favorable. Under conditions of strong overvaluation, subjects appear to be thinking something such as, "This person makes me feel really good about myself, but either he or she is an insincere flatterer or a poor judge of character, so I don't find him or her attractive." Because attraction, unlike self-centered hedonic feelings, is an interpersonal variable, people's levels of attraction are likely to be tempered by relationship concerns.

IMPLICATIONS OF TWO LEVELS OF PROCESSING FOR THE MEASUREMENT OF SELF-ESTEEM

If people have two conceptual systems for adapting to the world, with one based on schemata derived primarily from emotionally significant experiences and the other based on more abstract, verbal beliefs, it follows that people may have different assessments of their self-worth in the two systems. These would consist of an explicit evaluation, directly accessible via verbal report, and an implicit self-assessment that can only be inferred. We shall refer to the two kinds of self-esteem as *explicit* and *implicit* self-esteem. The existence of two kinds of self-esteem has important methodological implications, for it suggests that self-report measures of self-esteem are limited. This conclusion is supported by a series of studies by Savin-Williams and Jacquish (1981) that examined the relations between behavioral, self-report, and judges' ratings of self-esteem. They found only modest correspondence between the different procedures. Self-report measures inform us only of a person's conscious, explicit appraisals, which may or may not coincide with the person's implicit self-evaluation in the experiential system that, according to CEST, is the more important influence on the person's behavior and emotions. Lest we be misunderstood, we do not mean to deny the importance of self-report measures of self-esteem. That people's conscious, explicit assessments are important is well substantiated by a great deal of research that has demonstrated that such measures are significantly and coherently associated with many other variables of interest. This association is to be expected, of course, because of the often considerable overlap between the two systems.

Casual observation reveals that people differ in the degree of correspondence between their two kinds of self-esteem. We are all aware of people who profess a positive self-evaluation and attempt to impress others with their superiority, yet demonstrate in their behavior and emotional reactions that they are defensive, insecure, and lacking in confidence, all hallmarks of low implicit self-esteem. More extreme examples include people with delusions of grandeur and those with a diagnosis of narcissistic personality.

Given that implicit and explicit self-esteem may fail to correspond, it would be extremely useful to be able to measure them independently. There is no problem in measuring explicit self-esteem, as there are many sophisticated, reliable questionnaires for doing so. The problem is not so readily solved with respect to measuring implicit self-esteem; however, a variety of approaches appear promising.

According to CEST, schemata in the experiential system can be inferred from behavior and emotions. Thus, one promising approach to measuring implicit self-esteem is to obtain samples of everyday behavior and emotions. In research using this approach, we have had subjects keep daily records of events that raised and lowered their self-esteem (Epstein, 1983; Losco & Epstein, 1978; O'Brien & Epstein, 1988). Although this procedure relies on self-report, the reporting is much more objective than when subjects report general impressions in self-report inventories. Results support that the two procedures are not equivalent. The two are only modestly correlated; furthermore, our subjects often expressed surprise at the difference between the two measures. In some cases, subjects had a more favorable implicit self-picture than self-report measures indicated, whereas in other cases the discrepancy was in the opposite direction.

McClelland and his associates (e.g., McClelland, Koestner, & Weinberger, 1989; Weinberger & McClelland, 1990) have proposed a distinction between "implicit" and "self-attributed" motives that is highly consistent with the operational principles of the experiential and rational systems. Of particular interest with respect to measurement, they have demonstrated that self-report measures, which are assumed to measure explicit motives, have different correlates from indirect measures such as responses to specially constructed Thematic Apperception Tests (TATs), which are assumed to measure implicit motives. According to their findings, responses to TATs provide a better predictor of real-life behavior, whereas self-report measures are more strongly associated with cognitive responses (e.g., other self-report measures). So far, the procedure with TATs has produced impressive results for the measurement of a variety of motives, including achievement, affiliation, and power. It would be interesting to use the procedure for measuring the implicit assessment of self and the implicit motive for self-enhancement.

Measuring cognitive processes under conditions of memory load or time pressure (e.g., Gilbert et al., 1988; Swann et al., 1990) may provide another route for assessing implicit needs and schemas. Under cognitive load, subjects are unable to employ the purposeful attention and cognitive effort required by the rational system and are forced to rely on the more primitive and automatic information processing of the experiential system. A related, simpler procedure that we have found promising in exploratory research is to have people list their first three thoughts in response to how they would react in certain situations. The first thought is often nonrational and consistent with the operation of the experiential system, whereas the third thought usually reflects deliberative judgment, consistent with the operation of the rational system.

Other techniques that could be explored for measuring implicit appraisals of the self are dichotic listening tasks, subthreshold measures, priming procedures, and a variety of projective techniques, including drawings of the self and specially constructed word-association tests.

In a highly influential article on the self-concept from a social–cognitive perspective, Markus (1977) introduced a reaction-time technique for measuring accessibility of self-schemata. People who were faster at identifying words as self-descriptive were assumed to be schematic on domains related to those words. Although the technique is a questionable measure of accessibility of certain schemata (because a person's level of conflict in a domain confounds effects of delayed reactions), it may nevertheless be able to provide useful information on implicit self-esteem. A person with a favorable, unconflicted assessment of self would be expected to acknowledge positive and deny negative attributes more rapidly than someone who is defensively high on self-esteem, that is, high on explicit and low on implicit self-esteem. Physiological recording could be used in conjunction with reaction-time methods, much in the manner of lie detection.

Interesting as many of the aforementioned measures appear to be, a caveat is in order regarding the reliance on verbal self-assessments in any form, including those that examine reaction times and physiological responses to words. Because words are not the preferred medium of the experiential system, it is possible that many of the important schemata that influence emotions and behavior are not encoded in words. How serious this concern is, only future research will tell.

APPLICATION OF THE MODEL TO ADAPTIVE AND MALADAPTIVE BEHAVIOR

CEST's view that self-enhancement interacts with other equally important needs is useful for understanding abnormal as well as normal behavioral patterns. In this section, we discuss issues involved in balancing the four basic needs and how the model can be applied to a number of self-esteem issues concerning normal and abnormal adjustment.

BALANCING THE FOUR BASIC NEEDS IN NORMAL AND ABNORMAL ADJUSTMENT

Given four equally important needs, what are the consequences of satisfying one need with respect to satisfying the others? If one need is satisfied, does it mean that fulfillment of the others is necessarily reduced? The answer provided by CEST is that people with poor adjustment sacrifice some needs in order to fulfill others, but that well-adjusted people tend to solve the problem in a synergistic manner. Let us consider this issue further using self-esteem as an example. Poorly adjusted people whose self-esteem is threatened may be driven to affirm their self-worth by making insistent demands for appreciation, respect, and admiration from others. By doing so, they alienate others, thereby sacrificing the need for relatedness. They may also cope with feelings of inferiority by exaggerating their accomplishments and virtues to the extent that they invalidate a realistic model of the world. Finally, because of a lack of confidence, low self-esteem people may avoid potentially rewarding experiences or, alternatively, force themselves to engage in joyless or self-defeating activities in order to prove their superiority (Adler, 1954). The overall result is that they sacrifice all other basic needs in a desperate attempt to bolster self-esteem.

A further consideration that has received some support (e.g., Epstein, 1992) is that the attempt to fulfill one need at the expense of the other needs is likely to boomerang even with respect to the single need, because all the needs are interconnected. Thus, failing to solve one tends to contribute to failing to solve the others. In sum, attempting to shore up one of the basic needs at the expense of the others, except as a temporary expedient, is a self-defeating strategy.

Contrast the zero-sum, neurotic strategy discussed above with a synergistic strategy that is assumed to be a fundamental attribute of successful adjustment. Highly functioning people satisfy the four basic needs in a manner such that satisfying one need is harmonious with, rather than in conflict with, satisfying the other needs. For example, they establish rewarding relationships with others that contribute to, rather than compromise, self-acceptance. They achieve realistic accomplishments in a way that elicits approval and admiration rather than enmity from others. They receive genuine enjoyment from their strivings, rather than being duty-driven. Ultimately, a stable, positive sense of self in the experiential system must rest on real-life experience, which means realistic accomplishments, rewarding relationships with enhancing partners, and a meaningful, coherent, and emotionally satisfactory life-style.

SELF-ENHANCING ILLUSIONS

Are illusions necessary for mental well-being? Several psychologists have recently concluded that they are and have suggested that reality awareness is therefore not a useful criterion of mental health. Their conclusion is based on widespread evidence in laboratory studies that normal individuals often exhibit a self-enhancing bias in evaluating themselves and an optimism-enhancing bias in evaluating events (see the reviews in Snyder & Higgins, 1988; Taylor & Brown, 1988).

CEST provides a different perspective for viewing these findings, namely, that they can be accounted for by the interaction of multiple needs. It is not that reality awareness is an inappropriate criterion of mental health, but that it is not the *only* criterion and cannot be evaluated independently of the contribution of other equally important needs. As noted earlier, given a compromise between the basic needs to maintain an accurate, cohesive model of the world and to enhance self-esteem, most people can be expected to exhibit a favorable, but moderate, bias in their self-assessments. Relatedly, given the needs to maintain a favorable pleasure–pain balance and to maintain a realistic model of the world, a compromise between the two needs should foster a moderate optimistic bias. It is important to note that under many circumstances, moderately favorable biases are likely to contribute to positive affective states without any accompanying disadvantages. Where there is something to gain by being accurate, research has demonstrated that the biases tend to disappear (e.g., Epstein & Meier, 1989). Thus, it is not at all surprising that most people adopt strategies that maximize positive affect and minimize negative affect in ways that do not seriously interfere with fulfillment of their other needs, including the need to maintain a realistic, coherent model of the world.

THE REASONS PEOPLE MAINTAIN NEGATIVE SELF-VIEWS

Since it obviously feels better to view oneself favorably rather than unfavorably, why do some people maintain negative self-assessments? CEST suggests that the other basic needs contribute in important ways to maintaining negative self-views. First, the most obvious need that can account for maintaining a negative self-view is the need to maintain the stability and coherence of a person's conceptual system. Because a person's implicit evaluation of his or her worthiness is a fundamental construct in the person's self-system, its invalidation could destabilize the entire personality structure, generating overwhelming anxiety. Even a negative self-system is less distressing than one that is under pressure of disorganizing. Thus, people have a vested interest in maintaining their basic negative as well as positive beliefs (Epstein, 1973, 1980, 1992; Losco & Epstein, 1978). This view is similar to the finding of Swann, Stein-Seroussi, and Giesler (1992) that people with low self-images tend to choose self-verifying partners for "pragmatic and epistemic reasons." The maintenance of a low self-image to prevent the disorganization of the self (the motivation cited by CEST) corresponds to the epistemic motivations cited by Swann's subjects.

Second, the need for maximizing pleasure and minimizing pain, strange as it may seem, also contributes to the maintenance of a negative view of the self. Painful as a low base level of self-acceptance is, it is less distressing than sudden, phasic decreases in self-esteem (Epstein, 1992). Expressed otherwise, by evaluating the self negatively, people can reduce the sting of negative evaluations, rejection, and failure. As noted elsewhere (Epstein, 1992), the situation is analogous to one in which people invest their entire capital in insurance, thereby permanently depriving themselves of the opportunity for leading an enjoyable life, but providing them with security with respect to future misfortunes. One has to be desperately afraid of disappointment to engage in such a bargain, but it should be understood that the bargain is automatically made in the experiential system and is not the result of a conscious, deliberative process in the rational system.

The remaining need that can contribute to the maintenance of a negative self-view is the need for relatedness. According to CEST, and consistent with the views of Sullivan (1953) and Bowlby (1988), people's schemata about their relations with significant others in childhood generalize to their adult relationships. According to Sullivan, a child with an unsatisfactory relationship with a caretaker has two alternative ways of construing the situation: Either the child is bad and the caretaker is good, or the caretaker is bad and the child is good. Because the child's very life depends on relatedness, he or she has little choice. To view the caretaker as bad leads to feelings of hopelessness, rage, and insecurity. To view the self as bad, while unpleasant, at least provides hope and a sense of control. If the child can change his or her own "bad" behavior, then there is the possibility of being accepted by the caregiver on whom the child is dependent. Thus, the most common outcome of an unsatisfactory relationship with parents is that the child is strongly motivated to view the self as bad. This self-view and its related behavior patterns tend to become integrated into an enduring relationship pattern maintained into adulthood.

AN EXAMPLE OF SUCCESSFUL ADJUSTMENT

An example from a young woman's personal story illustrates poignantly how self-esteem interacts with the other basic needs, how certain kinds of emotionally significant experiences at particular ages can affect the balance among them, and how improved adjustment is often associated with a harmonious fulfillment of previously conflicting needs:

> I remember coming home from school all excited about a project or a grade and showing [my father]. But he did not want to be bothered with it . . . . He used to tell me he was surprised I had any friends because I had no personality. I heard this at least once a week . . . . [And when I applied to colleges] he would constantly tell me that with my grades I was going nowhere and no college would ever want me . . . . I lived in an all girls' dormitory my first semester. I went out a lot with friends from home and the girls on my floor started coming over a lot to hang out and to ask me if they could go out with me. I asked them why they wanted to be with me as I had no personality. They told me I had the most dominant personality on the floor. That was the happiest day of my life and the worst day of my life. The resentment toward my father brewed . . . . I thought I could never forgive him for hurting me so badly all those years.

Interpreted by CEST, when the information from her college friends contradicted her father's negative feedback, the woman needed to reframe her models of her father and herself (which were interrelated). She could no longer continue to believe that she was as worthless as her father had said. But disbelieving him meant confronting the possibility of forever losing an important relationship, a thought that led to acute feelings of distress, betrayal, and resentment. Her reframing was timed at college because of her greater independence from her father in combination with the pleasure, favorable assessment, and the validation of her new assessments that she received from her friends, which apparently outweighed the pain of rejecting and being rejected by him. Thus, all four basic needs and beliefs were implicated in the changed view of self. The young woman's story also illustrates how the different needs interact over the life course. Early in life, the need to maintain a positive relationship with her father was prepotent and constrained her need for self-enhancement. Later on, her reduced dependence on him, the increased support from others, her continued need to view the world accurately, and the pleasure she obtained from her new way of assessing herself and others' opinions of her combined to allow her to discount her father's appraisal. The result was that the woman gradually raised her self-esteem in an adaptive way that fulfilled all four experiential motives.

SUMMARY

In this chapter, we have suggested that a theory of self-esteem belongs within a broader theory of personality. CEST, as a global theory of personality that emphasizes the self-concept, provides a useful framework for examining self-esteem. Research conducted within this framework demonstrated that in order to understand people's reactions to evaluations, it is necessary to consider two levels of information processing and needs other than enhancement and verification. We suggested solutions to the problem of measuring self-esteem at both the explicit and the implicit level. Finally, we demonstrated how the principles of CEST can clarify the role of self-esteem in good and poor adjustment.

ACKNOWLEDGMENTS. Preparation of this chapter and the research reported in it were supported, in part, by NIMH research grant MH 01293 and Research Scientist Award 5 K05 00363 to Epstein.

REFERENCES

Adler, A. (1954). *Understanding human nature*. New York: Fawcett.

Allport, G. W. (1961). *Pattern and growth in personality*. New York: Holt, Rinehart & Winston.

Ansbacher, H. L., & Ansbacher, R. R. (1956). *The individual psychology of Alfred Adler: A systematic presentation in selections from his writings*. New York: Harper & Row.

Aronson, E. (1968). A theory of cognitive dissonance: A current perspective. In L. Berkowitz (Ed.), *Advances in experimental social psychology*, Vol. 4, (pp. 1–34). New York: Academic Press.

Bargh, J. A. (1989). Conditional automaticity: Varieties of automatic influence in social perception and cognition. In J. S. Uleman & J. A. Bargh (Eds.), *Unintended thought* (pp. 3–51). New York: Guilford Press.

Bargh, J. A. (1990). Auto-motives: Preconscious determinants of social interaction. In E. T. Higgins & R. M. Sorrentino (Eds.), *Handbook of motivation and cognition*, Vol. 2., *Foundations of social behavior* (pp. 93–130). New York: Guilford Press.

Bowers, K S., & Meichenbaum, D. (Eds.). (1984). *The unconscious reconsidered*. New York:, John Wiley.

Bowlby, J. (1969). *Attachment and loss*, Vol. 1, *Attachment*. New York: Basic Books.

Bowlby, J. (1988). *A secure base: Parent–child attachment and healthy human development*. New York: Basic Books.

Carnelley, K. B., Pietromonaco, P. R., & Jaffe, K. (1994). Depression, working models of others, and relationship functioning. *Journal of Personality and Social Psychology, 66*, 127–140.

Chaiken, S. (1980). Heuristic versus systematic information processing and the use of source versus message cues in persuasion. *Journal of Personality and Social Psychology, 39*, 752–766.

Chaiken, S. (1987). The heuristic model of persuasion. In M. P. Zanna, J. M. Olson, & C. P. Herman (Eds), *Social influence: The Ontario Symposium*, Vol. 5 (pp. 3–39). Hillsdale, NJ: Erlbaum Associates.

Epstein, S. (1973). The self-concept revisited, or a theory of a theory. *American Psychologist 28*, 404–416.

Epstein, S. (1979). Natural healing processes of the mind. I. Acute schizophrenic disorganization. *Schizophrenia Bulletin, 5*, 313–321.

Epstein, S. (1980). The self-concept: A review and the proposal of an integrated theory of personality. In E. Staub (Ed.), *Personality: Basic issues and current research* (pp. 82–132). Englewood Cliffs, NJ: Prentice-Hall.

Epstein, S. (1983). The unconscious, the preconscious and the self-concept In J. Suls & A. Greenwald (Eds.), *Psychological perspectives on the self*, Vol. 2 (pp. 219–247).

Epstein, S. (1990). Cognitive–experiential self-theory. In L. A. Pervin (Ed.), *Handbook of personality: Theory and research* (pp. 165–191). New York: Guilford Press.

Epstein, S. (1991). Cognitive–experiential self-theory: An integrative theory of personality. In R. Curtis (Ed.), *The relational self: Convergences in psychoanalysis and social psychology* (pp. 111–137). New York: Guilford Press.

Epstein, S. (1992). Coping ability, negative self-evaluation, and overgeneralization: Experiment and theory. *Journal of Personality and Social Psychology, 62*, 826–836.

Epstein, S., & Meier, P. (1989). Constructive thinking: A broad coping variable with specific components. *Journal of Personality and Social Psychology, 57*, 332–349.

Erikson, E. H. (1959). Identity and the life cycle: Selected papers. *Psychological Issues, 1*, 5–165.

Erikson, E. H. (1963). *Childhood and society*, 2nd ed. New York: Norton.

Fairbairn, W. R. D. (1954). *An object relations theory of the personality*. New York: Basic Books.

Fazio, R. H. (1990). Multiple processes by which attitudes guide behavior: The MODE model as an integrative framework. In M. P. Zanna (Ed.), *Advances in experimental social psychology*, Vol. 23 (pp. 75–110). New York: Academic Press.

Festinger, L. (1957). *A theory of cognitive dissonance*. Palo Alto, CA: Stanford University Press.

Fiske, S. T., & Taylor, S. E. (1991). *Social cognition*, Vol. 2. New York: McGraw-Hill.

Gilbert, D. T., Pelham, B. W., & Krull, D. S. (1988). On cognitive busyness: When person perceivers meet persons perceived. *Journal of Personality and Social Psychology, 54*, 733–739.

Greenwald, A. G., & Pratkanis, A. R. (1984). The self. In R. S. Wyer, Jr., & T. K Srull (Eds.), *Handbook of social cognition*, Vol. 3 (pp. 129–178). Hillsdale, NJ: Erlbaum Associates.

Janoff-Bulman, R. (1992). *Shattered assumptions*. New York: Free Press.

Kahneman, D., & Tversky, A. (1984). Choices, values, and frames. *American Psychologist, 39*, 341–350.

Kihlstrom, J. F. (1987). The cognitive unconscious. *Science, 237*, 1145–1152.

Kohut, H. (1971). *The analysis of the self*. New York. International Universities Press.

Losco, J., & Epstein, S. (1978). Reactions to favorable and unfavorable evaluations in everyday life as a function of level of self-esteem. Paper presented at Eastern Psychological Association, Washington, DC.

Markus, H. (1977). Self-schemata and processing information about the self. *Journal of Personality and Social Psychology, 35*, 63–78.

Markus, H., & Wurf, E. (1987). The dynamic self-concept: A social psychological perspective. In M. R. Rosenszweig & L. W. Porter (Eds.), *Annual review of psychology*, Vol. 38 (pp. 299–337). Palo Alto, CA: Annual Reviews.

McCann, I. L., & Pearlman, L. A. (1990). *Psychological trauma and the adult survivor: Theory, therapy, and transformation.* New York: Brunner/Mazel.

McClelland, D. C., Koestner, R., & Weinberger, J. (1989). How do self-attributed and implicit motives differ? *Psychological Review, 96,* 690–702.

Nisbett, R. E., & Wilson, T. D. (1977). Telling more than we can know: Verbal reports on mental processes. *Psychological Review, 84,* 231–259.

Petty, R. E., & Cacioppo, J. T. (1986). The elaboration likelihood model of persuasion. *Advances in Experimental Social Psychology. 19,* 123–205.

O'Brien, E. J., & Epstein, S. (1988). *The multidimensional self-esteem inventory.* Odessa, FL: Psychological Assessment Resources.

Rogers, C. R. (1951). *Client-centered therapy: Its current practice, implications and theory.* Boston: Houghton Mifflin.

Rogers, C. R. (1959). A theory of therapy, personality, and interpersonal relationships, as developed in the client-centered framework. In S. Koch (Ed.), *Psychology: A study of a science,* Vol. 3 (pp. 184–256). New York: McGraw-Hill.

Savin-Williams, R. C., & Jacquish, G. A. (1981). The assessment of adolescent self-esteem: A comparison of methods. *Journal of Personality, 49,* 324–335.

Shrauger, J. S. (1975). Responses to evaluation as a function of initial self-perceptions. *Psychological Bulletin, 82,* 581–596.

Snyder, C. R., & Higgins, E. T. (1988). Excuses: Their effective role in the negotiation of reality. *Psychological Bulletin, 104,* 23–35.

Steele, C. M. (1988). The psychology of self-affirmation: Sustaining the integrity of the self. In L. Berkowitz (Ed.), *Advances in experimental social psychology,* Vol. 21 (pp. 261–302). New York: Academic Press.

Straumann, T. J., & Higgins, E. T., (1987). Automatic activation of self-discrepancies and emotional syndromes: When cognitive structures influence affect. *Journal of Personality and Social Psychology, 53,* 1004–1014.

Sullivan, H. S. (1953). *The interpersonal theory of psychiatry.* New York: Norton.

Swann, W. B. (1990). To be adored or to be known? The interplay of self-enhancement and self-verification. In E. T. Higgins & R. M. Sorrentino (Eds.), *Handbook of motivation and cognition,* Vol. 2, *Foundations of social behavior* (pp. 408–448). New York: Guilford Press.

Swann, W. B., & Read, S. J. (1981). Acquiring self-knowledge: The search for feedback that fits. *Journal of Personality and Social Psychology, 41,* 1119–1128.

Swann, W. B., Griffin, J. J., Predmore, S., & Gaines, B. (1987). The cognitive–affective crossfire: When self-consistency confronts self-enhancement. *Journal of Personality and Social Psychology, 52,* 881–889.

Swann, W. B., Pelham, B. W., & Krull, D. S. (1989). Agreeable fancy or disagreeable truth? Reconciling self-enhancement and self-verification. *Journal of Personality and Social Psychology, 57,* 782–791.

Swann, W. B., Hixon, J. G., Stein-Seroussi, A., & Gilbert, D. T. (1990). The fleeting gleam of praise: Cognitive processes underlying behavioral reactions to self-relevant feedback. *Journal of Personality and Social Psychology, 59,* 17–26.

Swann, W. B., Stein-Seroussi, A., & Giesler, R. B. (1992). Why people self-verify. *Journal of Personality and Social Psychology, 57,* 392–401.

Taylor, S. E., & Brown, J. D. (1988). Illusion and well-being: Some social psychological contributions to a theory of mental health. *Psychological Bulletin, 103,* 193–210.

Taylor, S. E., & Crocker, J. (1981). Schematic bases of social information processing. In E. T. Higgins, C. P. Herman, & M. P. Zanna (Eds.), *Social cognition: The Ontario Symposium,* Vol. 1 (pp. 89–134). Hillsdale, NJ: Erlbaum Associates.

Tesser, A. (1988). Toward a self-evaluation model of social behavior. In L. Berkowitz (Ed.),

Advances in experimental social psychology, Vol. 21 (pp. 181–227). New York: Academic Press.

Uleman, J. S. (1989). A framework for thinking intentionally about unintended thoughts. In J. S. Uleman & J. A. Bargh (Eds.), *Unintended thought* (pp. 425–429). New York: Guilford Press.

Weinberger, J., & McClelland D. C. (1990). Cognitive versus traditional motivational models, irreconcilable or complementary? In E. J. Higgins & R. M. Sorrentino (Eds.), *Handbook of motivation and cognition* (pp. 562–597). New York: Guilford Press.

Westen, D. (1990). Psychoanalytic approaches to personality. In L. A. Pervin (Ed.), *Handbook of personality: Theory and research* (pp. 21–65). New York: Guilford Press.

CHAPTER 2

HUMAN AUTONOMY

THE BASIS FOR TRUE SELF-ESTEEM

EDWARD L. DECI AND RICHARD M. RYAN

INTRODUCTION

Over and over, investigators have found self-esteem to be central in a broad network of constructs associated with motivation, performance, and well-being. Esteeming oneself—thinking well of oneself—has often been found to relate to more effective behavior and better adjustment than has low self-regard.

The concept has had great appeal and has been widely studied, in part because it is easy to understand and measure and because its relation to other variables has seemed straightforward: Put quite simply, more is better. Recent research and theory have indicated, however, that the concept is more complex than this. As it turns out, more is not necessarily better. Baumeister, Heatherton, and Tice (1993), for example, reported that high-self-esteem individuals developed egoistic illusions that led them to perform less well than low self-esteem individuals. Furthermore, Kernis, Grannemann, and Barclay (1989) reported that people with unstable high self-esteem were more angry and aggressive than people with low self-esteem.

EDWARD L. DECI AND RICHARD M. RYAN • Department of Psychology, University of Rochester, Rochester, New York 14627.

Efficacy, Agency, and Self-Esteem, edited by Michael H. Kernis. Plenum Press, New York, 1995.

With these and other such findings, it has become increasingly clear that a reconsideration of the concept of self-esteem, using a more refined analysis is essential. Our approach to such an analysis has been to distinguish between contingent self-esteem and true self-esteem basing this distinction on the differentiated analysis of self contained within self-determination theory (Deci & Ryan, 1991).

Contingent self-esteem refers to feelings about oneself that result from—indeed, are dependent on—matching some standard of excellence or living up to some interpersonal or intrapsychic expectations. A man who feels like a good and worthy person (i.e., has high self-esteem) only when he has just accomplished a profitable business transaction would have contingent self-esteem. If he were very successful, frequently negotiating such deals, he would have a continuing high level of self-esteem; yet that high level would be tenuous, always requiring that he continue to pass the tests of life, always requiring that he match some controlling standard.

A high level of contingent self-esteem is thus a kind of aggrandizement of oneself associated with being *ego-involved* in some types of outcomes and dutifully achieving them (Ryan, 1982). Often, contingent self-esteem involves social comparison because, to the extent that one has to live up to externally imposed criteria to feel worthy, one is likely to esteem oneself in accord with how one measures up relative to others. If the basis of a woman's feeling good about herself is financial success, she may always feel wanting until she has matched Ross Perot. And if the basis of a man's feeling good about himself is looking like the media-popularized muscular hunk, he may always feel wanting until he has a body like Arnold Schwarzenegger's. Having such social-comparison demands operative, of course, ensures that contingent self-esteem will be a powerful motivator.

Contingent self-esteem tends to be associated with a kind of narcissism that has one anxiously focused on one's own agenda, whether that agenda is being feminine, famous, fashionable, fabulously wealthy, or far out. To the extent that attaining such a goal determines a person's self-esteem, one can well imagine that the person will use whatever means are available to match the standards, including rationalization, self-deception, and other such defensive processes that have been linked to less positive mental health.

In contrast, *true self-esteem* is more stable, more securely based in a solid sense of self. A woman who is true to herself would have a high level of true self-esteem simply by being who she is. Her self-worth would essentially be a given and would have developed as she acted autonomously within the context of authentic relationships (Ryan, 1993). Her worth would not need to be continually put to the test, so she would not typically be engaged in a process of self-evaluation. The fact of being focused on one's worth—of continually evaluating oneself—implies that one's self-esteem is contingent rather than true.

With a more secure sense of self, and a high level of true self-esteem, the more vacuous or narcissistic goals such as money and fame would be less important and would not be the basis for one's feelings of self-worth. Similarly, the insidious and internalized requirements of fulfilling parents' expectations would not be the basis of one's feelings of self-worth. Instead, one's worth would be an integrated aspect of one's self and would be reflected in agency, proactivity, and vitality (Ryan & Frederick, 1994).

People with high true self-esteem, of course, would have goals and aspirations, and they would attempt to accomplish those outcomes by devoting their personal resources to them, often wholeheartedly. And their emotions would surely be affected by the outcomes of their efforts. They would probably feel pleased or excited when they succeed and disappointed when they fail. But their feelings of worth as people would not fluctuate as a function of those accomplishments, so they would not feel aggrandized and superior when they succeed or depressed and worthless then they fail.

When asked to complete a self-esteem scale, people with high true self-esteem would, of course, come out high, even though they do not typically engage in such self-evaluations. And herein lies a problem for self-esteem research, because people with contingent self-esteem, who have been succeeding, would also come out high, yet the nature of the self-regard held by these two types of individuals would be quite different.

The distinction between true self-esteem and contingent self-esteem is based on the distinction between an integrated or true self and an unintegrated or false self as outlined in self-determination theory (Deci & Ryan, 1991; Ryan, 1993). It suggests, as will be elaborated later, that an integrated sense of self develops as one acts agentically within a context that allows satisfaction of the three fundamental psychological needs for autonomy, competence, and relatedness (e.g., Ryan, 1993). True self develops as one acts volitionally (i.e., autonomously), experiences an inner sense of efficacy (i.e., competence), and is loved (i.e., feels related to) for who one is rather than for matching some external standard.

The problem is that all too often people in one's socializing environment make their love or esteem contingent on living up to some standards, so one may feel forced to give up autonomy and a true sense of self, while taking on a socially implanted self. As that happens, one's sense of self-worth becomes contingent on continuing to live up to those implanted standards.

The point, then, is that people develop more of a true self and have truer self-esteem when they are supported and loved as they behave agentically from their own perspective, whereas they develop more of a false self and have more contingent self-esteem when they are pressured to meet others' standards and are loved only for matching those standards. In turn, true self-esteem is the basis for further agentic activity, whereas contingent self-esteem is the basis for being controlled by the demands placed on people by the social world (or by internalized versions of those demands).

Because being autonomous and having a more integrated sense of self have been associated with more positive mental health, whereas being controlled and having a less integrated sense of self have been associated with more negative mental health (e.g., Kasser & Ryan, in press; Ryan, Rigby, & King, 1993), one can begin to understand why high self-esteem does not always have positive consequences. Self-esteem that is true would be expected to have positive consequences, whereas self-esteem that is contingent would be expected to have less positive, and at times negative, consequences.

A DIFFERENTIATED VIEW OF SELF

At the heart of self-determination theory is the concept of self, which is based in the active, integrative processes of the organism that underlie human development and have also been referred to as the "organization principle" (Piaget, 1971), the "actualizing tendency" (Rogers, 1951), and the "synthetic function of the ego" (Freud, 1923/1962). As development proceeds, through the organismic integration process, one's intrinsic or core self is elaborated and refined, and this ever-changing set of integrated processes and structures is referred to as "self" (i.e., as true self or integrated self). In other words, self develops through the ongoing, synthetic resolution of the interaction between the active, integrative organism and the challenges of the environment, and only those psychic elements that have been integrated are considered part of the self.

Development of self, through organismic integration, is theorized to be a motivated process. One integrates intrapsychic and interpersonal material out of the needs to be autonomous, competent, and related. Because integration operates in the service of these needs, social contexts that permit their satisfaction are theorized to facilitate the development of self and a feeling of true self-worth, whereas social contexts that do not are expected to impair the development of self and prompt the internalization of a contingent sense of one's worth.

Behavior that emanates from one's integrated sense of self is said to be "autonomous" or "self-determined"; it has what deCharms (1968) referred to as an "internal perceived locus of causality." As one behaves autonomously, acting with an internal perceived locus of causality, the behavior promotes further development of self and a stronger sense of true self-worth. Thus, being autonomous is both an input to and a manifestation of the development of an integrated self and true self-esteem. In our theory, the term *human agency* refers to those motivated behaviors that emanate from one's integrated self. To be agentic is thus to be self-determined.

Our view of self as being based in organismic integration has a very important set of corollaries that have been implicit in our discussion thus far. Specifically, it means that (1) not all intrapsychic processes are part of the self, (2) not all motivated behaviors are autonomous, and (3) not all positive self-evaluations are healthy. Because we restrict the term *self* (i.e., true or integrated self) to those processes and structures that have been integrated with one's intrinsic self or phenomenal core, there are many elements of a person's psychic makeup that do not constitute self but rather are separate from and may conflict with one's self. Because we restrict the term *self-determined* to behaviors that emanate from one's true self (and have an internal perceived locus of causality), there are many intentional behaviors regulated by processes within the person that are not truly agentic or autonomous but rather are pressured or controlled (and have an external perceived locus of causality). And because we restrict the term *true self-esteem* to feelings associated with the autonomous or integrated aspects of oneself, there are many reports of high self-esteem that are not well-grounded and stable but rather are tenuous and linked to performing up to some demands or controls.

The development of self entails both the maintenance and the elaboration of one's intrinsic self—of one's curiosity, proactivity, integrative tendency, and inherent interests—and the integration of other intrapsychic or interpersonal material with that which is intrinsic. Acting from one's self, which describes being autonomous, can thus be either intrinsically motivated or regulated by integrated processes.

To summarize, motivated behavior varies along a continuum describing the degree to which it is autonomous and emanates from the self rather than being controlled and pressured by some nonintegrated force. True self-esteem is associated with acting agentically from one's integrated self, whereas contingent self-esteem is associated with being controlled and needing to live up to some socially imposed standards.

In order to explore empirically the functioning of self and self-determination, we have anchored these concepts in motivational and regulatory processes. In other words, we have explicated the types of motivational or regulatory processes that are theorized to be associated with self and self-determination, and those that are not, and we have explored the antecedents, correlates, and consequences of those different types of motivational or regulatory processes, as a way of providing empirical grounding for our theory of self. We therefore turn to a more thorough consideration of the regulatory bases of behavior, describing research that is pertinent to true vs. contingent self-esteem.

THE REGULATION OF BEHAVIOR

The concept of *intention* or purpose is key to understanding the regulation of behavior (e.g., Heider, 1958; Lewin, 1951). People are said to be motivated to the extent that they intend to accomplish something—that is, to the extent that they have a purpose. Motivated behaviors are mediated by intentions.

Some actions—actions such as defensively withdrawing from others—may *not* be experienced as intentional, and if they are not, they would not properly be termed motivated. In our theory, such an action is referred to as *amotivated,* and it is theoretically related to what Heider (1958) has called "impersonal causation," Rotter (1966) has designated an "external locus of control," Bandura (1977) has labeled "low self-efficacy," and Seligman (1975) has termed "learned helplessness." There is ample evidence that amotivation and impersonal causation are associated with low self-esteem, and self-determination theory, like each of the theories just mentioned, would predict just that.

Self-determination theory differs from these other theories, however, by distinguishing types of motivated behavior and thus being able to differentiate the concept of self-esteem. By conceptualizing motivated behavior as falling along the autonomous–controlled continuum, the theory can explain why the qualities of motivated actions vary and people have secure vs. tenuous self-esteem.

Both autonomous and controlled behaviors are intentional, but only autonomous actions emanate from one's true sense of self. An example of intentional activity that is self-determined would be a developer who acquires a building with a nonpressured sense of choice, believing he can save it from the wrecker's ball and preserve a small piece of history. In contrast, an example of intentional activity that is coerced or controlled would be a real estate developer who acquires yet another building because he feels internal pressure to one-up a primary rival. In the first example, the developer would be behaving with a sense of freedom and choice, in accord with an integrated value and based on a nonpressured consideration of consequences. His behavior would be autonomous; it would emanate from an integrated sense of self. In the second example, however, the developer would be responding to the intense press for acclaim and aggrandizement; he would be ego-involved in acquiring the building, and his self-esteem would no doubt be contingent on his success.

As Ryan (1982) demonstrated, being motivated by ego involvements does not represent self-determination, for it undermines intrinsic motivation, which is the prototype of self-determination. Rather, ego involvement is an instance of being controlled by a nonintegrated internal force. Succeeding at an activity in which one is ego-involved bolsters self-esteem, but of course it would be contingent self-esteem.

The distinction between autonomous and controlled activity is important when considering the concept of human agency. To be truly agentic means to be autonomous; it means acting from one's integrated self. Yet theorists who have not made this critical distinction treat all intentional behavior as though it were agentic. For example, Bandura (1989), in his self-efficacy theory, asserted that the critical antecedents of intentional behavior are contingency beliefs and efficacy beliefs and that when one has such beliefs, one will be agentic. The problem with this view, of course, is that people can be highly self-efficacious, believing they can achieve whatever outcomes they desire, but at the same time be controlled by (i.e., ego-involved in) those outcomes. Using deCharms's terminology, such people would be self-efficacious "pawns," but they would not in a true sense be agentic. They would likely have high self-esteem, but it would be contingent. Human agency and true self-esteem require autonomy; they require that one be "an origin not a pawn" (deCharms, 1968). Being competent is simply not sufficient for human agency or true self-esteem (e.g., Koestner & McClelland, 1990).

INTRINSIC AND EXTRINSIC MOTIVATION

The prototype of autonomous behavior—of behavior emanating from one's self—is intrinsically motivated. It is performed out of interest and requires no "separable" consequence, no external or intrapsychic prods, promises, or threats (Deci, 1975). Csikszentmihalyi (1975) used the term "autotelic" to describe this behavior, for which the only necessary reward is the spontaneous experience of interest and enjoyment. Intrinsic motivation entails curiosity, exploration, spontaneity, and interest in one's surroundings. It is readily evident in mastery strivings (White, 1959) and assimilation (Piaget, 1971).

Intrinsically motivated behaviors are experienced as wholly volitional, as representative of and emanating from one's integrated sense of self. They are the behaviors that people perform interestedly when they are free from demands, constraints, or homeostatic urgencies.

In contrast, extrinsically motivated behaviors are performed instrumentally to attain some separable consequence. Initially, extrinsically motivated behaviors would not occur spontaneously and would therefore have to be prompted by a request or by some promised consequence. Such behaviors, because they are dependent on a separable consequence, are typically less autonomous.

In our conceptualization, however, extrinsically motivated behaviors can vary in the extent to which they are autonomous vs. controlled. We employ a developmental analysis—using the concept of organismic integration—to elaborate different types of extrinsic motivation that vary in their degree of self-determination (Deci & Ryan, 1985; Ryan, Connell, & Deci, 1985). Because intrinsically motivated behaviors are by definition self-determined, their behavioral and experiential qualities serve as a gauge against which extrinsically motivated behaviors can be compared to index their degree of self-determination.

Extrinsically motivated behaviors can become self-determined through the natural developmental tendencies to *internalize* and *integrate* meaningful aspects of one's social context. Internalization entails transforming external regulatory processes into internal regulatory processes (Meissner, 1981; Schafer, 1968), and integration is the means through which these values and regulations become integrated with one's self (Deci & Ryan, 1991).

According to self-determination theory, people tend naturally to internalize the regulation of socially sanctioned activities to feel related to others and efficacious within their social world, and they tend to integrate those regulatory processes to maximize their experience of autonomy or self-determination. Put differently, individuals seek to feel competent, related to others, and autonomous in their actions by taking in and integrating the regulation of those behaviors that were initially externally prompted within a social milieu (Deci & Ryan, 1985, 1991). However, these processes may function more or less effectively, in part as a function of the social context, resulting in more vs. less integration of regulations and thus more vs. less self-determination of actions. When a value or regulatory process has been taken in but not accepted as one's own, we say it has been "introjected."

EXTRINSIC MOTIVATION: A DIFFERENTIATED VIEW

There are four types of extrinsic regulation, resulting from different degrees of internalization and integration.

External regulation describes behaviors that have not been internalized but instead are prompted and sustained by contingencies overtly external to the individual. Examples would be engaging in a behavior explicitly to attain a reward or avoid a punishment. Externally regulated behaviors are intentional, but they are dependent on external contingencies and are thus described as being controlled by those contingencies rather than being autonomous or fully agentic.

Introjected regulation refers to behaviors that are motivated by internal prods and pressures, resulting from regulatory processes having been introjected but not integrated. This type of regulation is operative when one behaves because one thinks one *should* or because one would feel guilty if one did not. When a regulation has been introjected, it is internal to the person in the sense that it no longer requires overtly external prompts, but it is still external to the person's sense of self. Introjected regulation describes a type of internal motivation in which actions are controlled or coerced by internal standards and contingent self-esteem. It is thus not autonomous and is said to have a relatively external perceived locus of causality (deCharms, 1968; Ryan & Connell, 1989).

The strength of introjected regulations derives from one's feelings of worth being dependent on performing as the introjects demand. When people behave because their "self-esteem" is contingent, they feel pressured or coerced to behave, and they are said to be ego-involved.

Identified regulation occurs when a behavior is accepted as personally important or valuable. By identifying with the underlying value of an activity and thus having begun to incorporate it into one's sense of self, the person is moving toward being self-determined for an extrinsic or instrumental activity.

Integrated regulation is the most autonomous form of extrinsic motivation and results from the integration of identified values and regulations into one's coherent sense of self. When a person has fully integrated an extrinsic regulatory process, he or she will be self-determined with respect to that behavior. As an example, consider a professional football player who had initially identified with being both a rugged athlete and a composer of romantic music. He would no doubt have experienced tension between these identifications, but if he were to make the necessary changes—for example, giving up his "tough-guy" image and setting aside enough of his time to immerse himself in music—he could integrate the two values with each other and with other aspects of the self. A creative synthesis would occur, and the two identifications would no longer be cause for psychological stress. In such a case, the musical athlete would have elaborated his true sense of self, and his self-esteem would no longer be contingent on matching standards in either domain.

According to self-determination theory, integrated extrinsic regulation, together with intrinsic motivation, represent the bases for self-determined functioning, which in its fullest sense is characterized by total involvement of the self. Thus, being intrinsically motivated and integrated would be accompanied by the experience of true self-esteem.

Various questionnaires have been developed to assess the strength of each of these types of regulation. For example, Ryan and Connell (1989) developed one for the academic domain that they used in a study of children of late-elementary-school age. They also collected other data from the children and their parents. Analyses revealed that the children's introjected (i.e., relatively controlled) regulatory style and their identified (i.e., relatively autonomous) regulatory style were correlated equally with parents' reports of how motivated their children were and with the children's self-reports of how hard they tried. However, introjected regulation was positively correlated with anxiety about school and self-blaming in response to failure, whereas identified regulation was positively correlated with enjoyment of school and with proactive responses to failure. This finding suggests, then, that although people can be highly internally motivated by either introjects or identifications, there are quite different affective accompaniments of each. Motivation based in introjects is not self-determined, for although it is powerful, it does not have a solid foundation in the self. Thus, as the data showed, to the extent that people were introjected, they tended to be anxious and to feel worthless when they failed. When they succeed, they would no doubt experience heightened self-esteem, but it would not be the type of self-esteem that is central to stable, healthy adjustment. It would not be true self-esteem.

In contrast, when people have identified with a value or regulation and thus have begun to integrate it, they are more autonomous, more self-assured, more able to feel a sense of enjoyment without having their feelings of self-worth contingent on outcomes. When they fail, they simply get on with figuring out how to do better next time. Their sense of themselves is more solid and true.

ASPIRATIONS, AUTONOMY, AND WELL-BEING

With a secure sense of self, people would be expected to have less narcissistic goals, to behave more autonomously, and to display more positive mental health. Several recent studies have confirmed this expectation. These studies have employed two strategies. Some have compared the correlates of intrinsic aspirations vs. extrinsic aspirations; others have compared the correlates of people's strivings that are more autonomous vs. more controlled.

In two recent sets of studies, Kasser and Ryan (1993, in press) assessed the aspirations of over 500 subjects from three groups of college students, one group of low self-esteem 18-year-olds, and one group of mixed self-esteem adults. Taken together, the studies compared three types of intrinsic aspirations with three types of extrinsic ones. Personal growth, meaningful relationships, and community contributions were considered intrinsic because achieving these aspirations tends to be a reward in its own right and because these aspirations are theoretically congruent with intrinsic needs, growth tendencies, and a secure sense of self. In contrast, financial success, fame, and physical attractiveness were considered extrinsic aspirations, for they are primarily instrumental to other rewards rather than being rewards in their own right. Money brings all manner of goods and services, as well as power; fame brings adulation and privilege; attractiveness brings attention and approval. These goals not only are extrinsic, but also tend to be very controlling, and they relate to the desires of a looking-glass self (Cooley, 1902). They are typical bases of self-evaluation that people adopt from the social order; they are the external criteria for feeling worthy, and thus they are the assets people flaunt to feel better than others. Through attaining these goals, people can bolster their feelings of worth, piling affirmation on an insecure foundation.

Kasser and Ryan found that the relative importance people placed on each of the three *intrinsic* aspirations was positively correlated with a variety of indicators of mental health and well-being, including self-actualization (Jones & Crandall, 1986), vitality (Ryan & Frederick, 1994), global social functioning (Shaffer et al., 1983), and social productivity (Ikle, Lipp, Butters, & Ciarlo, 1983), and it was negatively correlated with indicators of ill-being, including anxiety (Spielberger, Gorsuch, & Lushene, 1970), depression (Radloff, 1977), physical symptoms (Derogatis, Lipman, Rickels, Uhlenhuth, & Covi, 1974), and conduct disorders (Herjanic & Reich, 1982). In contrast to these results, the relative importance people placed on each of the three *extrinsic* aspirations—money, fame, and attractiveness—was negatively correlated with the indicators of well-being and positively correlated with the indicators of ill-being. It therefore seems that having one's sense of self associated with long-term goals that are more intrinsic has clear mental health advantages, relative to goals that are extrinsic to the person and mediated by their visibility to others.

It is worth noting that Kasser and Ryan (1993, in press) also assessed subjects' beliefs about the likelihood of being able to attain the goals, and they found that feeling more able to attain the extrinsic goals was also associated with indicators of poor mental health, whereas feeling more able to attain the intrinsic goals was associated with indicators of good mental health. This underscores the point that we made earlier, namely, that just having high efficacy expectations with regard to goals is not enough to ensure positive well-being and true self-esteem; those efficacy expectations must be associated with greater autonomy (in this case, intrinsic aspirations) for the expectations to have clear benefits.

In another set of studies, Sheldon and Kasser (in press) had subjects report their strivings using a method developed by Emmons (1986). They also asked the subjects to rate the reasons they strive for those goals, using the type of measure developed by Ryan and Connell (1989) to assess the degree of autonomy. In the Sheldon and Kasser studies, subjects' autonomous vs. controlled reasons for pursuing their goals were related to the well-being variables of self-actualization, vitality, empathy (Davis, 1980), and openness to experience (Costa & McCrae, 1985). Each measure of well-being was significantly correlated with the relative autonomy of one's strivings, and being more autonomous in one's strivings was also correlated with life satisfaction and self-theory coherence (Harter & Monsour, 1992).

These various studies suggest that aspirations and strivings that are theoretically linked to contingent self-esteem are associated with poorer mental health than those that are theoretically linked to true self-esteem. Recognizing the difference between the type of self-esteem that is tenuously contingent on outcomes and the type that is securely based in being true to oneself can therefore provide the basis for an account of why high self-esteem does not always have positive consequences.

SELF-DETERMINATION AND THE SOCIAL CONTEXT

Considerable research has focused on social-contextual conditions that enhance vs. diminish self-determination and the development of self. Because true self-esteem is theorized to be associated with behaving autonomously, as an expression of one's self, we briefly review research exploring the contextual conditions that enhance vs. undermine the two types of autonomous behavior, namely, intrinsic and integrated.

In making predictions about and interpreting the results of the research, we considered the theoretical relation of the contextual conditions to the three fundamental psychological needs—the needs for competence, autonomy, and relatedness (Deci & Ryan, 1985; Ryan, 1993). Social conditions that afford opportunities to satisfy these three needs are predicted to facilitate intrinsic motivation, the integration of extrinsic motivation, and thus a true sense of self-esteem. In contrast, social conditions that obstruct satisfaction of these needs—for example, conditions in which love is given contingently, so one must give up autonomy to obtain love—are expected to impair intrinsic motivation and interrupt integration of extrinsic motivation, thus resulting in either contingent or low self-esteem.

The earliest studies were laboratory experiments that manipulated specific events (e.g., Deci, 1971). With a few limiting conditions, the experiments showed that material rewards (Deci, 1971, 1972), threats of punishment (Deci & Cascio, 1972), evaluations (Smith, 1974), deadlines (Amabile, DeJong, & Lepper, 1976), imposed goals (Mossholder, 1980), and good-player awards (Lepper, Greene, & Nisbett, 1973) all tended to be controlling (i.e., to be experienced as pressure to perform in specific ways), and thus they undermined intrinsic motivation. On the other hand, providing choice (Zuckerman, Porac, Lathin, Smith, & Deci, 1978) and acknowledging feelings (Koestner, Ryan, Bernieri, & Holt, 1984) tended to be experienced as autonomy-supportive (i.e., as encouragement for self-initiation and choice), and thus they maintained or enhanced intrinsic motivation.

Subsequent experimental work (i.e., Harackiewicz, 1979; Ryan, 1982) refined these early results, indicating that although, on average, certain events are controlling and others autonomy-supportive, the style and language with which the events are administered significantly influence their effects. For example, Ryan, Mims, and Koestner (1983) found that although performance-contingent rewards tend to be experienced as controlling, they can have positive effects if administered in a noncontrolling, autonomy-supportive way.

Laboratory studies exploring the conditions that promote competence found that optimal challenge (Danner & Lonky, 1981) and positive feedback (Deci, 1971) enhanced intrinsic motivation, although these effects require that the interpersonal context (i.e., the style and locution of administration) be autonomy-supportive rather than controlling (Fisher, 1978; Ryan, 1982). To be self-determined and to develop true self-esteem, people need to feel that their successes are truly their own—they must feel autonomous rather than controlled. Thus, positive feedback that is controlling (e.g., praising people for "doing as they should") can rob them of the opportunity to feel good about their accomplishments because it places the causes of their successful actions in sources external to the self.

This and related research thus provides further evidence that although personal control over outcomes (i.e., self-efficacy) is important, it is not sufficient for intrinsic motivation; the feelings of competence must be accompanied by perceived autonomy for people to be intrinsically motivated (Deci & Ryan, 1991; Ryan, 1993). A person can develop a strong sense of contingent self-esteem by consistently being efficacious in the accomplishment of introjected goals, but if the behavior is not self-determined, it will not enhance intrinsic motivation or promote true self-esteem.

Several field studies have also explored autonomy-supportive vs. controlling interpersonal climates. Deci, Schwartz, Sheinman, and Ryan (1981) developed a measure of autonomy support within the classroom that assesses the degree to which teachers attempt to motivate learning in a controlling vs. an autonomy-supportive manner. These researchers, as well as Ryan and Grolnick (1986), found that in autonomy-supportive classrooms, where teachers tended to consider the students' frame of reference, students displayed greater curiosity and more independent mastery attempts than students in more controlling classrooms. Importantly, they also developed higher self-esteem in the autonomy-supportive classrooms.

The finding that autonomy support plays an important role in facilitating self-determination and personal satisfaction is not limited to the classroom, however. Grolnick and Ryan (1989), using an interview procedure, found that parental autonomy support (vs. control) affected their children's degree of intrinsic motivation for learning, and Kasser, Ryan, Zax, and Sameroff (in press) found that involved, autonomy-supportive parents tended to have children who developed intrinsic aspirations, whereas cold and controlling parents had children who placed more value on extrinsic aspirations.

As mentioned, not only are individuals naturally intrinsically motivated, but also they have an innate tendency to internalize the regulation of extrinsically motivated behaviors that are useful for effective functioning in the social world. Internalization allows people to feel related to others and to feel competent in dealing within the social matrix. Internalization can, however, take the form of mere introjection or, alternatively, of greater integration. Although people may feel both related and competent when their behavior is regulated by introjects, they will feel autonomous only when the regulation is self-determined—that is, only when internalized regulatory processes have been fully integrated.

Our research has shown that internalization and integration are facilitated by the autonomy support and interpersonal involvement of significant adults. For example, Grolnick and Ryan (1989) found that parental autonomy support and involvement influenced children's being autonomously self-regulating in doing their schoolwork. When parents were more autonomy-supportive and involved, the students displayed greater internalized motivation and were rated by teachers as being more competent and better adjusted.

Deci, Eghrari, Patrick, and Leone (1994) reported that supporting self-determination—by providing a meaningful rationale, acknowledgment of the person's feelings, and an interpersonal style that emphasized choice rather than control—led to greater internalization than being non-supportive of self-determination. This study, which was a laboratory experiment, thus complements the Grolnick and Ryan (1989) field study. However, the experiment of Deci et al. (1994) also showed that internalization that had occurred in the conditions that supported self-determination was integrated, as reflected by positive correlations between the amount of time subjects subsequently spent with the target activity and self-reports of perceived choice, personal importance of the activity, and enjoyment, whereas internalization that had occurred in the more controlling conditions was introjected, as reflected by negative correlations between the amount of time subjects subsequently spent with the target activity and the same three affective self-report variables. In other words, people who internalized regulations in autonomy-supportive contexts engaged in the stipulated activity while feeling free and enjoying the activity. However, people who internalized regulations in controlling contexts engaged in the activity subsequently despite not feeling free and not enjoying it. They engaged in the activity because they felt they had to, presumably because their feelings of self-worth were contingent on doing so.

To summarize, the data indicate that socializing agents who are controlling (i.e., who pressure people to perform up to standards) promote introjection, whereas those who are autonomy-supportive (i.e., who take the individuals' perspectives, support self-initiation, and offer choice) promote integration. When the context is pressuring, individuals take in those pressures and controls and use them on themselves. The introjected demands become standards that the people use to evaluate themselves— much like others in the social context had initially done to them. Simply stated, introjects provide the rules for achieving contingent, rather than true, self-esteem.

CONCLUSIONS

Self-esteem, which has been widely studied, has generally been interpreted as comprising any positive evaluations individuals have about themselves. As well, it has generally been expected to have positive correlates. Recent work, however, has indicated that its correlates are not always positive, thus highlighting the importance of differentiating the concepts of true self-esteem vs. contingent self-esteem. We have done that, doing so on the basis of the differentiated conception of self (viz., integrated or true self vs. introjected or false self) contained within self-determination theory.

True self, herein defined, refers only to those regulatory processes and other psychic elements that are either intrinsic or have been integrated with one's intrinsic or core self. When one feels esteem for those aspects of oneself, one experiences true self-esteem, and this type of self-esteem will be enhanced only when one's actions are self-determined—that is, only when one acts with an internal perceived locus of causality.

In contrast, regulatory processes that have merely been introjected, that have been taken in but not integrated with one's intrinsic or core self, underlie controlled rather than self-determined actions, and they gain their potency from one's unstable sense of self. With the aim of shoring up one's ego, one may persist at an activity in a pressured way, acting with an external perceived locus of causality. Although successful completion of such activities will lead to positive feelings about oneself, those feelings represent contingent rather than true self-esteem.

Social contexts in which socializing agents are genuinely related to and autonomy-supportive of the target individual facilitate the development of true self-esteem. Being related to and autonomy-supportive of another—of one's child or student, for example—means valuing the other for who he or she is and taking that other's frame of reference. It means accepting the other's point of view by acknowledging feelings and providing choice. In essence, it means beginning by accepting and relating to the self of the other. It is precisely the acceptance of *self*—first by others and then by oneself—that supports the development and maintenance of true self-esteem. By acting from one's true self, by acting from one's innate potentials and phenomenal core, one will feel a sense of personal integrity and agency. One will experience true self-esteem.

ACKNOWLEDGMENT. Preparation of this chapter was facilitated by research grant HD19914 from the National Institute of Child Health and Human Development.

REFERENCES

Amabile, T. M., DeJong, W., & Lepper, M. R. (1976). Effects of externally imposed deadlines on subsequent intrinsic motivation. *Journal of Personality and Social Psychology, 34,* 92–98.
Bandura, A. (1977). Self-efficacy: Toward a unifying theory of behavioral change. *Psychological Review, 84,* 191–215.
Bandura, A. (1989). Self-regulation of motivation and action through internal standards and goal systems. In L. Pervin (Ed.), *Goal concepts in personality and social psychology.* Hillsdale, NJ: Erlbaum Associates.
Baumeister, R. F., Heatherton, T. F., & Tice, D. M. (1993). When ego threats lead to self-

regulation failure: Negative consequences of high self-esteem. *Journal of Personality and Social Psychology, 64,* 141–156.

Cooley, C. (1902). *Human nature and the social order.* New York: Scribner.

Costa, P. T., Jr., & McCrae, R. R. (1985) *The NEO Personality Inventory manual.* Odessa, FL: Psychological Assessment Resources.

Csikszentmihalyi, M. (1975). *Beyond boredom and anxiety.* San Francisco: Jossey-Bass.

Danner, F. W. & Lonky, E. (1981). A cognitive–developmental approach to the effects of rewards on intrinsic motivation. *Child Development, 52,* 1043–1052.

Davis, M. H. (1980). A multidimensional approach to individual differences in empathy. *JSAS Catalog of Selected Documents in Psychology, 10,* 85.

deCharms, R. (1968) *Personal causation: The internal affective determinants of behavior.* New York: Academic Press.

Deci, E. L. (1971). Effects of externally mediated rewards on intrinsic motivation. *Journal of Personality and Social Psychology, 18,* 105–115.

Deci, E. L. (1972). Intrinsic motivation, extrinsic reinforcement, and inequity. *Journal of Personality and Social Psychology, 22,* 113–120.

Deci, E. L. (1975). *Intrinsic motivation.* New York: Plenum Press.

Deci, E. L. & Cascio, W. F. (1972). Changes in intrinsic motivation as a function of negative feedback and threats. Paper presented at the meeting of the Eastern Psychological Association, Boston, April 1972.

Deci, E. L., & Ryan, R. M. (1985). Intrinsic motivation and self-determination in human behavior. New York: Plenum Press.

Deci, E. L., & Ryan, R. M. (1991). A motivational approach to self: Integration in personality. In R. Dienstbier (Ed.), *Nebraska symposium on motivation,* Vol. 38, *Perspectives on motivation* (pp. 237–288). Lincoln: University of Nebraska Press.

Deci, E. L., Schwartz, A. J. , Sheinman, L., & Ryan, R. M. (1981). An instrument to assess adults' orientations toward control versus autonomy with children: Reflections on intrinsic motivation and perceived competence. *Journal of Educational Psychology, 73,* 642–650.

Deci, E. L., Eghrari, H., Patrick, B. C., & Leone, D. R. (1994). Facilitating internalization: The self-determination theory perspective. *Journal of Personality, 62,* 119–142.

Derogatis, L. R., Lipman, R. S., Rickels, K., Uhlenhuth, E. H., & Covi, L. (1974). The Hopkins Symptom Checklist (HSCL): A self report symptom inventory. *Behavioral Science, 19,* 1–15.

Emmons, R. A. (1986). Personal strivings: An approach to personality and subjective well-being. *Journal of Personality and Social Psychology, 51,* 1058–1068.

Fisher, C. D. (1978). The effects of personal control, competence, and extrinsic reward systems on intrinsic motivation. *Organizational Behavior and Human Performance, 21,* 273–288.

Freud, S. (1923/1962). *The ego and the id.* New York: Norton (original work published in 1923).

Grolnick, W. S., & Ryan, R. M. (1989). Parent styles associated with children's self-regulation and competence in school. *Journal of Educational Psychology, 81,* 143–154.

Harackiewicz, J. (1979). The effects of reward contingency and performance feedback on intrinsic motivation. *Journal of Personality and Social Psychology, 37,* 1352–1363.

Harter, S., & Monsour, A. (1992). Developmental analysis of conflict caused by opposing attributes in the adolescent self-portrait. *Developmental Psychology, 28,* 251–260.

Heider, F. (1958). *The psychology of interpersonal relations.* New York: John Wiley.

Herjanic, B., & Reich, W. (1982). Development of a structured psychiatric interview for children: Agreement between child and parent on individual symptoms. *Journal of Abnormal Child Psychology, 10,* 307–324.

Ikle, D. N., Lipp, D. O., Butters, E. A., & Ciarlo, J. (1983). *Development and validation of the adolescent community mental health questionnaire.* Denver: Mental Systems Evaluation Project.

Jones, A., & Crandall, R. (1986). Validation of a short index of self-actualization. *Personality and Social Psychology Bulletin, 12,* 63–73.

Kasser, T., & Ryan, R. M. (1993). A dark side of the American dream: Correlates of financial success as a central life aspiration. *Journal of Personality and Social Psychology, 65,* 410–422.

Kasser, T., & Ryan, R. M. (in press). Further examining the American dream: Differential correlates of intrinsic and extrinsic goals. *Personality and Social Psychology Bulletin.*

Kasser, T., Ryan, R. M., Zax, M., & Sameroff, A. J. (in press). The relation of maternal and social environments to late adolescents' materialistic and prosocial aspirations. *Developmental Psychology.*

Kernis, M. H., Grannemann, B. D., & Barclay, L. C. (1989). Stability and level of self-esteem as predictors of anger arousal and hostility. *Journal of Personality and Social Psychology, 56,* 1013–1022.

Koestner, R., & McClelland, D. C. (1990). Perspectives on competence motivation. In L. A. Pervin (Ed.), *Handbook of personality: Theory and research* (pp. 527–548). New York: Guilford Press.

Koestner, R., Ryan, R. M., Bernieri, F., & Holt, K. (1984). Setting limits on children's behavior: The differential effects of controlling versus informational styles on intrinsic motivation and creativity. *Journal of Personality, 52,* 233–248

Lepper, M. R., Greene, D., & Nisbett, R. E. (1973). Undermining children's intrinsic interest with extrinsic rewards: A test of the "overjustification" hypothesis. *Journal of Personality and Social Psychology, 28,* 129–137.

Lewin, K. (1951). Intention, will, and need. In D. Rapaport (Ed.), *Organization and pathology of thought* (pp. 95–153). New York: Columbia University Press.

Meissner, W. W. (1981). *Internalization in psychoanalysis.* New York: International Universities Press.

Mossholder, K. W. (1980). Effects of externally mediated goal setting on intrinsic motivation: A laboratory experiment. *Journal of Applied Psychology, 65,* 202–210.

Piaget, J. (1971). *Biology and knowledge.* Chicago: University of Chicago Press.

Radloff, L. (1977). The CES-D scale: A self-report depression scale for research in the general population. *Applied Psychological Measurement, 1,* 385–401.

Rogers, C. (1951). *Client centered therapy.* Boston: Houghton-Mifflin.

Rotter, J. B. (1966). Generalized expectancies for internal versus external control of reinforcement. *Psychological Monographs, 80* [1 (entire No. 609)], 1–28.

Ryan, R. M. (1982). Control and information in the intrapersonal sphere: An extension of cognitive evaluation theory. *Journal of Personality and Social Psychology, 43,* 450–461.

Ryan, R. M. (1993). Agency and organization: Intrinsic motivation, autonomy and the self in psychological development. In J. Jacobs (Ed.), *Nebraska symposium on motivation: Developmental perspectives on motivation,* Vol. 40 (pp. 1–56). Lincoln: University of Nebraska Press.

Ryan, R. M., & Connell, J. P. (1989). Perceived locus of causality and internalization: Examining reasons for acting in two domains. *Journal of Personality and Social Psychology, 57,* 749–761.

Ryan, R. M., & Frederick, C. M. (1994). *A theory and measure of vitality.* Unpublished manuscript. Rochester, NY: University of Rochester.

Ryan, R. M., & Grolnick, W. S. (1986). Origins and pawns in the classroom: Self-report and projective assessments of individual differences in children's perceptions. *Journal of Personality and Social Psychology, 50,* 550–558.

Ryan, R. M., Mims, V., & Koestner, R. (1983). Relation of reward contingency and interpersonal context to intrinsic motivation: A review and test using cognitive evaluation theory. *Journal of Personality and Social Psychology, 45,* 736–750.

Ryan, R. M., Connell, J. P., & Deci, E. L. (1985) A motivational analysis of self-determination and self-regulation in education. In C. Ames & R. E. Ames (Eds.), *Research on motivation in education: The classroom milieu* (pp. 13–51). New York: Academic Press.

Ryan, R. M., Rigby, S., & King, K. (1993). Two types of religious internalization and their relations to religious orientations and mental health. *Journal of Personality and Social Psychology, 65,* 586–596.

Schafer, R. (1968). *Aspects of internalization.* New York: International Universities Press.

Seligman, M. E. P. (1975). *Helplessness: On depression, development, and death.* San Francisco: Freeman.

Shaffer, D., Gould, M. S., Brasic, J., Ambrosini, P., Fisher, P., Bird, H., & Aluwahlia, S. (1983). A children's global assessment scale (CGAS). *Archives of General Psychiatry, 40,* 1228–1231.

Sheldon, K. M., & Kasser, T. (in press). Coherence and congruence: Two aspects of personality integration. *Journal of Personality and Social Psychology.*

Smith, W. E. (1974). *The effects of social and monetary rewards on intrinsic motivation.* Unpublished doctoral dissertation. Ithaca, NY: Cornell University.

Spielberger, C. D., Gorsuch, R. L., and Lushene, R. (1970). *Test manual for the state–trait anxiety inventory.* Palo Alto, CA: Consulting Psychologists Press.

White, R. W. (1959). Motivation reconsidered: The concept of competence. *Psychological Review, 66,* 297–333.

Zuckerman, M., Porac, J., Lathin, D., Smith, R., & Deci, E. L. (1978). On the importance of self-determination for intrinsically motivated behavior. *Personality and Social Psychology Bulletin, 4,* 443–446.

CHAPTER 3

NOT ALL HIGH (OR LOW) SELF-ESTEEM PEOPLE ARE THE SAME

THEORY AND RESEARCH ON STABILITY OF SELF-ESTEEM

KEEGAN D. GREENIER, MICHAEL H. KERNIS, AND STEFANIE B. WASCHULL

INTRODUCTION

Self-esteem is a central construct in clinical, developmental, personality, and social psychology, and its role in psychological functioning has been studied for nearly a century. Though there have been periods in which research on self-esteem fell into disfavor (cf. Wylie, 1974), in the last decade there has been a resurgence of interest. This resurgence has yielded significant advances in our understanding, as revealed in the other chapters in this volume, as well as in other recent compilations (e.g., Baumeis-

KEEGAN D. GREENIER • Department of Psychology, University of Georgia, Athens, Georgia 30602. MICHAEL H. KERNIS • Department of Psychology and Institute for Behavioral Research, University of Georgia, Athens, Georgia 30602 STEFANIE B. WASCHULL • Athens Area Technical Institute, Athens, Georgia 30601.

Efficacy, Agency, and Self-Esteem, edited by Michael H. Kernis. Plenum Press, New York, 1995.

ter, 1993a). Nonetheless (and perhaps not surprisingly), significant controversies remain. At their core, these controversies revolve around the essence of what it means to be either high or low in self-esteem. For example, is high self-esteem a precious commodity that must be zealously defended and promoted in order to survive? Or does it reflect a global and secure sense of one's self-worth that is not readily threatened? Likewise, to what extent is low self-esteem indicative of maladjustment? Is it inevitably associated with an absence of self-protective and self-enhancement strategies?

In this chapter, we elaborate on these controversies and show how consideration of individual differences in stability of self-esteem may help to reconcile them. Specifically, we will review evidence indicating that among high self-esteem individuals (high SEs), self-esteem instability reflects fragility in one's positive self-feelings and is associated with heightened tendencies to defend and promote these positive self-feelings. In addition, we will present research showing that among low self-esteem individuals (low SEs), self-esteem instability is importantly related to various indices of psychological difficulties and maladjustment. In so doing, we aim to demonstrate that a full understanding of the role of self-esteem in psychological functioning requires consideration of both its level and its stability. We begin by focusing on the construct of stability of self-esteem and how it is assessed. We then discuss some contemporaneous factors and early childhood experiences that we believe promote unstable self-esteem (for a more extended discussion of these issues, see Kernis & Waschull, in press).

DEFINING SELF-ESTEEM INSTABILITY

Our analysis begins with the assertion that self-esteem instability is a dimension distinct from level of self-esteem along which people can be characterized. Specifically, self-esteem instability refers to the magnitude of short-term fluctuations that people experience in their contextually based feelings of self-worth.[1] In contrast, level of self-esteem refers to people's characteristic or relatively stable baseline feelings of self-worth (see also Rosenberg, 1986: Savin-Williams and Demo, 1983).

It has long been recognized that people possess both characteristic

[1] Actually, self-esteem instability has been defined in terms of both short-term and long-term fluctuations (for a discussion of these two forms, see Kernis & Waschull, in press; Rosenberg, 1986). In our work, we focus on short-term fluctuations, and so we limit our discussion to that type of self-esteem instability.

self-feelings that are relatively stable and transcend specific contexts and more transient self-feelings that are contextually based and subject to momentary fluctuations. James (1890/1950 p. 306), for example, wrote of "a certain average tone of self-feeling which each one of us carries about with him, and which is independent of the objective reasons we may have for satisfaction and discontent" (i.e., self-esteem level). At the same time, he argued that one's feelings of self-worth fluctuate as a function of the ratio of one's successes to one's pretensions (i.e., self-esteem instability) (cf. Harter, 1983). More recently, Rosenberg (e.g., 1986) distinguished "baseline" global self-feelings that are subject to only gradual change over an extended period of time (self-esteem level) from "barometric" self-feelings, which are subject to rapid, moment-to-moment fluctuations (self-esteem instability). Despite this long-time recognition, there have been few attempts, prior to our research, to empirically assess and examine the psychological implications of both components of self-esteem (for one example, see Rosenberg, 1986). We now turn to how we assess self-esteem instability in our research.

ASSESSING SELF-ESTEEM INSTABILITY

To measure individual differences in self-esteem instability, we obtain multiple assessments of individuals' *current* global self-esteem in naturalistic contexts made once or twice daily for periods ranging from 5 days to 1 week. In our research with adults, we use a modified version of the Rosenberg (1965) Self-Esteem Scale in which we direct participants to respond on the basis of how they feel about themselves at the moment that they are completing the form. We then calculate the standard deviation of each individual's total scores across these multiple assessments; the greater the standard deviation, the more unstable is the person's self-esteem.[2]

To assess level of self-esteem in adults, we administer the Rosenberg (1965) Self-Esteem Scale on a separate occasion in a group setting as part of a battery of self-report measures. Although not part of Rosenberg's original instructions, we now direct people to respond on the basis of how they typically, or generally, feel about themselves. In our research with adults to date, the zero-order correlation between stability and level of self-esteem has ranged from 0.15 to the high 0.20s. This means that unstable self-esteem is not the exclusive province of either low or high SEs.

---

[2]We refer to individuals with stable or unstable self-esteem for convenience only. Self-esteem instability is both conceptualized and operationalized as a continuous dimension along which people vary.

Moreover, we have found no evidence that self-esteem instability is most extreme among individuals with moderate self-esteem (compared to those with high or low self-esteem). These two findings are important, because they substantiate the claim that stability and level of self-esteem are distinct dimensions along which individuals can be characterized.

WHY DO PEOPLE VARY IN THE EXTENT TO WHICH THEIR SELF-ESTEEM IS UNSTABLE?

A natural question to ask at this point is why people vary in the extent to which their self-esteem is unstable. Although most of our work has been directed toward documenting the "consequences" of possessing unstable self-esteem, we have recently turned our attention to possible precursors or determinants, or both, of self-esteem instability. In this section, we briefly discuss several contemporaneous factors that may underlie or promote unstable self-esteem. We then turn to the role of early childhood experiences. A more thorough treatment of these issues can be found in Kernis and Waschull (in press).

CONTEMPORANEOUS FACTORS

Ego Involvement

In our view, one important factor that is associated with individual differences in self-esteem instability is the extent to which people are ego-involved in their everyday activities. Specifically, we believe that people whose self-esteem or self-worth is continually "on the line" will be likely to possess unstable self-esteem. For these people, feelings of self-worth are highly dependent on the degree to which they act and are perceived as acting competently, are popular, and so forth. Most of us encounter information pertaining to these aspects of ourselves quite frequently, sometimes many times on any given day. On some occasions, information contained in evaluative events may be quite positive (e.g., task success, a compliment about one's appearance); on other occasions, the information can be quite negative (e.g., a broken date without adequate explanation, task failure, a direct insult during an argument). Moreover, people often engage in self-evaluative processes in the absence of explicit externally provided feedback (e.g. "Do I look as pretty as I did yesterday?").

The hallmark of being ego-involved is the linking of one's feelings of self-worth to these types of specific, frequently experienced, and potentially inconsistent, evaluative information (deCharms, 1968; Ryan, 1982). Consequently, when the contextually based self-esteem of ego-involved individuals is tracked over time, it should reveal considerable fluctuations. Stated differently, the more weight people place on specific evaluative information (either externally provided or internally generated) in determining their feelings of global self-worth, the more likely these feelings are to fluctuate.

Given that individuals' specific self-evaluations are affected by various forms of evaluative information (e.g., Kernis & Johnson, 1990), these considerations suggest the following: (1) The greater the importance that people report placing on specific self-evaluations as determinants of their global feelings of self-worth, the more these feelings should fluctuate; (2) greater fluctuations in specific self-evaluations should relate to more unstable global self-esteem; and (3) the combination of placing high importance on, and experiencing considerable fluctuations in, specific self-evaluations should relate to especially unstable global self-esteem.

These hypotheses were recently tested by Kernis, Cornell, Sun, Berry, and Harlow [1993 (Study 2)]. Participants first indicated the extent to which self-perceived competence, social acceptance, and physical attractiveness were important determinants of their feelings of self-worth. They then indicated their day-to-day self-evaluations along each of these dimensions over a 4-day period. As hypothesized, compared to people with stable self-esteem, people with unstable self-esteem indicated that self-evaluations of competence and physical attractiveness (but, unexpectedly, not social acceptance) were more important determinants of their feelings of self-worth, and they fluctuated more in their day-to-day self-appraisals along each of the three dimensions. Furthermore, for the dimension of competence, the combination of high importance and large fluctuations in day-to-day self-judgments was related to especially unstable self-esteem. The same pattern emerged among people who viewed themselves relatively favorably along each of the other two dimensions. For those individuals with relatively unfavorable self-evaluations, greater fluctuations were related to more unstable self-esteem regardless of the amount of importance placed on them. Thus, compared to individuals with stable self-esteem, individuals with unstable self-esteem are more likely to link their contextually based feelings of global self-worth to how they "measure up" on specific self-evaluative dimensions.

Additional support for our assertion that unstable self-esteem is associated with heightened ego involvement comes from a study by Waschull and Kernis (1993). In this study, the relations between stability and level of self-esteem, intrinsic motivation, and reasons for anger were examined in a sample of 5th-grade children. Here we focus on the findings for reasons for anger.

Level of self-esteem was assessed by the Global Self-worth subscale of the Harter (1985) Perceived Competence Scale for Children. To assess stability of self-esteem, items on this scale were modified so that they reflected momentary self-esteem, and they were administered twice daily for a period of 5 days. In addition, participants read five scenarios of aversive peer-related interpersonal events that each constituted an instrumental thwarting as well as a potential threat to self-esteem. The perpetrator in each scenario was always of the same sex as the respondent. Two reasons for becoming angry were presented under each vignette, in this form: "Some kids would become angry because . . . but other kids would become angry because . . . ." One reason reflected the potential self-esteem-threatening consequences of the behavior (e.g., ". . . because I would *feel* weak"): the other represented the instrumental thwarting consequences of the behavior (e.g., ". . . because I would have to wait longer"). Participants were asked to first decide which child they were more like and then to decide whether the reaction was "sort of true" or "really true" of them (for more details regarding this measure, see Waschull & Kernis, in press).

If self-esteem instability is associated with heightened ego involvement, children with unstable self-esteem should be especially sensitive to the self-esteem-threatening qualities of aversive events. Hence, they should be more likely (than children with stable self-esteem) to indicate that they would become angry because of the self-esteem-threatening aspects of the events depicted in the scenarios. The results strongly supported this prediction. Specifically, both unstable self-esteem and low self-esteem were correlated with children reporting that they would become angry more because of the self-esteem-threatening implications of the aversive events. Most important, however, regression analyses indicated that only unstable self-esteem was a unique predictor.

Although the results of these studies are consistent with the proposition that unstable self-esteem is associated with heightened ego involvement, we recognize that additional, more direct, support is warranted. Such support will we hope, become available in the near future.

Impoverished Self-Concepts

Consideration of factors related to unstable self-esteem suggests one other candidate worthy of investigation—a poorly developed self-concept. That is, having a poorly developed self-concept could lead individuals to rely on, and be more affected by, specific evaluative information, thereby contributing to unstable self-esteem (e.g., Baumgardner, 1990; Campbell, 1990). Stated differently, the less people know about themselves (who they are, what they like and dislike, what their strengths and weaknesses are), the less well-anchored their feelings of self-worth may be. The distinction made by Paulhus and Martin (1988) between functional flexibility (i.e., the capacity to perform various social behaviors as dictated by the situation) and situationality (i.e., viewing one's behavior as being dependent on the situation) is also relevant here. Specifically, to the extent that unstable self-esteem is associated with poorly defined self-concepts, it should relate to diminished functional flexibility (since one is less sure of one's capabilities) and to enhanced situationality (since one is likely to depend on the situation for guidance on how to act).

We have yet to systematically examine the extent to which self-esteem instability is related to an impoverished or poorly developed self-concept. Nonetheless, we mention it here because of the great conceptual and intuitive appeal that it has. Moreover, as will become clear, linking unstable self-esteem to an impoverished self-concept enriches the theoretical framework for interpreting some of our research findings.

Our discussion to this point has focused on "contemporaneous" factors that may promote or underlie unstable self-esteem. However, it is important also to focus on developmental factors that may foster unstable self-esteem. Specifically, are there early childhood experiences that promote unstable self-esteem, perhaps by fostering an ego-involved orientation or interfering with the development of a well-defined self-concept? In the following section, we consider this very important issue.

Early Childhood Experiences

Kernis and Waschull (in press) suggested that early childhood experiences that involve substantial amounts of noncontingent and/or controlling feedback (from parents, teachers, and other significant others) are likely to promote the development of unstable self-esteem. The essence of noncontingent feedback is that it is not under the recipient's control (Berglas, 1985). Furthermore, noncontingent feedback is not a direct function of the recipient's abilities and performances, but is instead based on such things as the recipient's ascribed characteristics (e.g., being a Boy Scout) criteria established by the evaluator but unknown to the recipient, and the evaluator's mood (Berglas, 1985).

Noncontingent feedback can contribute to poorly developed self-concepts, ego involvement, and/or unstable self-esteem in several, related ways (Berglas, 1985). First, it may prevent recipients from achieving a clear understanding and appreciation of their own capabilities and limitations. Second, because the source's conveyed sentiments are unreliable, recipients may lack clearly defined "reflected appraisals" of their self-worth (Felson, 1985; Mead, 1934). Third, since some forms of noncontingent feedback link specific evaluative information to one's overall self-worth (e.g., "Good boys behave themselves in public"), self-worth is more likely to fluctuate as a function of specific evaluative information.

Feedback that is experienced as controlling, that is, as "pressure to think, feel, or behave in specified ways" (Deci & Ryan, 1985, p. 95), is also likely to undermine a stable sense of one's self-worth (Berglas, 1985; Deci & Ryan, 1987). As a consequence of such felt pressure, one's actions and internal states become governed primarily by specific contingencies, rather than by an awareness of one's organismic needs and the desire to fulfill them (Deci & Ryan, 1985) (for a discussion of the distinction between unconditional and conditional positive regard, see also Rogers, 1959). Over time, an excessive focus on one's success or failure at navigating these contingencies is likely to contribute to feelings of overall self-worth that fluctuate in tune with performance–contingency (mis)matches (see also Chapter 2).

To summarize our discussion so far, we have suggested that stability and level of self-esteem are distinct components of self-esteem along which individuals can be characterized. In addition, we have argued and presented evidence suggesting that unstable self-esteem is associated with a heightened tendency to be ego-involved in everyday activities, and we have speculated that it is associated with an impoverished self-concept. Finally, we have speculated on early childhood experiences that may promote unstable self-esteem. We turn now to a discussion of how a consideration of self-esteem instability can help to reconcile the different views of high and low self-esteem that were alluded to at the beginning of the chapter.

THE ESSENCE OF HIGH SELF-ESTEEM

One predominant view of high SEs, consistent with humanistically oriented theories (e. g., Rogers, 1961), is that they feel that they are worthwhile individuals, are satisfied with and like themselves, and have confidence in their skills and abilities, yet are accepting of their weaknesses. Implicit in this view is that high SEs' feelings of self-worth are built on solid foundations that do not require continual validation (see also

Chapter 2). Moreover, their feelings of self-worth are thought to not be questioned or modified with each adverse experience that life inevitably presents to them.

In contrast, according to others (mostly experimentally oriented social/personality psychologists), high SEs are threatened by a wide variety of negative self-relevant events, and to minimize their impact, high SEs employ a variety of self-protective strategies. Furthermore, adherents of this view suggest that in response to positive events, high SEs are especially likely to engage in a variety of self-enhancement strategies. Rather than viewing high self-esteem as based on a solid foundation, these researchers appear to be implying that high self-esteem is a precious commodity that must be continually promoted and defended in order to survive.

In support of this latter view, research has shown that compared to low SEs, high SEs are more likely to display self-serving attributions (Fitch, 1970), self-handicap to enhance the potentially positive implications of good performance (Tice, 1991), set inappropriately risky goals when ego-threatened (Baumeister, Heatherton, & Tice, 1993), actively create less fortunate others with whom they can compare favorably (Gibbons & McCoy, 1991), and derogate outgroup members, especially when their ingroup has been criticized (Crocker, Thompson, McGraw, & Ingerman, 1987). Findings such as these paint a picture of high SEs that suggests that they are not very secure in their feelings of self-worth and -liking.

Which view of high self-esteem is more accurate? Although the types of reactions described in the preceding paragraph have typically been ascribed to high SEs in general, we suggest that they will especially be manifested among unstable high SEs. That is, to the extent that unstable high SEs are highly ego-involved (and less certain of their self-worth and who they are), they have a very precious resource—their favorable feelings of self-worth—that is fragile and highly vulnerable to challenge. Consequently, unstable high SEs will be highly invested in maintaining and enhancing their favorable self-feelings, as well as in minimizing their negative self-feelings. In contrast, stable high SEs are thought to have a well-anchored sense of their self-worth that is not dependent on the attainment of specific outcomes or on validation by others (consistent with the first perspective on high self-esteem). These people should be little threatened by negative evaluative events, nor should they especially revel in their successes (again, see also Chapter 2).

In sum, we believe that among high SEs, tendencies to self-enhance and self-protect will be exaggerated among individuals whose self-esteem is unstable. We turn now to our research that has addressed this issue.

SELF-ENHANCEMENT

Findings from several of our studies indicate that unstable high SEs are especially likely to respond in ways that highlight and magnify positive self-feelings and self-evaluations. For example, Kernis, Grannemann, and Barclay (1992) examined the relationship of stability and level of self-esteem to college students' endorsement of performance-inhibiting factors after they received feedback about their scores on an important examination. The nature of these performance-inhibiting factors was either motivational (e.g., "I could not get 'psyched up' to study for this exam"), power (e.g., "I did not get enough sleep the night before"), or task-difficulty (e.g., "The amount of material covered on this exam was too much") (based on Darley and Goethals, 1980). If people indicate that these factors interfered with their performance *after* finding out that they succeeded, this can be considered self-enhancing because they are implying that they did well despite the difficulties (Kelley, 1972: Kernis et al., 1992). As anticipated, compared to stable high SEs, unstable high SEs who performed well were more self-enhancing, in that they were more likely to indicate that such performance-inhibiting factors (specifically motivational factors) were operative. Likewise, in a recent study in which reactions to interpersonal evaluations were examined [Kernis et al., 1993 (Study 1)], unstable high SEs who received positive feedback (compared to their stable high SE counterparts) viewed the evaluator as especially competent and likeable and experienced enhanced levels of positive affect.

How do stable and unstable high SEs evaluate their own behaviors and self-characteristics? We recently administered Harter's Self-Perception Profile for College Students to a sample of approximately 100 undergraduate women. The Self-Perception Profile assesses self-evaluations in 12 domains: scholastic competence, intellectual ability, creativity, job competence, athletic competence, physical appearance, peer acceptance, close friendships, romantic relationships, relationships with parents, morality, and sense of humor. Regression analyses revealed significant Level × Stability interactions for scholastic competence, intellectual ability, job competence, close relationships, and relationships with parents, and marginal interactions ($p < 0.08$) for physical appearance, peer acceptance, and morality (Berry, Kernis, & Cornell, 1994). Although the effects were typically not very large, predicted values yielded highly consistent patterns across the various subscales—among high SEs, instability tended to relate to more positive self-evaluations. Rather than reflecting solidly based self-judgments that stem from a well-developed sense of self-worth, these highly positive self-evaluations are thought to reflect motivated efforts to shore up positive self-feelings through positive self-evaluations.

Finally, we recently examined the extent to which stability and level of self-esteem are related to both pride in oneself as a person and pride in one's behavior, as measured by the *Test of Self-Conscious Affect* (Tangney, Wagner, & Gramzow, 1989). Pride in self (alpha pride) and pride in behavior (beta pride) are assessed in terms of the favorability of reactions to hypothetical positive events. Consistent with our framework, unstable high SEs (more so than stable high SEs) responded in a self-enhancing manner by exhibiting greater pride in self and pride in behavior.

WHAT ABOUT SELF-PROTECTION?

Due to the precarious nature of their positive self-feelings (brought on by heightened ego involvement and perhaps relatively impoverished self-concepts), unstable high SEs are also expected to be highly threatened by negative self-relevant events. Consequently, unless unstable high SEs somehow "neutralize" the threatening information, they may feel compelled to negatively revise their self-feelings. Will unstable high SEs attempt to minimize the threat by recognizing, accepting, and working on whatever weaknesses they may possess? We see this as highly unlikely, because such reactions will only feed into their fragile feelings of self-worth. Rather, it seems more likely that they will locate the source of the threat as external to themselves and attack it. In so doing, consciously experienced declines in self-worth can be attenuated or avoided altogether. In brief, our framework holds that in response to threats, unstable high SEs will be highly defensive and actively attempt to undermine the threat's legitimacy.

Before proceeding further, it is important to distinguish elements of self-protective strategies that are primarily "internally or self-directed" (i.e., that pertain to remedial possibilities such as attributions to lack of effort) from those that are primarily "externally" directed (e.g., attacks on the source of the threat). Internally directed self-protective efforts are more adaptive, by and large, than those that are externally directed because the consequences they produce are more under the actor's control. For example, attributing failure to a lack of effort signifies that future occurrences can be prevented through increased diligence, and it is associated with more sophisticated problem-solving strategies (Dweck & Leggett, 1988) and lower negative affect (Kernis, Brockner, & Frankel, 1989a; Kernis & Grannemann, 1990). In contrast, attributing failure to an unfair exam provides little if any insight into remedial strategies that can prevent future failures (cf. Dweck & Leggett, 1988) and instead is likely to be associated with heightened negative affect (Arkin & Maruyama, 1981). For the present purposes, an important point is that our use here of the term "defensiveness" refers to externally directed, but not internally directed, self-protective strategies. For further discussion of this distinction, see Kernis, and Waschull (in press).

One manifestation of defensiveness is a heightened tendency to become angry or hostile. That is, anger and hostility are often instigated by threats of an interpersonal nature, such as insults or undue criticism. In such instances, anger and hostility can serve to ward off other negative self-feelings or to restore one's damaged self-esteem or public self-image (Felson, 1984; Feshbach, 1970). Moreover, they are often associated with externalization, or assignment of blame to the instigator (Averill, 1982). The preceding discussion suggests that unstable high SEs may be especially prone to experience anger and hostility, but is that the case? To address this question, Kernis, Grannemann, and Barclay (1989) first assessed stability and level of self-esteem and then had participants complete a variety of self-report measures of anger/hostility proneness. Consistent with our assertion that unstable high SEs are much more likely than stable high SEs to engage in defensive self-protective strategies, the results revealed that unstable high SEs scored especially high on these various anger/hostility proneness inventories, whereas stable high SEs scored especially low.

Similar defensive reactions among unstable high SEs, this time in response to explicit negative interpersonal feedback, were observed in a study referred to earlier [Kernis et al., 1993 (Study 1)]. Specifically, unstable high SEs, more so than stable high SEs, judged a negative evaluator to be highly incompetent and unlikeable.

An important issue that should be raised at this point is whether or not the self-enhancement and defensive strategies engaged in by unstable high SEs are successful. Research on depressive symptomatology (Kernis, Grannemann, & Mathis, 1991; Kernis, Waschull, Greenier, Whisenhunt, & Berry, in press; Roberts & Monroe, 1992; Whisenhunt, Waschull, & Greenier, 1993; for an extended discussion of this research, see Kernis & Waschull, 1994) suggests that they are not. Specifically, in several samples, unstable high SEs exhibited higher levels of depressive symptomatology than did stable high SEs. Thus, despite all their efforts to self-enhance and self-protect, unstable high SEs still exhibited greater dysphoria than did stable high SEs. At first glance, this might seem surprising. It makes sense, however, if one recognizes that such strategies are not necessarily successful. In fact, from our perspective, dependence on such strategies reflects a basic weakness in the foundation of unstable high SEs' positive self-feelings. This weakness, accompanied by a heightened tendency to invest their self-worth in everyday activities, is thought to make unstable high SEs more prone to depressive symptoms than stable high SEs.

Earlier, we suggested that there are two broad perspectives on the essence of high self-esteem. One perspective holds that high SEs have a well-anchored sense of positive self-worth that is secure and that does not require constant validation. The other perspective holds that high self-esteem is a precious commodity that must be continually defended and promoted in order to survive. Consideration of the role of stability of self-esteem reveals that there is some truth to each of these perspectives. Specifically, the evidence reviewed in this section indicates that among high SEs, self-esteem instability is related to especially favorable reactions to positive events and to defensive reactions to negative events. Stated differently, among high SEs, instability reflects fragility in positive self-feelings, which promotes self-enhancing and externally directed (i.e., defensive) self-protective strategies. Thus, for unstable high SEs, self-esteem does appear to be a precious commodity.

On the other hand, the more stable an individual's high self-esteem, the less reactive he or she will be to specific positive or negative self-relevant events. Rather, stable high self-esteem reflects a well-developed sense of one's self-worth that is characterized by genuine self-acceptance and self-liking. Stated differently, the positive self-feelings of stable high SEs do not require constant buffering or bolstering, for they are securely based. Thus, it appears that the essence of high self-esteem varies considerably as a function of the extent to which it is stable or unstable.

Our characterization of the difference between stable and unstable high SEs bears some similarity to an earlier distinction that was made between "true" and "defensive" high SEs (Horney, 1950). On the one hand, true high SEs are thought to have secure positive self-feelings that they accurately report. On the other hand, defensive high SEs are thought to harbor inner negative feelings of self-worth, but because of high approval needs, they report feeling positively about themselves. Defensive high SEs are typically distinguished from true high SEs by their high scores on a measure of social desirability, such as the Social Desirability Scale of Crowne and Marlowe (1960) (e.g., Schneider & Turkat, 1975). Compared to true high SEs, defensive high SEs are more likely to present themselves in positive ways and to have more adverse reactions to negative self-relevant events (e.g., Schneider & Turkat, 1975). These reactions are similar to the outcomes that are associated with unstable high self-esteem. However, we believe that unstable high SEs differ in important ways from their defensive high self-esteem counterparts. First, unstable high SEs are not thought to harbor ill feelings toward themselves that they are unwilling to admit. Instead, unstable high SEs are thought to have positive self-feelings that are fragile and that require constant validation. Second, if in fact unstable high SEs are more defensive in the traditional sense, they should be consistently positive in their contextually based self-feelings, which they obviously are not. Finally, self-esteem instability does not significantly correlate with scores on the Social Desirability Scale of Crowne and Marlowe (1960) (Kernis et al., 1992), nor do stability and level of self-esteem interact in the prediction of scores on that measure. These considerations indicate that the constructs of self-esteem instability and defensive self-esteem are not synonymous. Rather, they indicate that each construct has valuable (though separate) contributions to make to our understanding of self-esteem processes.

THE ESSENCE OF LOW SELF-ESTEEM

As was the case for high self-esteem, there seem to be two different perspectives on the essence of low self-esteem. One perspective, which has predominated for many years (cf. Harter, 1983), holds that low SEs exhibit a wide variety of maladaptive cognitive, affective, motivational, and behavioral patterns. Specifically, low SEs are thought to have quite negative self-views, to be readily accepting (cognitively, at least) of unfavorable feedback, to be highly prone to experience negative affect, to exhibit ineffective strategies in the face of adversity, and to show little if any propensity to self-enhance and self-protect (e.g., Harter, 1993; Kernis et al., 1989a; Watson & Clark, 1984). In contrast, another perspective has recently emerged in which low SEs are characterized as cautious and uncertain (rather than highly maladjusted) individuals whose behavioral styles are geared toward minimizing exposure of their deficiencies (Baumeister, Tice, & Hutton, 1989). Proponents of this latter viewpoint assert that the self-evaluations and self-concepts of low SEs are characterized more by uncertainty and neutrality than by negativity (Baumeister, 1993b: Baumeister et al., 1989; Campbell, 1990) and that low SEs do embrace positive self-aspects (Swann, Pelham, & Krull, 1989) as well as engage in some forms of self-protective strategies and "indirect" forms of self-enhancement (Brown, Collins, & Schmidt, 1988; Tice, 1991).

From our perspective, the degree of maladjustment and the propensity to engage in self-protective strategies among low SEs is thought to vary substantially as a function of stability of self-esteem. We should acknowledge at the outset that our position on this issue has evolved considerably over time (see Kernis, 1993; Kernis et al., 1992, 1993). Given space limitations, we discuss this evolution only briefly here (for a full discussion, see Kernis & Waschull, in press). Our initial position was that among low SEs, self-esteem instability would relate to greater resiliency and more adaptive, internally directed, self-protective efforts. Specifically, we believed that among low SEs, unstable self-esteem is a manifestation of a desire to avoid continuously negative self-feelings. This desire was thought to promote the use of self-protective strategies and possibly "indirect" self-enhancement strategies such as aligning themselves with successful others (so-called "basking in reflected glory") (Cialdini & Richardson, 1980; Tesser, 1988). However, in agreement with others (e.g., Baumeister et al., 1989; Brown et al., 1988; Tice, 1991), we argued that low SEs (even unstable low SEs) typically do not engage in direct self-enhancement strategies due to concerns about whether a positive identity can be successfully defended.

Our early work was generally supportive of this position. Specifically, among low SEs, self-esteem instability related to greater self-protective excuse-making following failure (Kernis et al., 1992) and to lower subsequent depressive symptomatology (Kernis et al., 1991). These findings were taken as support for the view that compared to stable low SEs, unstable low SEs are more resilient and are more likely to engage in internally directed self-protective strategies (Kernis, 1993). Furthermore, in several studies, we found no evidence that self-esteem instability related to greater use of direct self-enhancement strategies among low SEs. Specifically, among low SEs who succeeded on an exam, self-esteem instability did not relate to greater endorsement of performance-inhibiting factors (as it did among high SEs) (Kernis et al., 1992). Also, among low SEs, self-esteem instability did not relate to more favorable reactions to positive interpersonal feedback (as it did among high SEs) [Kernis et al., 1993 (Study 1)], nor did it relate to more positive self-evaluations along specific dimensions or to measures of pride in self and pride in behavior (as it did among high SEs) (see Kernis & Waschull, in press).

However, our more recent work has suggested that among low SEs, self-esteem instability is related to psychological difficulties that may be quite pervasive. Specifically, compared to stable low SEs, unstable low SEs are more likely to (1) believe that negative interpersonally based feedback is accurate [Kernis et al., 1993 (Study 1)]; (2) have attachment styles that involve either a negative self or other model (Waschull, Greenier, & Kernis, 1993); (3) score higher on a measure of neuroticism but lower on measures of agreeableness and conscientiousness (Berry, Kernis, & Cornell, 1993); (4) rate themselves less favorably on various specific self-dimensions (Berry et al., 1994); (5) experience greater depressive symptomatology (Kernis et al., 1994; Whisenhunt et al., 1993), especially when they report experiencing high numbers of daily hassles (Kernis et al., 1994); and (6) exhibit less self-serving and self-protective attributional styles (Kernis et al., 1994), as measured by the Attributional Styles Questionnaire (Peterson, Semmel, von Baeyer, Abramson, Metalsky, & Seligman, 1982).

Findings such as these have led us to seriously question whether unstable low SEs are generally more resilient than stable low SEs. Furthermore, they have led us to search for answers as to why unstable low self-esteem is related to such a wide variety of adverse outcomes. Kernis and Waschull (in press) suggested several possibilities. First, given their generally negative specific self-evaluations, unstable low SEs may lack the necessary skills and resources to refute the validity of negative self-relevant events and to redirect their focus onto more positive self-aspects (something that unstable high SEs may be better able to do) (see also Spencer, Josephs, & Steele, 1993). This lack of skills and resources may be particularly detrimental if they are more highly ego-involved (and perhaps less certain about their self-concepts) than stable low SEs. A second possibility is that unstable low SEs may periodically experience positive self-feelings that they perceive as not being available to them permanently. These intermittent elevations in self-feelings may tease unstable low SEs with a temporary experience of positive self-regard that lets them know what they are missing. Consequently, subsequent declines in self-feelings may be particularly painful for them and thus be associated with various adverse outcomes. A third possibility is that unstable low SEs vacillate between adaptive functioning and poor self-regulation, perhaps depending on whether they are currently experiencing predominantly positive or negative fluctuations in temporary self-esteem. This last possibility would help to account for our findings that sometimes unstable low SEs seem to fare better than stable low SEs, whereas at other times they seem to fare worse.

These speculations suggest some important avenues for future research to take. The first avenue would be to systematically examine the extent to which self-esteem instability (in combination with self-esteem level) is related to a wide range of coping strategies. The second avenue would be to systematically assess the proposed relations between self-esteem instability (again, in combination with level) and ego involvement, self-concept impoverishment, functional flexibility, and situationality. A third avenue would be to examine more precisely the nature of the short-term fluctuations that people with unstable self-esteem exhibit. Systematic research focused on these and related issues would substantially increase our understanding of self-esteem instability in general and among low SEs in particular.

As we pointed out earlier, researchers and theorists differ in their views of what it means to have low self-esteem. Some view low self-esteem as reflecting pervasive psychological difficulties, whereas others take a more benign view. Here again, self-esteem instability may be important in reconciling these conflicting positions. Admittedly, at this time, the role of self-esteem instability among low SEs is somewhat unclear. Stated differently, given the disparity in findings across our studies, it seems premature to reach definitive conclusions about the overall role of self-esteem instability among low SEs. However, our research to date does indicate that the role of self-esteem instability is different for low than for high SEs. Specifically, it is only among high SEs that unstable self-esteem is associated with greater tendencies to engage in direct self-enhancement.

SUMMARY AND CONCLUSIONS

People differ not only in whether their level of self-esteem is high or low but also in the extent to which their self-esteem is stable or unstable. These individual differences in stability of self-esteem can be traced to at least two factors (although more evidence is clearly needed): the extent to which people invest their feelings of self-worth in everyday outcomes and the extent to which their self-concepts are impoverished. Specifically, it seems likely that the more people invest their feelings of self-worth and the less well developed their self-concepts, the more unstable their self-esteem will be. Developmentally, early childhood environments that impose substantial amounts of noncontingent or controlling feedback or both are thought to promote unstable self-esteem, heightened tendencies toward ego involvement, and perhaps more uncertain or impoverished self-concepts (see also Chapter 2).

It is important to recognize that stability of self-esteem, ego involvement, and perhaps self-concept impoverishment [or lack of self-concept clarity, to use the terminology of Campbell (1990)] are parts of a system that are likely to have reciprocal influences on one another. For example, just as heightened ego involvement may contribute to unstable self-esteem, fluctuations in self-esteem may be likely to heighten ego involvement. Thus, more often than not, a particular component can be conceptualized as either a predictor or a criterion variable in relation to another component. Typically, we have chosen to enter this system by measuring individual differences in self-esteem stability: we then examine how these individual differences (in combination with individual differences in level of self-esteem) relate to a variety of other psychological phenomena.

As we have described in this chapter, some of the controversies in the self-esteem literature can be resolved by taking into account individual differences in stability of self-esteem. This possibility is most clear with regard to how high self-esteem is conceptualized. On the other hand, an important agenda for future research is to better understand the implications of self-esteem instability among low SEs. On the positive side, achieving this understanding is likely to yield more complete answers to the questions of when and why low self-esteem is associated with maladaptive and distressing psychological outcomes. We hope that this chapter will stimulate other researchers to assist in this endeavor.

REFERENCES

Arkin, R. M., & Maruyama, G. M. (1981). Attribution, affect, and college exam performance. *Journal of Educational Psychology, 71,* 85–93.

Averill, J. R. (1982). *Anger and aggression: An essay on emotion.* New York: Springer-Verlag.

Baumeister, R. (Ed) (1993a). *Self-esteem: The puzzle of low self-regard.* New York: Plenum Press.

Baumeister, R. (1993b). Understanding the inner nature of low self-esteem: Uncertain, fragile, protective, and conflicted. In R. Baumeister (Ed.), *Self-esteem: The puzzle of low self-regard* (pp. 201–218). New York: Plenum Press.

Baumeister, R. F., Tice, D. M., & Hutton, D. G. (1989). Self-presentational motivations and personality differences in self-esteem. *Journal of Personality, 57,* 547–579.

Baumeister, R. F.. Heatherton. T. F., & Tice, D. M. (1993). When ego threats lead to self-regulation failure: The negative consequences of high self-esteem. *Journal of Personality and Social Psychology, 64,* 141–156.

Baumgardner, A. H. (1990). To know oneself is to like oneself: Self-certainty and self-affect. *Journal of Personality and Social Psychology, 58,* 1062–1072.

Berglas, S. (1985). Self-handicapping and self-handicappers: A cognitive/attributional model of interpersonal self-protective behavior. In R. Hogan & W. H. Jones (Eds.), *Perspectives in personality,* Vol. 1 (pp. 235–270). Greenwich, CT: JAI Press.

Berry, A. J., Kernis, M. H., & Cornell, D. P. (1993). *Examining the relationships between stability and level of self-esteem and the "big five" personality dimensions.* Paper presented at the annual convention of the Southeastern Psychological Association, Atlanta, March 1993.

Berry, A. J., Kernis, M. H., & Cornell, D. P. (1994). *Stability and level of self-esteem and domain specific self-evaluations.* Paper presented at the annual convention of the Southeastern Psychological Association, New Orleans, March 1994.

Brown, J. D., Collins, R. L., & Schmidt, G. W. (1988). Self-esteem and direct versus indirect forms of self-enhancement. *Journal of Personality and Social Psychology, 55,* 445–453.

Campbell, J. D. (1990). Self-esteem and clarity of the self-concept. *Journal of Personality and Social Psychology, 59,* 538–549.

Cialdini, R. B., & Richardson, K. D. (1980). Two indirect tactics of image management: Basking and blasting. *Journal of Personality and Social Psychology, 39,* 406–415.

Crocker, J., Thompson, L. L., McGraw, K. M., & Ingerman, C . (1987). Downward comparisons, prejudice, and evaluation of others: Effects of self-esteem and threat. *Journal of Personality and Social Psychology, 52,* 907–916.

Crowne, D. P., & Marlowe, D. (1960). A new scale of social desirability independent of psychopathology. *Journal of Consulting Psychology, 24,* 349–354.

Darley, J. M., & Goethals, G. R. (1980). People's analyses of ability-linked performances. In

L. Berkowitz (Ed.), *Advances in experimental social psychology* (Vol. 13, pp. 1–37). San Diego: Academic Press.

deCharms, R. (1968). *Personal causation: The internal affective determinants of behavior.* New York: Academic Press.

Deci, E. L., & Ryan, R. M. (1985). *Intrinsic motivation and self-determination in human behavior.* New York: Plenum Press.

Deci, E. L., & Ryan, R. M. (1987). The support of autonomy and the control of behavior. *Journal of Personality and Social Psychology, 53,* 1024–1037.

Dweck, C. S., & Leggett, E. L. (1988). A social–cognitive approach to motivation and personality. *Psychological Review, 95,* 256–273.

Felson, R. B. (1984). Patterns of aggressive social interaction. In A. Mummendey (Ed.), *Social psychology of aggression: From individual behavior to social interaction* (pp. 107–126). Berlin: Springer-Verlag.

Felson, R. B. (1985). Reflected appraisal and the development of self. *Social Psychology Quarterly, 48,* 71–77.

Feshbach, S. (1970). Aggression. In P. H. Mussen (Ed.), *Carmichael's manual of child psychology,* Vol. 2 (pp. 159–259). New York: John Wiley.

Fitch, G. (1970). Effects of self-esteem, perceived performance, and choice on causal attributions. *Journal of Personality and Social Psychology, 16,* 311–315.

Gibbons, F. X., & McCoy, S. B. (1991). Self-esteem, similarity, and reactions to active versus passive downward comparison. *Journal of Personality and Social Psychology, 60,* 414–424.

Harter, S. (1983). Developmental perspectives on the self-system. In E. M. Hetherington (Ed.), *Handbook of child psychology,* Vol. 4. New York: John Wiley.

Harter, S. (1985). *Manual for the self perception profile for children.* University of Denver, Denver, CO.

Harter, S. (1993). Causes and consequences of low self-esteem in children and adolescents. In R. Baumeister (Ed.), *Self-esteem: The puzzle of low self-regard* (pp. 87–116). New York: Plenum Press.

Horney, K. (1950). *Neurosis and human growth: The struggle toward self-realization.* New York: Norton.

James, W. (1890/1950). *The principles of psychology.* New York: Dover (original work published in 1890).

Kelley, H. H. (1972). Causal schemata and the attribution process. In E. E. Jones, D. E. Kanousa, H. H. Kelley, R. E. Nisbett, S. Valins, & B. Weiner (Eds), *Attribution: Perceiving the causes of behavior.* Morristown, NJ: General Learning Press.

Kernis, M. H. (1993). The roles of stability and level of self-esteem in psychological functioning. In R. Baumeister (Ed.), *Self-esteem: The puzzle of low self-regard* (pp. 167–182). New York: Plenum Press.

Kernis, M. H., & Grannemann, B. D. (1990). Excuses in the making: A test and extension of Darley and Goethals' attributional model. *Journal of Experimental Social Psychology, 26,* 337–349.

Kernis, M. H., & Johnson, E. K. (1990). Current and typical self-appraisals: Differential responsiveness to evaluative feedback and implications for emotions. *Journal of Research in Personality, 24,* 241–257.

Kernis, M. H., & Waschull, S. B. (in press). The interactive roles of stability and level of self-esteem: Research and theory. In M. P. Zanna (Ed.), *Advances in experimental social psychology,* Vol. 27. San Diego: Academic Press.

Kernis, M. H., Brockner, J., & Frankel, B. S. (1989). Self-esteem and reactions to overgeneralization. *Journal of Personality and Social Psychology, 57,* 707–714.

Kernis, M. H., Grannemann, B. D., & Barclay, L. C. (1989). Stability and level of self-esteem as predictors of anger arousal and hostility. *Journal of Personality and Social Psychology, 56,* 1013–1023.

Kernis, M. H., Grannemann, B. D., & Mathis, L. C. (1991). Stability of self-esteem as a moderator of the relation between level of self-esteem and depression. *Journal of Personality and Social Psychology, 61,* 80–84.

Kernis, M. H., Grannemann, B. D., & Barclay, L. C. (1992). Stability of self-esteem: Assessment, correlates, and excuse making. *Journal of Personality, 60,* 521–644.

Kernis, M. H., Cornell, D. P., Sun, C. R., Berry, A. J., & Harlow, T. (1993). There's more to self-esteem than whether it is high or low: The importance of stability of self-esteem. *Journal of Personality and Social Psychology, 65,* 1190–1204.

Kernis, M. H., Waschull, S. B., Greenier, K. D., Whisenhunt, C. R., & Berry, A. J. (1994). Self-esteem and vulnerability to depressive symptoms: Moderators and mediators (in prep.).

Mead, G. H. (1934). *Mind, self, and society.* Chicago: University of Chicago Press.

Paulhus, D. L., & Martin, C. L. (1988). Functional flexibility: A new conception of interpersonal flexibility. *Journal of Personality and Social Psychology, 55,* 88–101.

Peterson, C., Semmel, A., von Baeyer, C., Abramson, L. Y., Metalsky, G. I., & Seligman, M. E. P. (1982). The attributional style questionnaire. *Cognitive Therapy and Research, 6,* 287–300.

Roberts, J. E., & Monroe, S. M. (1992). Vulnerable self-esteem and depressive symptoms: Prospective findings comparing three alternative conceptualizations. *Journal of Personality and Social Psychology, 62,* 804–835.

Rogers, C. R. (1959). A theory of therapy, personality, and interpersonal relationships, as developed in the client-centered framework. In S. Koch (Ed.), *Psychology: A study of science,* Vol. 3 (pp. 184–256). New York: McGraw-Hill.

Rogers, C. R. (1961). *On becoming a person: A therapist's view of psychotherapy.* Boston: Houghton Mifflin.

Rosenberg, M. (1965). *Society and the adolescent self-image.* Princeton, NJ: Princeton University Press.

Rosenberg, M. (1986). Self-concept from middle childhood through adolescence. In J. Suls & A. G. Greenwald (Eds.), *Psychological perspectives on the self,* Vol. 3 (pp. 107–135). Hillsdale, NJ: Erlbaum Associates.

Ryan, R. M. (1982). Control and information in the interpersonal sphere: An extension of cognitive evaluation theory. *Journal of Personality and Social Psychology, 43,* 450–461.

Savin-Williams, R. C., & Demo, D. H. (1983). Situational and transituational determinants of adolescent self-feelings. *Journal of Personality and Social Psychology, 44,* 824–833.

Schneider, D. J., & Turkat, D. (1975). Self-presentation following success and failure: Defensive self-esteem models. *Journal of Personality, 43,* 127–135.

Spencer, S. J., Josephs, R. A., & Steele, C. M. (1993). Low self-esteem: The uphill struggle for self-integrity. In R. Baumeister (Ed.), *Self-esteem: The puzzle of low self-regard* (pp. 21–37). New York: Plenum Press.

Swann, W. B., Pelham, B. W., & Krull, D. S. (1989). Agreeable fancy or disagreeable truth?: Reconciling self-enhancement and self-verification. *Journal of Personality and Social Psychology, 57,* 782–791.

Tangney, J. P., Wagner, P., & Gramzow, R. (1989). *The test of self-conscious affect.* Fairfax, VA: George Mason University.

Tesser, A. (1988). Toward a self-evaluation maintenance model of social behavior. In L. Berkowitz (Ed.), *Advances in experimental social psychology,* Vol . 21 (pp. 181–227). San Diego: Academic Press.

Tice, D. M. (1991). Esteem protection or enhancement? Self-handicapping motives and attributions differ by trait self-esteem. *Journal of Personality and Social Psychology, 60,* 711–725.

Waschull, S. B., & Kernis, M. H. (in press). Level and stability of self-esteem as predictors of children's intrinsic motivation and reasons for anger. *Personality and Social Psychology Bulletin.*

Waschull, S. B., Greenier, K. D., & Kernis, M. H. (1993). *Unstable self-esteem: Familial antecedents and adult relationships.* Presented at the annual convention of the Southeastern Psychological Association, Atlanta. March 1993.

Watson, D., & Clark, L. A. (1984). Negative affectivity: The disposition to experience aversive motivational states. *Psychological Bulletin, 96,* 469–490.

Whisenhunt, C. R., Waschull, S. B., & Greenier, K. D. (1993). Role of self-esteem stability in the relationship between self-esteem and depression. Paper presented at the annual convention of the Southeastern Psychological Association, Atlanta, March 1993.

Wylie, R. (1974). *The self-concept,* Vol. 1. Lincoln: University of Nebraska Press.

Chapter 4

TOWARD A DUAL-MOTIVE DEPTH PSYCHOLOGY OF SELF AND SOCIAL BEHAVIOR

Jeff Greenberg, Tom Pyszczynski, and Sheldon Solomon

INTRODUCTION

Motivational constructs involving the defense and enrichment of the self have been employed either separately or in combination in a wide variety of analyses of human behavior throughout the history of psychology. Whereas the defensive orientation has traditionally been the domain of psychoanalytical theorists, the growth orientation has been espoused most prominently by proponents of humanistic psychology. Interestingly, there currently seems to be a resurgence in analyses relying on these two distinct types of motives in contemporary academic psychology. Although our own terror management theory and research focuses exclusively on defensive motivation, we recognize that defensive concerns are not the only forces impinging on human behavior. The primary purpose of this chapter is therefore to expand our conceptualization to consider the role of growth and enrichment motives in human behavior and to explore the interplay

Jeff Greenberg • Department of Psychology, University of Arizona, Tucson, Arizona 85721.   Tom Pyszczynski • Department of Psychology, University of Colorado–Colorado Springs, Colorado Springs, Colorado 80933.   Sheldon Solomon • Department of Psychology, Skidmore College, Saratoga Springs, New York 12866.

Efficacy, Agency, and Self-Esteem, edited by Michael H. Kernis. Plenum Press, New York, 1995.

of such motives with the defensive terror management motives that have been the focus of our previous work. Consideration of these motive systems in tandem will ultimately produce a richer, more balanced, and more complete understanding of human behavior than could be provided by exclusive reliance on terror management theory in its original form. In the following pages, we present a theoretical and empirical overview of terror management theory, a conceptualization of the nature and functioning of a separate growth-oriented enrichment motive system, and a consideration of the interplay between the two systems.

TERROR MANAGEMENT THEORY

Terror management theory (Greenberg, Pyszczynski, & Solomon, 1986; Solomon, Greenberg, & Pyszczynski, 1991) was originally developed in an attempt to formulate a simple, internally consistent analysis of human motivation based on the writings of Ernest Becker (1962, 1973, 1975). Becker's work, in turn, was an effort to synthesize key converging insights from the diverse fields concerned with understanding human behavior: anthropology, biology, economics, philosophy, political science, psychology, and sociology. The theory we developed reflects both the interdisciplinary nature and the ambitiousness of Becker's work. It also shares with Becker's writings an existential perspective that focuses on threatening aspects of reality that the reader, like many past readers of our work, may find no less distressing than we ourselves find them to be. We believe, however, that this perspective provides unique insights into a variety of aspects of human behavior.

Terror management theory (Greenberg et al., 1986; Solomon et al., 1991) is concerned with the consequences of a motivational system directed toward self-preservation in an organism intelligent enough to be aware of its own vulnerabilities and ultimate mortality. Because of the sophisticated cognitive abilities through which we, as a species, are able to anticipate future events and become conscious of our own existence, we are aware of our inherent physical limitations, of the ongoing potential for catastrophic events (e.g., brain tumors, lethal viruses), and of our inevitable demise even in the absence of such events. Because this awareness runs directly contrary to the basic animal instinct for self-preservation and continued existence, humans have an enormous potential for anxiety. Indeed, Becker (1973) argued that direct uncensored recognition of death and tragedy would leave individuals paralyzed with terror.

Following Becker (1973), Berger and Luckmann (1967), and Rank (1941/1958), the theory proposes that cultural worldviews have evolved to help individuals manage this terror by denying that life is a purposeless biological accident and that death is absolute annihilation for the individual. Cultural worldviews accomplish this by imbuing existence with order, stability, and permanence. An example of this in Western cultures would be the treatment of time. In a sense, all an individual experiences is an ongoing stream of consciousness, which presumably ends at death. Yet the individual within Western culture conceptualizes his or her experiences in terms of calendar and clock designations. So there are years, months, days, and hours that are largely arbitrary designations—11:00 P.M., Monday, March 14, 1994—and there will be another year, and another Monday, and another March 14th. These are shared cultural conceptions of ongoing conscious experience that facilitate the belief that life has order, stability, and permanence.

In addition to these basic anchoring conceptions of reality, three sets of cultural constructs play especially important roles in terror management. First, all cultures infuse the universe with meaning by offering explanations for the origin of human beings and the place of humans within the cosmic scheme of things. Second, all cultures provide prescriptions for feeling good and valuable, largely through the provision of valued social roles, behavior, and attributes. Finally, all cultures offer safety and hope of literal or symbolic immortality to those who meet the prescriptions of value. Literal immortality consists of notions of an afterlife (e.g., spirit, souls); symbolic immortality consists of extensions of the self, such as prosperous children, permanent marks on reality (e.g., buildings, monuments), enduring achievements (e.g., a great painting or novel), and identification with ideologies and entities that transcend death (e.g., a political ideal, one's country, the cosmos).

This analysis suggests that in order to function with minimal anxiety, humans need (1) faith in a relatively benign cultural worldview (meaning) and (2) the belief that one is living up to the standards of value prescribed by that worldview (value). We refer to meaning and value as the dual components of the cultural anxiety buffer, which functions at the individual psychological level through the acquisition and maintenance of self-esteem (i.e., the belief that one is a valuable member of a meaningful universe).

A number of basic implications emerge from this analysis. Although the need for self-esteem is posited to be universal, because self-esteem is derived from cultural standards of value, the behaviors and attributes that provide self-esteem will vary widely across cultures. Because of the vital roles that self-esteem and the cultural worldviews play in managing existential terror, a great deal of personal and interpersonal behavior is directed toward the maintenance and defense of these structures. Given

that both the worldview and self-esteem are ultimately cultural construc-
tions, they require continual validation from others and are very vulnerable to challenge from others. Finally, challenges to either component of
the cultural anxiety buffer engender anxiety and compensatory defensive
responses.

From the perspective of terror management theory, most human social behavior can thus be seen as oriented toward the maintenance of either
the meaning or the value components of the cultural anxiety buffer. Our
analysis is in accord with the commonly held assumption that the pursuit
of a positive self-image is a superordinate goal toward which a great deal
of human behavior aspires (e.g., Carver and Scheier, 1981; Steele, 1988;
Tesser, 1988). From our depth perspective, however, the pursuit of both
self-esteem and faith in one's worldview is ultimately rooted in the need
for protection from existential terror that results from awareness of the
inevitability of death and the ever-present potential for tragedy. For a more
detailed discussion of the hierarchical relationship among these and other
social motives, see Pyszczynski, Greenberg, Solomon, and Hamilton (1990)
and Solomon et al. (1991).

RESEARCH ON THE PSYCHOLOGICAL FUNCTION
OF CULTURAL WORLDVIEWS

The Mortality Salience Effect

One basic hypothesis derived from the theory is that when people are
reminded of their own mortality, their need for faith in their worldviews
is increased. If the cultural worldview protects people from anxiety concerning death, then making mortality salient should engender a more
tenacious affinity for their cultural worldviews. Support for this hypothesis has been obtained in a series of studies showing that asking subjects
to contemplate their own death leads to especially favorable reactions to
those who validate their worldviews and especially unfavorable reactions
to those who challenge their worldviews (e.g., Greenberg et al., 1990;
Greenberg, Simon, Pyszczynski, Solomon, & Chatel, 1992a; Greenberg et
al., in press, a; Ochsmann & Reichelt, 1994; Rosenblatt, Greenberg, Solomon, Pyszczynski, & Lyon, 1989). More specifically, mortality salience
leads to more extreme punishments for moral transgressors and higher
rewards for those who uphold cultural values, more positive evaluations
of ingroup members (e.g., Christians) and more negative evaluations of
outgroup members (e.g., Jews, when evaluated by Christian subjects), and
more positive evaluations of those who praise the United States and more

negative evaluations of those who criticize the United States (by American citizens).[1]

We have also recently shown that mortality salience makes it more difficult for one to violate important cultural standards (Greenberg et al., in press, b). Specifically, reminding subjects of their mortality before asking them to work on problem-solving tasks that entailed using cultural icons (a flag and a crucifix) in a culturally inappropriate way led subjects to find the tasks more tension-producing and difficult and to take longer to solve them. This study provides the first direct evidence that mortality salience not only leads to negative judgments of others who challenge cultural norms but also increases subjects' resistance to violating such norms themselves.

Are Mortality Salience Effects Specific to Thoughts of One's Own Death?

The mortality salience treatment used in most of these studies asks subjects to answer two questions about death under the guise of a projective personality assessment: one regarding the feelings aroused in them by the thought of their own death and one concerning what will happen to them as they physically die and once they are physically dead. Control subjects have filled out either a similar questionnaire concerning food or television or no questionnaire at all. Clearly, this is a complex manipulation that may have a variety of potential confounds. However, comparison conditions and auxiliary measures in these studies indicate that mortality salience effects do not result from negative affect, heightened self-awareness, physiological arousal, or the priming of cultural values.

We have also recently conducted a series of studies in which we contrasted the effects of thinking about one's mortality with that of thinking about a variety of other aversive events, such as an examination in an important class, giving a speech in front of a large audience, worries about life after college, or intense physical pain. These studies have shown that

---

[1] A recent study (Simon, Harmon-Jones, Greenberg, Solomon & Pyszczynski, in press) found that these mortality salience effects are even stronger for mildly depressed individuals, perhaps because these individuals have more tenuous faith in their worldview and therefore must cling to it more tightly when confronted with mortality. Additionally, findings from two recent studies suggest that mortality salience will not always lead to derogation of different others (Greenberg et al., 1992a). Specifically, if tolerance is an important component of the individual's worldview or if the value of tolerance is primed, mortality salience does not engender such derogation. Presumably, the reason is that mortality salience motivates adherence to the values prescribed by one's worldview, as well as defense of that worldview.

although thoughts of one's mortality consistently lead to increased defense of the cultural worldview, thoughts of these other aversive events or even an actual failure experience do not (Greenberg et al., 1994, in press, a). Interestingly, this pattern has emerged even though these other aversive events often produce significant increases in anxiety or negative affect, whereas our mortality salience treatment consistently produces no such increase.

Finally, when the effects of thoughts of one's own mortality are contrasted with those of the death of a loved one, both types of death-related thoughts lead to increased defense of the cultural worldview (Greenberg et al., 1994). However, the salience of one's own mortality leads to significantly larger effects. Internal analyses suggest that the salience of the death of a loved one may produce increased worldview defense because it makes one's own death salient. Thus, the evidence available to date suggests that the mortality salience effects obtained in our research are indeed specific to the thoughts about one's own death.

Role of Affect and Consciousness in Mortality Salience Effects

Perhaps the most interesting finding from auxiliary measures in the mortality salience studies is that our mortality salience inductions consistently do not generate any negative affect. Our explanation for this is that the subjects' existing faith in their worldviews and sense of self-worth is sufficient to buffer them from any affective reaction to this relatively subtle treatment.[2] In psychoanalytical terms, the cultural worldview facilitates and bolsters the repression of the underlying terror (or potential terror) of death, which we presume accounts for the lack of negative affect in our studies following the mortality salience manipulation. This reasoning led us to consider the rather counterintuitive idea that the mortality salience effects produced in our studies might occur only when the thoughts of death are removed from conscious awareness—that is, when they are highly accessible but no longer in current working memory.

Consistent with this notion, all the mortality salience studies have

---

[2]Research findings on the anxiety-buffering function of self-esteem reported below are consistent with this notion. Additionally, we have recently obtained evidence that the cultural worldview also buffers anxiety regarding mortality (Pyszczynski, Becker, Vadeputte, Greenberg, & Solomon, 1994). In this study, subjects were led to support or refute the morality of the involvement of the United States in the Persian Gulf war and were then asked a set of questions about either death or television while their skin conductance was monitored. As expected, the death questions led to an increase in skin conductance in subjects led to question the morality of the United States, but not in subjects led to support the morality of the United States.

included a substantial delay and distraction between when the subjects think of mortality and when they fill out the dependent measures (subjects usually completed a mood measure and then read instructions and information about targets before evaluating them). In direct support of this analysis, three new studies (Greenberg et al., 1994), have shown that although the usual increased defense of the worldview occurs when subjects are distracted after the mortality salience induction, no such effects emerge when subjects are forced to keep death-related thoughts in mind until just before the dependent measures are assessed. In addition, a fourth study showed that the accessibility of death-related words is not increased directly after the mortality salience treatment, but is increased after a delay and distraction. Apparently, once death thoughts have successfully been removed from consciousness, suppression of such thoughts is relaxed and they become more accessible.

Presumably, then, when mortality thoughts are in consciousness, subjects are focused on getting those thoughts out of consciousness. Only after that has been accomplished does the individual engage in worldview defense. These findings provide what we view as an important first step toward the demonstration of the unconscious nature of processes involved in the operation of terror management motives.

RESEARCH ON THE FUNCTIONS OF SELF-ESTEEM

The second general hypothesis derived from terror management theory is that self-esteem serves as an anxiety buffer. A great deal of evidence is consistent with this hypothesis. First, a large correlational literature indicates that self-esteem is negatively correlated with various measures of anxiety and the physical and psychological consequences of anxiety. In addition, there is considerable evidence that people high in self-esteem perform better under stress than their low self-esteem counterparts. Furthermore, experimental evidence indicates that threats to self-esteem cause anxiety, that such anxiety triggers defense of self-esteem, and that these defenses effectively reduce the threat-engendered anxiety (for a review of this literature, see Solomon et al., 1991).

We have also provided more direct support for the self-esteem–anxiety hypothesis by showing that when self-esteem is momentarily bolstered or dispositionally high, subjects exposed to threatening stimuli exhibit less anxiety and less anxiety-related defense (Greenberg et al., 1992b; Greenberg et al., 1993). Specifically, increasing self-esteem led subjects to report less subjective anxiety in response to a graphic film depicting scenes of death, to exhibit less physiological arousal in response to the threat of painful electric shocks, and to exhibit lower levels of vulnerability-denying defensive distortions in their self-descriptions. This latter finding was replicated with a dispositional measure of self-esteem. Internal analyses in these studies ruled out the possibility that it was positive affect produced by the self-esteem boost rather than self-esteem per se that was responsible for the anxiety-buffering effects. In further support of the notion that self-esteem serves to protect the individual from mortality concerns, we have also recently found that a self-esteem boost or dispositionally high self-esteem reduces worldview defense and the delayed accessibility of death-related thoughts after mortality salience (Harmon-Jones, et al., 1994).

SELF-ESTEEM AND DEFENSIVENESS

If high self-esteem people are less anxious regarding vulnerabilities and threats, it makes sense that they would have less need for defenses. Consistent with this notion, along with vulnerability-denying defenses (Greenberg, et al., 1993), other research suggests that self-esteem-bolstering procedures can attenuate defenses such as the need to reduce dissonance (Steele, 1988; Steele & Liu, 1983) and to adjust perceptions of similarity to others to maintain positive self-evaluations (Tesser & Cornell, 1991). Similarly, Wicklund and Gollwitzer (1981) have shown that people who are unsure of their competence in a self-definitional domain behave in a biased, defensive manner, whereas those with a secure sense of their competence do not. These findings converge on the idea that self-esteem allows people to be less biased in their views of themselves and the world around them.

This, of course, is a central tenet of the theories of prominent humanistic psychologists such as Allport (1961), Maslow (1968), and Rogers (1959). It runs counter, however, to the currently popular notion that normal, psychologically healthy people are more biased in their beliefs than psychologically troubled individuals. This latter idea, which goes back at least as far as Freud, became popular in contemporary academic psychology largely because of the research of Alloy and Abramson (1979) suggesting that depressed people may be sadder but wiser. More recently, this idea has been effectively promoted by Taylor and Brown (1988), who reviewed a wide range of evidence that suggests that "normal" individuals consistently exhibit self-serving bias in their self-related judgments, judgments of control, and expectancies for the future.

There is likely to be some truth to both perspectives, although no empirical resolution to the apparent contradiction is currently available. One possibility is that "normal" people who score high on self-esteem scales are not necessarily truly high in self-esteem (cf. Horney, 1950).

Consistent with this possibility, Greenberg and Pyszczynski (1985) have shown that public failure can lead to inflated scores on a private disposi- tional measure of self-esteem, and Baumeister, Tice, and Hutton (1989) have demonstrated that high scores on dispositional self-esteem scales are sometimes a reflection of self-presentational concerns. Perhaps people tru- ly high in self-esteem, as described by the humanistic psychologists, do have more authentic views, but as Maslow (1968) argued, these people are rare. Potent laboratory self-esteem boosts may temporarily put people in a state akin to true high self-esteem people's chronic way of being and therefore temporarily reduce defensiveness.

From the perspective of the humanistic psychologists, it makes perfect sense that truly high self-esteem people could not be distinguished from others by how positively they view or report viewing themselves relative to others. However, they may be distinguishable on the basis of the sta- bility with which they hold those positive self-views. Indeed, recent work by Kernis and colleagues, described in Chapter 3 and elsewhere (e.g., Kernis, Grannemann, & Barclay, 1992), suggests that stability of self- esteem, rather than level of self-esteem, may be the key factor in determin- ing the utilization of psychological defenses.

Another approach to this issue is to suggest that high self-esteem individuals will be high in certain types of defense but not others. We (Greenberg et al., 1993) have recently argued that because self-esteem provides protection from deep-rooted anxieties, high self-esteem individ- uals engage in extensive defenses to protect their self-esteem. For the same reason, high self-esteem people will not have to be as defensive as others when confronted with threats not relevant to self-esteem, such as those regarding physical vulnerabilities and mortality. In contrast, low self- esteem individuals have little sense of personal value to defend and, as Swann's work (e.g., Swann, 1984) suggests, may actually derive some psychological benefits from their negative self-images. Yet that makes them vulnerable to a wide range of anxieties that they must defend against in other ways. We hope to investigate this possibility with research assess- ing the relationship between self-esteem and different types of defenses.

Summary

Terror management theory posits that culture serves to reduce the anxiety associated with the awareness of death through the provision of shared ideas about the nature of reality that imbue the universe with meaning and stability, and to offer the opportunity for literal or symbolic immortality, or both, through the satisfaction of appropriate standards of conduct associated with social roles. Self-esteem is the psychological mechanism by which culture serves its anxiety-buffering function. Empirical evidence supports the theory by (1) showing that self-esteem and faith in one's worldview do indeed serve anxiety-buffering functions and (2) demonstrating that mortality thoughts uniquely motivate defense of the worldview.

BEYOND TERROR: A GROWTH-ORIENTED ENRICHMENT MOTIVE SYSTEM

Although a substantial proportion of individual and social behavior quite readily can be seen as directed toward the maintenance of self-esteem and faith in the worldview, and as thus serving defensive terror management needs, clearly not all human behavior and psychological activity are guided solely by these concerns. Marx (1844), Nietzsche (1883/1982), Rank (1932/1989), and others have argued that sophisticated cognitive capabilities render humans conscious, and consequently creative, rather than purely reactive, organisms. It seems obvious that even beyond specific biologically based pleasurable experiences such as eating and sexual behavior, there are other phenomena that are not primarily defensive in nature, such as curiosity/exploratory behavior (e.g., Butler, 1953; Montgomery, 1953), effectance motivation (White, 1959), intrinsically motivated behaviors (e.g., Deci & Ryan, 1985), creativity (e.g. Menaker, 1982; Rank, 1936/1978), and phenomenological experiences associated with thrill-seeking and "flow" (Csikszentmihalyi, 1985). These and other related forms of behavior cannot be understood in the context of terror management theory in its present form.

As Rank (1932/1989), White (1959), Deci and Ryan (1991), and many others have suggested, these phenomena suggest the existence of a basic motive oriented toward the growth, expansion, and enrichment of the organism. This core motive is posited to underlie the human quest for knowledge and understanding and the perfection of various behavioral skills and competencies. From the first days of life, the human organism works relentlessly to take in information, make sense of it, and use it to guide subsequent thought and action. The child's joy and enthusiasm in response to discovery and developing new skills are prime manifestations of this motive system in action. Similarly, many adults retain a fascination with gathering information, understanding the causes of events around them, and developing skills. Indeed, the endeavor of science itself can be viewed as an institutionalized manifestation of this motivational system.

From an evolutionary perspective, an organismic growth/enrichment motivational system makes a great deal of sense. In order to survive long enough to reproduce and pass on its genes, an animal must be driven to explore, take in new information, and integrate that information with its existing conception of the world. Indeed, because an organism motivated entirely by defensive concerns would not be inclined to take the risks entailed in exploring its environment and developing new cognitive and behavioral capabilities, it would be unable to generate the novel behavior necessary to adapt to the demands of new and changing environments. Thus, it seems likely that a superordinate drive toward growth and enrichment would be just as important and basic as a drive toward self-preservation through defensive processes. Indeed, by guiding the organism, as the mythical Vulcans would say, to live long and prosper, a balance between these two motive systems would probably be most beneficial in terms of maximizing reproductive fitness.

It is not surprising, then, that these two motives have been employed either separately or in combination in a wide variety of analyses of human behavior from the beginning of this century to the present. Table 1 pro-

TABLE 1. Conceptions Reflecting Defense and Enrichment Motives

| Superordinate motives | Evolution by natural selection (inclusive fitness theory) | |
	Defense	Growth/Enrichment
James	Me (self as known)	I (self as knower/agent)
Freud	Superego functions/defense mechanisms	Eros
Rank	Fear of life and death	Separation/individuation (creative will)
G. Allport		Propriate striving
Maslow	Deficit motives	Growth motives (self-actualization)
Rogers	Defense (perceptual distortion and denial)	Self-actualizing tendency
N. O. Brown	Repressed functioning	Unrepressed living (play)
R. White		Effectance & competence motivation
Atkinson	Fear of failure	Motive for success
Duval & Wicklund	Objective self-awareness	Subjective self-awareness
Tedeschi	Defensive impression management	Assertive impression management
Deci & Ryan	Controlled functioning	Autonomous functioning
Sorrentino	Certainty orientation	Uncertainty orientation
Higgins	Negative outcome focus	Positive outcome focus
Solomon, Greenberg, & Pyszczynski	Terror management	Life-force—growth/enrichment

vides a list and categorization of some of the prominent theorists and researchers who have developed analyses using constructs that correspond to these motives. As Table 1 suggests, it would take far more than a section of a chapter for even a cursory attempt to review and compare these analyses; consequently, we will not do so here. It seems clear, however, that there is remarkable convergence on the importance of these two basic psychological constructs.

TOWARD A DUAL-MOTIVE DEPTH PSYCHOLOGY

Our current theoretical efforts to integrate defensive and growth motives are guided in large part by the work of Otto Rank (1932/1989, 1936/1978, 1941/1958) (for an overview of Rank's theorizing, also see Menaker, 1982) because it was Rank who first developed the ideas that evolved into terror management theory and also first grappled with the complex interplay of these two basic motive systems. We will therefore begin with a brief overview of Rank's analysis. For Rank, there is an inborn life force that provides vitality to all living organisms. This life force is manifested psychologically through the development and functioning of the creative will as children separate themselves from their parents (originally through the exertion of what Rank calls the "counterwill") in the service of individuation. Rank posited that the infant is not born with a sense of separateness and individuality; rather, this sense evolves with the development of cognitive abilities and growing opposition to parental control. This individuation process continues throughout childhood as the creative will becomes increasingly successful in guiding and controlling children's actions.

While this process involves growth toward self-actualization (achieving one's potential), according to Rank, it is also necessarily fraught with anxiety and guilt because individuation requires separation from the parents who were the child's primary security base and love objects. Here is perhaps the prototypical context in which the two driving forces, toward minimizing anxiety and toward growth, come into conflict—a phenomenon we will return to later.

According to Rank, this separation process results in a fear of life—a fear of asserting individuality and making unique claims of ability and of one's place in the world. Additionally, as children emerge as individuals as a consequence of the self-actualizing life force, they also become increasingly aware of their vulnerability to threats and the inevitability of death. Thus, death becomes the ultimate symbol of the loss of the very individuality the child has worked so hard to attain. Thus, the twin fears of life and death emerge as a result of a dialectical process of attachment and individuation.

The fear of life and death is then posited to instigate individuals' efforts to embed themselves in a larger framework of experience and to achieve death transcendence through the conventional vehicles of self-esteem within the context of the accepted cultural worldview (the core of our terror management analysis). Additionally, however, Rank argued that individuals also strive for immortality through the creative expression of their will, which serves to transform external reality to conform to desires that were originally imaginary in nature. This process is how Rank accounts for individual creativity and consequent social change, as well as constructive personality development.

We believe that Rank's perspective lays the groundwork for an integration of terror management with contemporary motivational analyses that posit an organismic tendency toward growth/enrichment.[3] We conclude this chapter with an overview of some preliminary implications of this integration.

UNIQUE ASPECTS OF THE ENRICHMENT SYSTEM

The growth- and enrichment-oriented motives are different from biological–homeostatic and symbolic–defensive motives in several important respects. Unlike these other motives, they do not stem from a sense of discomfort or distress that the organism is trying to minimize. Consequently, there is less of a sense of urgency about them. This, of course, is consistent with the contention of Maslow (1955) that growth-oriented motives are not oriented around the elimination of deficits.

Rather than operating in a drive-like, tension-reducing manner, growth-enrichment motives are fueled by acquisitive strivings for feelings of invigoration, mastery, and pleasure that result from the development and maximal engagement of one's cognitive and behavioral capacities. Such engagement of capacities produces integrative activity on the part of the organism (cf. Deci & Ryan, 1991), in which the new experience is taken in and incorporated into its existing representations, structures, or repertoires. This engagement–invigoration–integration process produces

---

[3]The only conceptual divergence we would at this point make from Rank is with regard to his distinction between fear of life (separation through individuation) and fear of death (loss of individuality). While we would grant that this distinction can be useful in certain contexts, we believe that both fears derive ultimately from annihilation anxiety because the fear of separation and individuation is likely to reflect the fear of losing the protection of the parents. Thus, we retain our contention that there is one root fear that underlies all other fears.

change or growth within the individual—an improvement in organization that advances simultaneously toward increases in both complexity and simplicity. Complexity increases in the sense that the internal representation of the reality becomes differentiated to encompass more and finer distinctions. Simplicity increases in the sense that the internal representation becomes more orderly and elegant; individual elements are organized into more coherent structures that increase the efficiency of the representation. Expansive activities are motivating because of the invigoration or pleasure or both that such engagement produces.

This capacity to experience invigoration or pleasure when one's capacities are maximally engaged is responsible, in part, for the motivation for both cognitive and behavioral mastery of one's world. It creates an incentive for exploration, the pursuit of novelty, and change. It no doubt varies among individuals, as a function of genetic, historical, and situational factors. Note that we emphasize that this capacity is only partly responsible for the pursuit of mastery because of the fairly obvious terror management functions that mastery can also serve. As we have maintained throughout this chapter, our beliefs about the nature of the world and sense of personal value or competence are the primary psychological mechanisms for the control of anxiety and dread.

EXPANSIVE AND DEFENSIVE CONCEPTIONS OF THE SELF

Whereas defensive, terror management motives are fundamentally symbolic in nature, pure growth–enrichment motives, although often expressed through symbols, are not. A person performing a task to enhance or protect self-esteem is concerned more with his or her own and other people's perceptions of his or her competence than with competence itself. Because it is the appearance and evaluative significance of the performance that really matters, defensive distortions, self-deceptions, and self-presentational tactics regarding the performance are useful strategies. In contrast, when enrichment motives are the primary force behind the behavior, the focus is on accurate understanding, enjoyment of the task, and developing one's skills; the evaluative and social implications of the performance are irrelevant.

Interestingly, a related distinction between these motives can be derived from William James (1890) and George Herbert Mead (1934) of the "I" and the "me" and the conceptions of Duval and Wicklund (1972) of subjective and objective self-awareness. For James and Mead, the I is the self as knower, the sense of agency (or, in Rank's terms, will) that we all experience, an organismic entity. The I is an emergent consequence of the person's psychological motives, processes, abilities, and potential. Duval and Wicklund refer to the state of the I unencumbered by the me as subjective self-awareness, a state in which attention is focused on the external environment. In contrast, the me is the self as known, the person's symbolic representation of self. Duval and Wicklund refer to the state of focusing on the me as objective self-awareness. Because of the dynamic and elusive nature of the I, the more static and self-knowable me is the focus of most contemporary empirical treatments of the self, whether the emphasis is on feelings about the self (e.g., self-esteem) or knowledge of the self (e.g., self-schemata).

Whereas the primary goal underlying growth–enrichment motives can profitably be viewed as maximization of the potential of the I, the primary goal underlying terror management can be viewed as maximization of the value of the me, toward preserving the me. It is tempting to argue that the goal of terror management is preservation of the I, but it is not, for the individual desiring immortality can only want to sustain what it knows, which is not the I, but rather the me. Thus, while the I strives to achieve its potential in the service of growth and enrichment, it simultaneously struggles to sustain the security of the me through the cultural worldview and a valued place for the me within it. Whereas the I ideally focuses on the environment toward enrichment without the burden of self-consciousness, self-consciousness necessitates defense of the me to mitigate the ever-present potential for terror. As noted earlier, self-consciousness, focus on the me, is a primary prerequisite for the emergence of the potential for existential terror.

Duval and Wicklund argued that self-awareness necessarily activates a self-evaluative process, in which one's current state is compared with internalized standards. Our analysis provides an explanation of why self-awareness leads to self-evaluation, a question not broached by other theories of self-awareness processes [beyond the assertion of Carver and Scheier (1981) that self-awareness serves a self-regulatory function]. We argue that with self-awareness comes awareness of one's vulnerability, creatureliness, and mortality. Because of the critical role that self-esteem plays in controlling the anxiety that this awareness produces, it leads to an assessment of the extent to which one is living up to one's internalized cultural standards of value, and instigates behavior to reduce any discrepancies in this respect that might be detected (for a more detailed analysis of the relationship between self-awareness and terror management, see Pyszczynski et al., 1990; Pyszczynski & Greenberg, 1992).

These ideas suggest that self-awareness will inevitably activate defensive concerns regardless of whether a behavior was originally initiated for growth–enrichment purposes. Once the activity becomes an arena for proving one's value, thus serving terror management needs, it begins to lose its value for growth or enrichment. We will pursue this issue of the interplay of the two motive systems further, but first we need to address a fundamental issue that sets our analysis apart from a number of other analyses that focus on defensive and nondefensive functioning.

WHY SO DEFENSIVE—IS IT SOCIETY OR REALITY?

Most analyses of defensive psychological functioning focus on defective social environments as the ultimate cause of personal distress and consequent compensatory responses (e.g., Allport, 1961; Brown, 1959; Deci & Ryan, 1985; Fromm, 1947; Higgins, 1989; Horney, 1950, Rogers, 1959). According to such analyses, controls, demands, and punishments of parents or society or both force the child to stifle his or her authentic organismic impulses and conform to societal demands. Interestingly, this view can also be seen in Rousseau (1755/1984), Marx (1844), and, to a certain extent, in the work of Freud (1929/1984). While it is clear that social environments can impede self-actualization, as Rank (1931/1961, 1936/1978), Becker (1973), and Marcuse (1955) and our terror management analysis point out, it is the realities of life and death rather than our parents or society that ultimately thwart our genuine desires. To cope with the real limitations and dangers of reality, we enslave ourselves, or as Rank (1941/1958 , p. 55) so eloquently put it, "Out of freedom, man creates a prison." From this perspective, then, defensive psychological activity is utterly necessary and cannot be avoided through the creation of utopian social conditions (this should not, however, in any way discourage concerted effort toward constructive social changes in the service of maximizing the realization of individual potential).

FREEDOM OR BALANCE?

Thus, we would argue that the ideal of a completely open person, free of defensiveness, autonomously striving for self-actualization, however appealing, is not possible. A delicate balance between the two systems may be the only realizable optimal condition that can be achieved. Whereas this analysis suggests that it is impossible to conceive of a functional human organism without defensive mechanisms to cope with uniquely human fears, it could also be argued that such an ideal would not even be desirable. Although in our terror management work we have emphasized the negative consequences of psychological defenses, there are most likely some positive consequences as well. Defensive concerns, and the pursuit of meaning and value they motivate, lead people to conform to social norms and standards. Although this is a mixed blessing at best, it certainly makes it possible for social organizations to function in an orderly manner. The Biblical story of the Tower of Babel vividly illustrates what would happen in the absence of shared meanings.

Perhaps more important, these defensive concerns also help to motivate highly valued accomplishments. The reality of the human dilemma and efforts to cope with it have contributed greatly to the creative accomplishments of many esteemed artists. Consider the paintings of Bosch, Van Gogh, and Munch; the music of Beethoven and Mahler, Charlie Parker and John Coltrane; the novels of Dostoyevsky, Hardy, and Joyce; and the films of Bergman and Fellini. All these works seem to be driven as much by efforts to battle fears and doubts as they are by desires to realize the creative potential of the artist. A purely autonomous, nondefensive human would probably not be capable of many of the achievements so highly valued in this and other cultures. The highest achievements seem to result from the interplay of defensive concerns and the expansion of one's capabilities.

Of course, we are not suggesting that existential fears are enjoyed by the individuals experiencing them or that they will inevitably lead to creative accomplishments; in the absence of a strong desire and capacity for growth and enrichment, such fears motivate only the most uncreative and often destructive conformity to social norms. Furthermore, such concerns weigh heavily on many people, contributing to anxieties and depressions that lead to nothing of value to anyone. Yet, great achievements often seem to result from the creative use of the individual's expansive potential to transcend fears through expressions of meaning and value.

Relationship between Defensive and Enrichment Motives

It seems clear from this analysis that the pursuit of self-esteem and the pursuit of self-expansion are guided by fundamentally different motives. Whereas the pursuit of self-esteem is defensive and symbolic, the quest for self-enrichment is acquisitive and direct. Whereas self-esteem concerns serve the minimization of negative affect and anxiety, self-enrichment motives serve a sense of mastery and positive affect. Whereas self-esteem pursuits are focused on the glorification of the me, self-enrichment motives aspire to the growth and fulfillment of the I. Of course, the I and the me are aspects of the same organism. Consequently, pursuing the growth and the enrichment of the I can lead to behaviors and accomplishments that, as a by-product, ultimately enhance self-esteem. Indeed, by encouraging the acquisition of skills and creative achievement, such activities may, ironically, provide a more durable basis of self-esteem—more stable high self-esteem in the terms of Kernis et al. (1992)—than activities specifically guided by self-esteem needs.

Unlike some other theories that contrast defensive and expansive motivation, we are not proposing two types of people, one type driven primarily by defensive concerns, the other by actualizing tendencies. Rather, both of these motive systems are posited to be driving forces in all people. Thus, for the present analysis, the question is: How do these systems combine and interact?

First, it is important to acknowledge that any given thought or action can serve either motive or both motives (cf. Deci & Ryan, 1985, 1991). For example, exercise can be used to develop one's physical abilities and feel good or to forestall heart disease and look attractive to others; one can buy a particular car to enjoy the "pure driving excitement" or to create a desired image; one can read a book to learn and enjoy or to feel good about oneself or to impress others. Indeed, the same type of behavior can reflect purely defensive functioning, purely expansive needs, or both.

Although a given behavior may serve only one of the motivational systems, as the preceding examples suggest, the two systems often push the individual in the same direction. As Deci and Ryan (1991) have noted, an individual can be conforming to societal standards and yet be functioning autonomously at the same time. When children truly internalize an external standard, they integrate that standard into the self, so that when living up to that standard, they are also engaging in autonomous self-directed action—doing what they authentically want to do. Deci and Ryan contrast such standards with introjected standards, which the child learns to obey but does not integrate into the self. The person conforming to such standards is functioning in a controlled way, serving only defensive needs by obeying introjected but ultimately external demands. In this latter case, defense and enrichment motives may be functioning in opposition to each other.

Thus, two instances of the same type of behavior that conforms to societal standards can reflect purely defensive functioning or both defensive and expansive needs. The behaviors, however, will not really be the same. Purely defensive behavior will have either a highly driven or passionless character, will be rigid and conventional, and will be associated with emotions such as anxiety, tension, and boredom. Behavior that also (or solely) serves enrichment motives will be more relaxed, flexible, playful, and creative and will be associated with positive affect and pleasure.

There is a complexity here, however, in that, as noted earlier, when behavior serves purposes other than enrichment, its value for subsequent enrichment may be somewhat diminished. We are of course referring to the literature on intrinsic motivation that indicates that when extrinsic goals are introduced in situations in which behavior is initially guided only by intrinsic interest, interest in the behavior and the relaxed quality of the behavior are often undermined. The classic example of such a situation is the finding that if rewards that are perceived to be controlling behavior rather than indicating the quality of one's performance are offered to perform intrinsically enjoyable tasks, interest in such tasks is reduced (for reviews, see Deci & Ryan, 1980, 1985). As suggested earlier, when we are self-aware, our behavior tends to become defensively driven, with the salient concern being self-evaluation rather than the intrinsic value of the activity. Thus, similar to external inducements, self-awareness leads to a shift in the perception of a task from something done for enjoyment to something done to prove or defend one's value. As soon as the activity becomes an indicator of one's value, it becomes critical for protection from deeply rooted fears; suddenly, it becomes a source of anxiety, and what was once play is now quite a serious matter.

Consistent with this reasoning, Plant and Ryan (1985) have shown that engaging in an activity when attention is focused on the self leads to a loss of intrinsic interest in the activity. In a related vein, studies have shown that presenting a task as a measure of intelligence also leads to a loss of intrinsic interest (e.g., Ryan, 1982; Ryan & Deci, 1989) and that giving subjects the opportunity to evaluate their task performance impairs the creativity of their performance (Szymanski & Harkins, 1992). It seems clear, then, that the conscious activation of defensive concerns does indeed tend to reduce an activity's enrichment value.

Variables that Influence the Dominance of Defensive vs. Enrichment Concerns

Given that either or both motive systems can be involved to varying degrees in specific activities, it is important to consider the factors that are likely to lead to one or the other motive's being particularly salient or influential in a specific behavioral context or for a specific person. We will briefly consider three such factors from the perspective of our dual-motive system conceptualization.

Effectiveness of the Cultural Anxiety Buffer

Terror management theory posits that the problem of mortality engenders an ever-present potential for terror that is averted by faith in a cultural worldview and one's value within the context of that worldview. If this premise is true, then a great deal of energy must be devoted to maintaining these constructs. As long as these components of the cultural anxiety buffer are secure, individuals are likely to focus much of their energy on growth and enrichment. However, when either of these constructs is threatened or undermined, defensive concerns with restoring and bolstering these constructs should dominate. We are not suggesting that no enrichment activities can occur in the face of threat or undermining, but that most of the individual's capabilities and energy will be devoted to bolstering the buffer. In general, then, the more an individual is having difficulty maintaining his or her sense of meaning and value, the more the person will be driven to restore those things and the less that person will enjoy activities for their own sake and strive toward growth and enrichment.

Our assumption here is that defense is generally prepotent. This is consistent with the argument of Maslow (1955) that deficiencies in such basic needs as safety, esteem, and belonging must be satisfied before the individual will pursue self-actualization. This is not to say that a person with urgent defensive concerns will not use his or her expansive capacities, but that these capacities will be used to facilitate the individual's quest for security.

Consider the example of a scientist striving to develop a better understanding of some issue—on the surface a fine example of growth–enrichment striving. However, if the individual is insecure about his or her current career status and has staked his or her reputation on a particular theoretical perspective, ideas and evidence consistent with that view will be emphasized and alternative ideas and evidence will be discounted, neglected, or distorted. The end result will not be an open-minded, creative, and accurate analysis, but an ego-saving exercise to shore up faith in one's anxiety-buffering sense of self-worth. Perhaps the work by Wicklund and Gollwitzer (1981), mentioned earlier, provides the best empirical evidence concerning this sort of process. These researchers have consistently found that people who feel incomplete with regard to self-definitional goals behave defensively, seeking to display superficial symbols of worth to prove their suitability for the desired self-definition.

Changes in Enrichment Potential over Time

Many roles and activities in people's lives, especially the more important ones, typically serve both terror management and enrichment needs. As individuals become more familiar with and more accomplished and invested in their roles or activities, these endeavors are likely to become increasingly useful for managing terror. However, the effects on enrichment value of increasing time spent in a given endeavor or relationship are more complex. At least two distinct types of changes occur in the potential for enrichment with the passage of time and increasing familiarity and experience. On the positive side, the longer one pursues a role or activity, the more complex and differentiated one's internal representation becomes and, consequently, the more one is able to notice and appreciate subtle aspects of the endeavor that might not be apparent to the novice. For example, the more experienced one is at listening to music, tasting wine, or watching basketball, the greater one's potential for appreciating the finer aspects of those perceptual experiences. Similarly, as one's skills in a given domain develop, the potential for creative use of those skills often expands in a logarithmic manner. It is the well-seasoned master musician, wine maker, or athlete who is most able to take his or her chosen endeavor to new heights of excellence.

On the negative side, prolonged pursuit of an activity or role can often lead to boredom and stagnation, resulting in a situation in which the activity or role mitigates negative affect sufficiently to be worth clinging to, but does little to provide positive affect and satisfaction. As something becomes more familiar, it often has fewer novel growth and enrichment possibilities to offer. The security benefits of what's known, on the other hand, tend to grow and linger. In the absence of alternative sources of meaning and value, people stick with roles that, although of little use for enrichment, still serve terror management functions. Unfortunately, long-term romantic relationships often seem to fall prey to this process. Early in the relationship, the partners learn from each other and help each other grow and enjoy the activities of life. But all too often, the shared experiences become routine and mundane, the passion is reduced, and, consequently, the relationship provides less and less enrichment, sometimes even stifling enrichment in other domains.

Both these processes are no doubt at work in most activities and roles. In many cases, these competing forces probably produce a curvilinear relationship between familiarity and enrichment potential, with this potential first increasing and later decreasing over time. However, as exemplified by the experienced master in many domains, this decrease in enrichment potential is not an inevitable characteristic of all endeavors. The precise nature of the relationship between enrichment potential and time or experience may depend on how well the activity or role was suited for the individual's unique interests and capacities in the first place, along with a host of environmental factors that might facilitate or inhibit the continuing enrichment value of such endeavors. However, regardless of the enrichment value of a role at a given point in time, the likelihood of abandoning that role will depend largely on the value of that role for terror management and the availability of alternative roles for serving that function.

REDUCING DEFENSIVENESS THROUGH ENRICHMENT

One final possibility worthy of consideration is that a life-style that provides one with many opportunities for enrichment may reduce the extent to which defensive concerns dominate one's daily affairs. Although we have emphasized the fragile nature of expansive motivation, and the ease with which expansive activities can be turned into arenas for self-aggrandization and thus terror management, it may be the case that throwing oneself into enrichment-oriented activity is useful, at least temporarily, for reducing the extent to which the fears that underlie defensive behavior become salient and thus exert a primary influence on behavior. When one is fully engaged in an enrichment or flow activity, one's attention is necessarily diverted from the self. To the extent that self-awareness is an important factor in setting defensive processes in motion, absorption in expansion-oriented activity may be a useful way of temporarily reducing the extent to which fears and other defensive concerns dominate one's life. The sad irony of this strategy is that to the extent that it is effective in providing relief from one's fears and defenses, it too may become utilized as a defensive form of distraction, and thus may eventually lose its utility for true enrichment. Still, at least in the short run, absorption in enrichment-oriented activities may be a useful means of escaping the hold that the existential realities of life have on most of us.

CONCLUSION: THE DYNAMIC DIALECTICAL BALANCE BETWEEN DEFENSE AND ENRICHMENT

At the most general level, this dual-motive depth psychology suggests that the best humans can hope for is a dynamic dialectical balance between defensive and expansive functioning that first emerges with cognitive and social development. This balance is precarious because of the complex relations between the two motive systems. When terror management concerns need to be addressed, enrichment strivings will be suppressed; when terror management is going well, enrichment can be the primary focus.

However, expansive strivings influence terror management in two opposite ways. The increasing sophistication of our cognitive abilities engendered by growth–enrichment motives is what created and amplifies our need for terror management. Rank argued that it is the development of consciousness that first allowed a linear conception of time that creates the problem of death (time ending). As we have argued, self-consciousness and increasing intellectual abilities create the potential for terror by allowing us to understand that the self is vulnerable to a wide variety of future threats including inevitable death. This phylogenetic sequence is then tragically recapitulated ontogenetically with each new child.

To the extent that the growth–enrichment motive has guided our cognitive development and understanding of ourselves and reality, it is what really got us into the existential jam in the first place. Indeed, the arts, the sciences, and the humanities have contributed greatly to the existential dilemma that terror management is purported to address. Thus, this theory itself is largely a product of the enrichment system (although our use of it is no doubt serving our own twisted terror management needs); if Western culture were driven by purely defensive concerns, Kierkegaard, Darwin, Rank, and others would probably never have attempted to do what they did and certainly would never have been lauded for doing so. And perhaps it would have been better that way, but we are driven on to explore and learn, at the same time trying to control our fears along the way.

Perhaps with knowledge and awareness of the horrors happening all over the globe, and cultural pluralism, all on the increase, our growth–enrichment concerns are beginning to outstrip our capacity for terror management over the life span. However, as Rank proposed, the same capacities that have created the potential for terror are also used to attempt to manage that terror, so we construct, patch up, and reconstruct conceptions of ourselves and the world that can help us sustain a sense of security and death transcendence. It is to be hoped that some new emerging forms of secular humanistic, artistic, religious, or spiritual conceptions of things will better provide meaning and value and the sense of identification with the continuity of life that are so sorely needed.

Rank has described a similar process occurring historically in the evolution of immortality ideologies. Perhaps this dialectical interplay also recapitulates throughout the individual life span; as turbulent internal and external events stimulate greater activation of one motive system, the other motive system must be employed to attempt to restore a healthy balance. Interestingly, Rank (1932/1989) argued that psychology is better at enhancing our awareness of the problem than it is at helping to solve it, because it deconstructs meanings without supplying a compelling ideology of meaning in place of the rubble it makes of existing ones (p. 192): "However, psychology, which is gradually trying to supplant religious and moral ideology, is only partially qualified to do this, because it is a preponderantly negative and disintegrating ideology. . . ."

In sum, we need our terror sufficiently mitigated to allow us to develop our capacities, just as the young child needs secure attachment to confidently explore his or her environment and develop his or her skills. As our growth–enrichment motives spur us on to greater cognitive abilities and understanding, however, the enormity of our vulnerabilities and mortality became all the more apparent; at that point, the hope is that those very capabilities can then be employed to better establish meaning and value to more effectively assuage our fears.

ACKNOWLEDGMENTS. Preparation of this chapter was supported in part by National Science Foundation Grant SBR9312546, a Faculty Development Grant from Skidmore College, and a grant from the Alexander von Humboldt Foundation.

REFERENCES

Alloy, L. B., & Abramson, L. Y. (1979). Judgement of contingency in depressed and non-depressed students: Sadder but wiser? *Journal of Experimental Psychology: General, 108,* 441–485.

Allport, G. W. (1961). *Pattern and growth in personality.* New York: Holt, Rinehart & Winston.

Baumeister, R. F., Tice, D. M., & Hutton, D. G. (1989). Self-presentational motivations and personality differences in self-esteem. *Journal of Personality, 57,* 547–579.

Becker, E. (1962). *The birth and death of meaning.* New York: Free Press.

Becker, E. (1971). *The birth and death of meaning, 2nd ed.* New York: Free Press.

Becker, E. (1973). *The denial of death.* New York: Free Press.

Becker, E. (1975). *Escape from evil.* New York: Free Press.

Berger, P. L., & Luckmann, T. (1967). *The social construction of reality: A treatise in the sociology of knowledge.* Garden City, NY: Anchor Books.

Brown, N. O. (1959). *Life against death: The psychoanalytic meaning of history.* New York: Viking.

Butler, R. A. (1953). Discrimination learning by rhesus monkeys to visual exploration motivation. *Journal of Comparative and Physiological Psychology, 46,* 95–98.

Carver, C. S., & Scheier, M. F. (1981). *Attention and self-regulation.* New York: Springer-Verlag.

Csikszentmihalyi, M. (1985). Emergent motivation and the evolution of the self. In D. Klieber & M. H. Maehr (Eds.) *Motivation in adulthood* (pp. 93–133). Greenwich, CT: JAI Press.

Deci, E. L. & R. M. (1980). The empirical exploration of intrinsic motivational processes. In L. Berkowitz (Ed.) , *Advances in experimental social psychology* (pp. 39–80). New York: Academic Press.

Deci, E. L., & Ryan, R. M. (1985). *Intrinsic motivation and self-determination in human behavior.* New York: Plenum Press.

Deci, E. L., & Ryan, R. M. (1991). A motivational approach to self: Integration in personality. In R. Dienstbier (Ed.), *Nebraska symposium on motivation,* Vol. 38, *Perspective on motivation* (pp. 237–288). Lincoln: University of Nebraska Press.

Duval, S., & Wicklund, R. A. (1972). *A theory of objective self-awareness.* New York: Academic Press.

Freud, S. (1929/1984). *Civilization and its discontents.* New York: W. W. Norton.

Fromm, E. (1947). *Man for himself: An inquiry into the psychology of ethics.* New York: Rinehart.

Greenberg, J., & Pyszczynski, T. (1985). Compensatory self-inflation: A response to the threat to self-regard of public failure. *Journal of Personality and Social Psychology, 49,* 273–280.

Greenberg, J., Pyszczynski, T., & Solomon, S. (1986). The causes and consequences of the need for self-esteem: A terror management theory. In R. F. Baumeister (Ed.), *Public self and private self*. New York: Springer-Verlag.

Greenberg, J., Pyszczynski, T., Solomon, S., Rosenblatt, A., Veeder, M., Kirkland, S., & Lyon, D. (1990). Evidence for terror management theory. II. The effects of mortality salience reactions to those who threaten or bolster the cultural worldview. *Journal of Personality and Social Psychology, 58*, 308–318.

Greenberg, J., Simon, L., Pyszczynski, T., Solomon, S., & Chatel, D. (1992a). Terror management and tolerance: Does mortality salience always intensify negative reactions to others who threaten one's worldview? *Journal of Personality and Social Psychology, 63*, 212–220.

Greenberg, J., Solomon, S., Pyszczynski, T., Rosenblatt, A., Burling, J., Lyon, D., Simon, L., & Pinel, E. (1992b). Why do people need self-esteem? Converging evidence that self-esteem serves an anxiety-buffering function. *Journal of Personality and Social Psychology, 63*, 913–922.

Greenberg, J., Pyszczynski, T., Solomon, S., Pinel, E., Simon, L., & Jordan, K. (1993). Effects of self-esteem on vulnerability-denying defensive distortions: Further evidence of an anxiety-buffering function of self-esteem. *Journal of Experimental Social Psychology, 29*, 229–251.

Greenberg, J., Pyszczynski, T., Solomon, S., Simon, L., & Breus, M. (1994). The role of consciousness and accessibility of death-related thoughts in mortality salience effects. *Journal of Personality and Social Psychology, 67*, 627–637.

Greenberg, J., Simon, L., Harmon-Jones, E., Solomon, S., Pyszczynski, T., & Lyon, D. (in press, a). Testing alternative explanations for mortality salience effects: Terror management, value accessibility, or worrisome thoughts? *European Journal of Social Psychology*.

Greenberg, J., Simon, L., Porteus, J., Pyszczynski, T., & Solomon, S. (in press, b). Evidence of a terror management function of cultural icons: The effects of mortality salience on the inappropriate use of cherished cultural symbols. *Personality and Social Psychology Bulletin*.

Harmon-Jones, E., Simon, L., Greenberg, J., Pyszczynski, T., Solomon, S., & McGregor, H. (1994). The interactive effects of self-esteem and mortality salience on worldview defense. Unpublished manuscript. Tucson: University of Arizona.

Higgins, E. T. (1989). Self-discrepancy theory: What patterns of self-beliefs cause people to suffer? In L. Berkowitz (Ed.), *Advances in experimental social psychology* (Vol. 22, pp. 93–136). Orlando, FL: Academic Press.

Horney, K. (1950). *Neurosis and human growth: 'The struggle toward self-realization*. New York: W. W. Norton.

James, W. (1890). *Psychology*. New York: Holt.

Kernis, M. H., Grannemann, B. D., & Barclay, L. C. (1992). Stability of self-esteem: Assessment, correlates, and excuse-making. *Journal of Personality, 60*, 621–644.

Marcuse, H. (1955). *Eros and civilization*. Boston: Beacon.

Marx, K. (1844). *Economic and philosophical manuscript of 1844* (M. Milligan, translator). New York: International Publications.

Maslow, A. (1955). Deficiency motivation and growth motivation. In M. R. Jones (Ed.), *Nebraska symposium on motivation*. Lincoln: University of Nebraska Press.

Maslow, A. (1968). *Toward a psychology of being*. Princeton, NJ: Van Nostrand.

Mead, G. H. (1934). *Mind, self, and society*. Chicago: University of Chicago Press.

Menaker, E. (1982). *Otto Rank: A rediscovered legacy*. New York: Columbia University Press.

Montgomery, K. C. (1953). Exploratory behavior as a function of "similarity" of stimulus situations. Journal of Comparative and Physiological Psychology, 46, 129–133.

Nietzsche, F. (1883/1982). *Thus spake Zarathustra* (T. Common, translator). New York: Random.

Ochsmann, R., & Reichelt, K. (1994). Evaluation of moral and immoral behavior: Evidence for terror management theory. Unpublished manuscript. Mainz, Germany: University of Mainz.

Plant, R. W., & Ryan, R. M. (1985). Intrinsic motivation and the effects of self-consciousness, self-awareness, and ego-involvement: An investigation of internally controlling styles. *Journal of Personality, 53*, 435–449.

Pyszczynski, T., & Greenberg, J. (1992). *Hanging on and letting go.* New York: Springer-Verlag.

Pyszczynski, T., Greenberg, J., Solomon, S., & Hamilton, J. (1990). A terror management analysis of self-awareness and anxiety: The hierarchy of terror. *Anxiety Research, 2,* 177–195.

Pyszczynski, T., Greenberg, J., Solomon, S., Sideris, J., & Stubing, M. (1993). Emotional expression and the inhibition of motivated cognitive bias: Evidence from cognitive dissonance and distancing from victims' paradigms. *Journal of Personality and Social Psychology, 64,* 177–186.

Pyszczynski, T., Becker, L., Vadeputte, D., Greenberg, J., & Solomon, S. (1994). The physiological effects of mortality salience and threatening or bolstering the cultural worldview. Unpublished manuscript. University of Colorado–Colorado Springs.

Rank, O. (1931/1961). *Psychology and the soul.* New York: Perpetual Books Edition (original work published in 1931).

Rank, O. (1932/1989). *Art and artist: Creative urge and personality development.* New York: W. W. Norton (original work published in 1932).

Rank, O. (1936/1978). *Truth and reality.* New York: W. W. Norton (original work published in 1936).

Rank, O. (1941/1958) . *Beyond psychology.* New York: Dover Publications (original work published in 1941).

Rogers, C. R. (1959). A theory of therapy, personality, and interpersonal relationships, as developed in the client-centered framework. In S. Koch (Ed.), *Psychology: A study of a science,* Vol. 3, *Formulations of the person and the social context* (pp. 185–256). New York: McGraw-Hill.

Rosenblatt, A., Greenberg J., Solomon, S., Pyszczynski, T., & Lyon, D. (1989). Evidence for terror management theory. I. The effects of mortality salience on reactions to those who violate or uphold cultural values. *Journal of Personality and Social Psychology, 57,* 681–690.

Rousseau, J. J. (1755/1984). Discourse on the origin and foundations of inequality among men. In R. D. Masters (Ed.), *The first and second discourses.* New York: San Martins (original work published in 1755).

Ryan, R. M. (1982). Control and information in the intrapersonal sphere: An extension of cognitive evaluation theory. *Journal of Personality and Social Psychology, 43,* 450–461.

Ryan, R. M., & Deci, E. L. (1989). When free-choice behavior is not intrinsically motivated: Experiments on internally controlling regulation. Unpublished manuscript. Rochester, NY: University of Rochester.

Simon, L., Harmon-Jones, E., Greenberg, J., Solomon, S., & Pyszczynski, T. (in press). Mild depression, mortality salience, and defense of the worldview: Evidence of intensified terror management in the mildly depressed. *Personality and Social Psychology Bulletin.*

Solomon, S., Greenberg, J., & Pyszczynski, T. (1991). A terror management theory of social behavior: The psychological functions of self-esteem and cultural worldviews. In M. P. Zanna (Ed.), *Advances in experimental social psychology* (pp. 91–159). San Diego: Academic Press.

Steele, C. M. (1988). The psychology of self-affirmation: Sustaining the integrity of the self. In L. Berkowitz (Ed.), *Advances in experimental social psychology* (pp. 261–302). San Diego: Academic Press.

Steele, C. M., & Liu, T. J. (1983). Dissonance processes as self-affirmation. *Journal of Personality and Social Psychology, 45,* 5–19.

Swann, W. B., Jr. (1984). Quest for accuracy in person perception: A matter of pragmatics. *Psychological Review, 91,* 457–477.

Szymanski, K., & Harkins, S. (1992). Self-evaluation and creativity. *Personality and Social Psychology Bulletin, 18,* 259–265.

Taylor, S. E., & Brown, J. D. (1988). Illusion and well-being: A social psychological perspective on mental health. *Psychological Bulletin, 103,* 193–210.

Tesser, A. (1988). Toward a self-evaluation maintenance model of social behavior. In L. Berkowitz (Ed.), *Advances in experimental social psychology* (pp. 181–227). San Diego: Academic Press.

Tesser, A., & Cornell, D. P. (1991). On the confluence of self processes. *Journal of experimental social psychology, 27,* 501–526.

White, R. (1959). Motivation reconsidered: The concept of competence. *Psychological Review, 66,* 297–334.

Wicklund, R. A., & Gollwitzer, P. M. (1981). Symbolic self-completion, attempted influence, and self-deprecation. *Basic and Applied Social Psychology, 2,* 89–114.

CHAPTER 5

THE EVALUATIVE ORGANIZATION OF SELF-KNOWLEDGE:

ORIGINS, PROCESSES, AND IMPLICATIONS FOR SELF-ESTEEM

CAROLIN J. SHOWERS

INTRODUCTION

Imagine two individuals, both of whom would describe their "social" selves with the same set of attributes: shy, loyal, awkward, lonely, cheerful, kind, energetic, respectful, nervous, and bored. Let's say that these two persons both find themselves talking to strangers at a formal reception, an experience that activates their perceptions of themselves as shy. Yet one of our characters, when he feels shy, thinks to himself, "Not only am I shy, I'm also often lonely and sometimes awkward." The second person, although she too knows that she is often lonely and sometimes awkward, may not necessarily bring these attributes to mind in this context. Instead,

CAROLIN J. SHOWERS • Department of Psychology, University of Wisconsin–Madison, Madison, Wisconsin 53706.

Efficacy, Agency, and Self-Esteem, edited by Michael H. Kernis. Plenum Press, New York, 1995.

she might think to herself, "I may be shy, but I'm also a loyal friend." Presumably, the latter thought moderates negative feelings about being shy by linking shyness to a positive belief about the self. In contrast, the first individual's stream of thought—shy, lonely, awkward—probably contributes to a very strong negative reaction in this situation.

This example illustrates that it is not just the content of one's beliefs about the self, but also how those beliefs are organized, that influence reactions to events. In particular, the evaluative organization of self-knowledge refers to the interconnectedness (associative links) between positive and negative items of information (Showers, 1992a,b). When beliefs that have the same evaluative valence are strongly associated, their affective impact should be enhanced. When beliefs of opposite valence are interconnected, the impact of any one belief should be minimized. If these associations are relatively stable, then over the course of many experiences, the evaluative organization of self-knowledge may have long-term consequences for global evaluations of the self (i.e., self-esteem) or mood. For instance, the person who thinks, "I'm shy, but loyal," may report higher self-esteem than the person who thinks, "I'm shy, lonely, and awkward," even though the basic content of their self-concepts is the same.

Measures of self-esteem typically assess the positivity of self-beliefs, not their organization. Self-esteem scales can be identified as one of two types. One type, for example, the Rosenberg (1965) scale, measures the positivity or negativity of highly generalized beliefs about the self. The other type, for example, the Tennessee Self-Concept Scale (Fitts, 1964), assesses domain-specific beliefs. Cognitive information-processing models of the self predict a close correspondence between these two types of measures, but in fact the correlations are weak (Hoge & McCarthy, 1984). However, the correspondence between such measures may improve if organizational factors, such as the relative importance of different domains, are taken into account (Pelham & Swann, 1989).

Cognitive models of the self typically go beyond trait measures of self-esteem to consider the accessibility as well as the content of positive or negative self-knowledge. The preferential accessibility of information in an individual's self-schemata has been demonstrated empirically using measures of response latency (Markus, 1977). Although the self-schema framework has not been applied directly to the study of self-esteem, cognitive models of depression have postulated the existence of negative self-schemata in depressed persons (Beck, 1976; Hammen, Marks, Mayol, & de Mayo, 1985; Segal, 1988). Moreover, Bargh and Tota (1988) demonstrated that negative self-referential constructs are automatically activated in depressed persons.

Most recently, cognitive models of the self have focused on the organization of self-knowledge as well as its content and accessibility. There are at least three ways in which organizational factors may influence global self-esteem. First, as suggested above, there may be meta-level organizational factors such as perceived importance, self-clarity, or self-complexity that moderate the relationship between positive or negative content and self-esteem (Campbell, 1990; Linville, 1985; Pelham & Swann, 1989). Second, organizational factors may influence the accessibility of positive and negative content. For our shy persons at the reception, the interconnectedness of specific items of information (shy, lonely, awkward, kind, loyal) makes this knowledge more or less accessible in the context described. Although the accessibility of information in a person's self-schemata is said to be due to the well-organized structure of the schemata, those organizational structures have not been studied explicitly (Higgins & Bargh, 1987; Higgins, Van Hook, & Dorfman, 1988; Segal, 1988; Spielman & Bargh, 1990). Third, organizational factors may contribute to the use of cognitive coping strategies that determine the impact of positive or negative events on self-esteem. For example, our two shy characters' streams of thought may represent two different coping strategies. The thought, "I'm shy, lonely, and awkward" suggests a process of over-generalization (Kernis, Brockner, & Frankel, 1989), whereas "I'm shy, but I'm loyal" tends to limit the impact of shyness across situations. Thus, the interconnectedness of positive and negative information may underlie the use of specific coping strategies or interpretive biases.

The role of organizational factors in determining global self-evaluation and affect has two important implications for theory, research, and applications related to self-esteem. First, it suggests that positive or negative content alone may not be a sufficient predictor of global self-esteem. Instead, two individuals who have the same positive or negative content of self-knowledge may experience very different levels of self-esteem, depending on how that knowledge is organized. Second, this model carries with it implications for how individuals whose self-concepts contain a great deal of negative information might be able to bolster self-esteem. Although a content-based approach to self-esteem might simply encourage these individuals to abandon their negative beliefs about the self, the model presented in this chapter suggests that it may be possible to enhance self-esteem by reorganizing positive and negative beliefs, without having to revise or deny presently held beliefs about the self. This approach may be especially valuable when the negative beliefs of a low self-esteem person are fairly accurate, as suggested by literature on depressive realism (Alloy & Abramson, 1988).

FORMAL MODEL AND INITIAL EVIDENCE

This model of the evaluative organization of the self emphasizes processes that contribute either to the *evaluative compartmentalization* of positive and negative self-knowledge or to its *evaluative integration.* The model assumes that the self is represented by multiple categories of information, or *self-aspects.* These self-aspects are idiographic, and they may represent roles, situations, moods, personality characteristics, activities, and the like. Each self-aspect contains a set of items of self-knowledge, assumed to be closely interconnected. The compartmentalization or integration of the current self-concept depends on the distribution of positively or negatively valenced items of information within and across self-aspects.

Section A in Table 1 illustrates the compartmentalized organization of knowledge about the self in social situations for the person in our example who thought, "I'm shy, lonely, and awkward." For this individual, items of the same valence are closely interconnected. The table suggests that this person may have one social self-aspect consisting of "social flaws" and another representing "social assets." These self-aspects are evaluatively compartmentalized, because each tends to contain similarly valenced items of information. When any negative self-aspect is activated, a person

TABLE 1. Examples of Evaluatively Compartmentalized and Evaluatively Integrative Organization for Two Individuals with the Same Content of the Self-Concept in the Social Domain

A. Evaluatively compartmentalized organization	
Social assets	Social flaws
+ Loyal	– Shy
+ Cheerful	– Lonely
+ Kind	– Awkward
+ Energetic	– Nervous
+ Respectful	– Bored

B. Evaluatively integrative organization	
Me with friends	Me with my boss
– Shy	– Lonely
+ Loyal	– Awkward
+ Kind	+ Cheerful
– Nervous	– Bored
+ Energetic	+ Respectful

with compartmentalized organization is likely to bring to mind other negative information about the self, intensifying the negativity of the experience. However, when positive self-aspects are activated, then compartmentalized organization should enhance the positivity of the experience. Over the course of many such experiences, the long-term impact of compartmentalized organization on global self-evaluations and affect should depend on the relative impact of the positive or the negative compartments.

For a person who has many positive experiences, positive compartments may be activated most frequently. These self-aspects may be perceived as highly important (i.e., central to the self), and they may even be chronically accessible (Bargh & Pratto, 1986; Higgins & King, 1981). This individual is described as *positive-compartmentalized,* and this type of organization should have positive implications for self-esteem. The compartmentalized individual whose pure negative self-aspects are important or frequently accessed is described as *negative-compartmentalized.* For this person, pure negative self-aspects likely intensify negative experience and tend to lower self-esteem. Although Pelham and Swann (1989) have already demonstrated that the relative importance of positive and negative self-aspects is a significant predictor of self-esteem, here I consider that feature of the self in conjunction with the organization of information within self-aspects in order to distinguish positive- and negative-compartmentalized types.

Section B illustrates the *evaluatively integrative* type of self-concept organization. The self-aspects labeled "me with friends" and "me with my boss" both contain mixtures of positive and negative information. The close interconnections between oppositely valenced items of knowledge in this type of organization should minimize the impact of negative knowledge, because negative items are likely to be linked to some more positive items of information. Conversely, if a positively valenced item of information is linked to negatives, then the impact of positive knowledge should be moderated as well.[1]

This model predicts that the effect of compartmentalized vs. integrative organization depends on the relative importance of positive and negative self-aspects. If an individual has a great deal of important negative self-knowledge, then negative compartments would likely be impor-

---

[1]The directionality of the interconnections between items of information is critical. An integrative thought that leads from a negative to a positive belief (e.g., "shy but loyal") need not imply the converse ("loyal but shy"). Clearly, it is the former associative link that is likely to be beneficial for self-esteem. The direction of integrative associations may be influenced by the motivational, cognitive, or affective processes that bring about a particular type of organization (see the section entitled "Origins of Evaluative Organization").

tant and frequently accessed. In this case, integrative organization (which links negative knowledge to positives) should be advantageous; over the course of many experiences, integrative organization should be associated with more positive self-evaluations (i.e., higher self-esteem) and mood. However, if the positive information about the self is most important and frequently accessed, then compartmentalized organization should be preferable to evaluative integration.

This prediction is most interesting if it can be shown that organizational factors explain differences in mood or self-esteem that cannot be accounted for by the sheer number of positive or negative beliefs in a person's self-concept. Although organizational factors may eventually alter the content of the self-concept by influencing the accessibility or interpretation of positive or negative beliefs, the strong prediction of this model is that organization will explain variance in mood or self-esteem when the positive or negative content of the self is held constant.

Evaluatively Integrative Thinking

The theoretical model can be tested by focusing either on the interconnectedness of positive and negative items of information or on representations of the category structure of the self. In two initial studies (Showers, 1992a), interconnectedness was assessed by having subjects generate spontaneous self-descriptions. Subjects were instructed to generate a list of items (characteristics, behaviors, or events) that described themselves in either academic or social situations. They were asked to list these items in the order in which they came to mind. This task may be thought of as a memory recall task, and it is assumed that each item listed is likely to be followed by an item to which it has strong associative links in memory.

On average, subjects generated 8.6 items describing themselves in academic situations and 9.1 items describing themselves in social situations. After completing their lists, subjects indicated the valence of each item and rated its perceived importance to their overall self-concept. The evaluative organization of each list was assessed by means of the Adjusted Ratio of Clustering (Murphy, 1979), an index of the tendency for items of similar valence to be clustered together in the lists. Hierarchical regressions were used to predict scores on the Rosenberg (1965) Self-Esteem Scale and the Positive and Negative Affect Scales (Watson, Clark, & Tellegen, 1988) from the clustering index, after controlling for the proportion of negative items listed and their perceived importance. Subjects who did not list at least two positive and two negative items were excluded from the regressions.

The results fit the predictions of the theoretical model. First, consider the subjects who were excluded from the regressions because they did not list a sufficient number of negative items. These subjects may be manifesting positive-compartmentalized organization. In doing the listing task, they listed information from their pure positive self-aspects only. Consistent with the model's predictions for positive compartmentalization, these individuals had significantly higher self-esteem than those subjects who were included in the regressions. The included subjects were those who had some important negative characteristics. The analyses showed that those who intermixed their positives and negatives (i.e., low clustering, integrative organization) had higher self-esteem than those whose lists contained clusters of positives and negatives (i.e., negative-compartmentalized organization).

For the lists describing the self in academic situations, a similar analysis showed that clustered organization (i.e., negative compartmentalization) was correlated with negative affect (but not low self-esteem). Although these results also fit the theoretical model, it is not clear why the academic lists predicted current affect and the social lists predicted cognitive self-evaluations (i.e., self-esteem). Perhaps this difference has to do with the relative stability of college students' academic and social selves; the organization of students' academic selves may reflect the ups and downs of recent events or transient moods. In contrast, college students' social selves may be more stable.

In a second task, subjects wrote paragraphs describing the most negative characteristics on their academic and social lists. Each sentence in the paragraphs was coded as representing a positive, negative, or integrative thought about that characteristic. An example of a positive statement about a negative characteristic is, "This is not really a problem for me." An integrative statement was a compound sentence that linked positive and negative beliefs, such as, "I'm outgoing with my friends, but shy around people I don't know very well." In a hierarchical regression analysis, the proportions of positive and integrative statements were used to predict self-esteem after the negativity and importance of the characteristic were held constant. Integrative thoughts, but not purely positive ones, were a significant predictor of self-esteem for both academic and social characteristics. Thus, among individuals who had important negative characteristics, evaluatively integrative thinking about that characteristic was associated with higher self-esteem. Again, those subjects with the highest self-esteem were excluded from these analyses because they did not list any purely negative characteristics.

It may seem surprising that integrative statements were associated with higher self-esteem, but positive statements were not. A pure positive statement about one's most negative characteristic in an important domain may be unrealistic. Such positive statements may represent (failed) attempts to deny or minimize the characteristic's negative implications (e.g., "This is no longer a problem for me"). Integrative statements typically acknowledge the negative facets of a characteristic, but also find the silver lining.

COMPARTMENTALIZED CATEGORY STRUCTURE

The listing and paragraph tasks examined evaluative organization within particular domains of the self, focusing on the interconnections (i.e., associative links) between items of information (Showers, 1992a). Alternatively, the evaluative organization of the self-concept may be assessed by looking at category structure across multiple self-aspects. Showers (1992b) assessed compartmentalized vs. integrative organization using a self-descriptive sorting task to examine the distribution of positive and negative items of self-knowledge across self-aspects. Each self-aspect is viewed as a category of information about the self. In compartmentalized organization, the self-aspect categories should contain mostly positive *or* mostly negative items of information, but not both. In integrative organization, the self-aspect categories should contain a mixture of positives and negatives. Table 1 illustrates these two types of category structures. Recall that the model predicts that the effects of compartmentalized organization on self-esteem should depend on the relative importance of the positive and negative self-aspects. An individual with the self-concept shown in Section A of Table 1, whose "social flaws" compartment is the important one, is negative-compartmentalized. For this person, compartmentalized organization should be correlated with lower self-esteem than the alternative integrative type of organization; however, if the "social assets" self-aspect is most important or frequently accessed, then this individual is positive-compartmentalized and his or her compartmentalized structure should be beneficial for self-esteem in comparison to the integrative type.

The sorting task used in Showers (1992b) was an adaptation of the self-descriptive sorting task developed by Linville (1985, 1987). In Study 3, subjects were given a stack of 40 index cards, each containing a potentially self-descriptive adjective. Of the 40 adjectives, 20 were positive and 20 were negative, as determined by pretesting. Subjects were asked: "Think about the different aspects of yourself or your life, and sort the cards into groups where each group represents an aspect of yourself or your life." They could use the same card in more than one group, and they could discard those that did not fit into any of their groups. After completing their sorts, subjects rated the positivity and the negativity of each self-aspect, as well as its importance, on 7-point Likert scales.

The measure of compartmentalization is Cramer's phi (Everitt, 1977), based on a χ^2 statistic. Phi represents the deviation from chance of the number of positive and negative adjectives in each self-aspect, where chance is determined by the overall proportion of positives and negatives across all self-aspects. Phi ranges from 0 (chance) to 1 (perfectly compartmentalized). A perfectly compartmentalized sort has groups that are uniformly positive and uniformly negative (Section A in Table 1). Low values of phi mean that the sort is evaluatively integrated, that is, that there is a mixture of positive and negatives in each group (Section B in Table 1). One advantage of the sorting task (compared to the listing task used in Showers, 1992a) is the most people include sufficient negatives in their sorts to permit estimation of phi. Typically, less than 5% of subjects are excluded for this reason.

The relative importance of positive and negative self-aspects is assessed by the Pelham and Swann (1989) measure of differential importance. This is the correlation, computed for each subject, of their positivity–negativity ratings and their importance ratings across the set of self-aspects generated in the sort. The differential importance score ranges from –1 to +1, where negative scores indicate that the most negative aspects are most important and positive scores mean that the most positive aspects are most important.

In order to test the predictions of the model, it is necessary to have a sample of subjects with a suitable range of differential importance (DI) scores. In random samples of college students, $M_{DI} = 0.52$, $SD_{DI} = 0.36$. Thus, a typical low DI score is near zero, meaning that positive and negative self-aspects are perceived to be similar in importance. However, the advantages of integrative thinking over negative compartmentalization should be greatest when negative self-aspects are perceived to be more important than positives (i.e., when DI is less than zero).

Compartmentalization was used to predict current self-esteem and depressed mood in a college student population, after controlling for the content of the self-concept (proportion of negative items in the sort, average positivity–negativity of self-aspects), DI, and their interactions. In order to increase the number of subjects with important negative self-aspects, subjects were selected for high or low proneness to depression (Alloy, Hartlage, Metalsky, & Abramson, 1989). The results confirmed the predictions of the theoretical model. For individuals whose positive self-aspects were important (high DI), compartmentalization was associated with higher self-esteem and lower levels of depression than more integrative organization. However, for individuals whose negative self-aspects were relatively important, the opposite was true. This finding seems consistent with the results of the listing-task studies; among individuals who have important negative characteristics, integrative thinking/organization is associated with higher self-esteem than negative compartmentalization. However, for those people whose positive self-knowledge is most important, positive-compartmentalized organization seems to be adaptive.

It is important to note that these findings were obtained when differences in the positive or negative content of the self were held constant. This means that organization explains differences in self-esteem beyond those that can be accounted for by the sheer number of positive or negative beliefs in the self-concept. In other words, individuals with the same amount of negative content, but different types of organization, may experience different levels of self-esteem. Thus, a person with many important negative beliefs about the self may be able to organize that knowledge in a way that minimizes its impact on the self, rather than trying to deny or change those beliefs.

A PROCESS MODEL OF EVALUATIVE ORGANIZATION

The studies described above provide evidence for a correlational relationship between evaluative organization and self-esteem or affect. However, the predictions of the theoretical model are based on a hypothesized process model in which the prior organization of self-knowledge influences reactions to events. In particular, the compartmentalized or integrated organization of the self may either intensify or moderate affective reactions to the events that activate certain self-aspects. In addition, organizational factors may influence global self-evaluations by their effects on the set of beliefs about the self that comes to mind whenever the individual reflects on a past experience or personal characteristic. Evidence for these kinds of processes may be sought in data on the changing self-perceptions of persons in a life transition (Showers & Ryff, 1993). The organization of the current self, as well as perceived changes in the self, may predict both immediate and long-term reactions to a life transition.

A data set collected by Ryff and Essex (1992) not only permitted a look at this process, but also provided the opportunity for an additional test of the basic theoretical model using a measure of evaluative organization that was conceptually similar to, but methodologically distinct from, the sorting task (Showers & Ryff, 1993). The sample in this study was women aged 55 and over who had relocated in the past year. They provided ratings of their current self-evaluations and their perceived self-change since moving in each of five life domains, and also responded to items assessing the psychological centrality (importance) of each of these domains. In addition, they completed measures of six dimensions of psychological well-being (Ryff, 1989) and the CES-D depression scale (Radloff, 1977). A measure of compartmentalized vs. integrative organization of the self was constructed for both current self-evaluations and perceived self-change. These measures were used to predict depression and psychological well-being in the year following the move.

In contrast to the idiographic measure of evaluative organization provided by the sorting task, the self-descriptions in this relocation study were assessed nomothetically for each of the five life domains. Participants rated their agreement with four positive or negative statements about themselves in each of the five domains. The items in each domain were averaged to create domain-specific self-evaluations for each person. According to the model of compartmentalization, individuals who have a compartmentalized view of themselves should be consistent and extreme in their ratings of items within any single domain. Thus, their domain-specific evaluations should be either extremely positive or extremely negative. Compartmentalization was estimated by the variability across an individual's domain-specific ratings, that is, the standard deviation of each individual's ratings across the five domains. The greater the standard deviation across domains, the more extremely positive and negative the domain-specific ratings must be. A measure of differential importance was calculated by correlating self-descriptive ratings with psychological centrality for each individual across five domains. Measures of compartmentalization and differential importance were calculated both for the individual's current self-evaluation and for their perceptions of self-change. The predictions of the theoretical model were tested in hierarchical regressions, holding constant measures of the overall positivity or negativity of current self-evaluations and ratings of self-change, as well as differential importance.

In this context, we expected that the critical feature of self-concept organization would be compartmentalization in ratings of self-change (as a result of relocation), rather than compartmentalization in current self-evaluations. During a life transition, many stresses may have to do with the novelty of the environment and choices associated with the transition. For this reason, the organization of beliefs about self-change (i.e., the pattern of improvements or losses across different self-aspects) may be more relevant to overall well-being and mood than the organization of beliefs about the current self. Although the absolute level of a person's current self-evaluations does predict a significant amount of variance in mood and well-being following the transition, when this effect is held constant, it is the organization of beliefs about self-change that carries significant weight. Using the self-change ratings, the predictions of the theoretical model were once again confirmed. For individuals whose positive domains of self-change were important, compartmentalization of perceived self-change was correlated with less depressed mood and greater self-acceptance and purpose in life. For individuals whose more negative domains of change were important, the opposite was true.

In the context of this life transition, individuals whose perceptions of self-change were positive-compartmentalized were those who experienced a great improvement in one or a few very important domains of the self in the year following their move. Those with a more integrative organization tended to see both positive and negative aspects to change within domains, and so they reported less extreme ratings of change. The regressions show that the positive-compartmentalized women (who experienced great improvement in at least one domain) had greater well-being in the year following the transition than those integrative individuals who experienced the same average improvement, spread more equally across domains. However, for negative-compartmentalized individuals, a great loss in an important domain was more devastating than more moderate losses in many domains (even though they amounted to the same average change). The disadvantage of the negative-compartmentalized perception of self-change may be that it becomes difficult to justify a move that caused such loss in a personally important domain. The advantage of the positive-compartmentalized organization may be that it provides individuals with one or more purely positive aspects of the self to fall back on in attempting to justify the decision to move. Having at least one very positive and personally important domain of improvement may bolster mood and self-evaluations when the transition becomes stressful or raises self-doubts.

Participants in the relocation study also rated their *feelings* (i.e., bothered, anxious, in control) about changes in each of the five life domains. Domain-specific analyses showed that compartmentalized individuals had more extreme positive feelings about changes in their most positive domains of change *and* more extreme negative feelings about changes in their most negative domain than did individuals with integrative organization. This was true regardless of the perceived importance of positive and negative domains (i.e., regardless of whether these individuals were positive-compartmentalized or negative-compartmentalized). However, when domain-specific feelings were used to predict general mood and well-being, their impact was moderated by differential importance (i.e., the relative importance of positive and negative domains). For individuals with high DI scores (positive self-aspects perceived to be more important than negatives), domain-specific feelings about the most positive domain of change were a significant predictor of CES-D depression and psychological well-being. However, for individuals with lower DI scores (positive and negative self-aspects perceived to be similarly important), domain-specific feelings about both the most positive *and* the most negative domain of change were needed to predict overall mood and well-being. Thus, although positive-compartmentalized individuals had extreme negative feelings about their most negative domains, these feelings about a relatively unimportant domain did not affect their overall mood or well-being. This finding supports the notion that compartmentalized individuals will have extreme affective reactions to specific events (either positive or negative), but that the impact of these feelings on overall mood and self-evaluation is moderated by the perceived importance of the self-aspects activated by the event.

STABILITY AND CERTAINTY

The evaluative organization of self-knowledge has potential implications for the stability as well as the level of self-esteem (cf. Kernis, 1993; Kernis, Grannemann, & Mathis, 1991). Positive-compartmentalized organization is probably associated with stable high self-esteem. A compartmentalized individual who has a great deal of important, positive self-knowledge and experiences mostly positive events may have only minimal access to any negative compartments. In this way, access to negative beliefs about the self (and therefore threats to self-esteem) should be minimized. However, the presence of pure negative self-aspects could make even the positive-compartmentalized individual vulnerable to a sudden shift in self-esteem, if one of the negative compartments were activated. This would probably require a shift in the perceived importance of that aspect in order to have a significant impact on self-esteem.

Persons with negative-compartmentalized organization may tend to have less stable self-esteem than those with positive compartmentalization. The reasoning here is that even depression-prone individuals (those most likely to be negative-compartmentalized) have DI scores that are near zero, rather than truly negative. This means that their positive and negative self-aspects are perceived to be fairly similar in importance, and they may be activated with similar frequency. Depending on whether a positive or a negative self-aspect is activated, perceptions of the self may be extremely positive or extremely negative. Thus, self-esteem may fluctuate accordingly. Those individuals whose negative self-aspects are perceived to be much more important than the positives (i.e., those for whom differential importance is clearly negative) are more likely to have stable low self-esteem.

Evaluatively integrative organization should buffer the impact of valenced outcomes and so should tend to prevent self-esteem from fluctuating in response to most events. Of course, this speculation is based on an assumption that the organization itself is stable. It is possible that integrative organization represents a relatively precarious defense against negative beliefs about the self and that this defense is easily shattered. If a major negative life event occurs, individuals with integrative organization may be vulnerable to reorganization of the self-concept into a more compartmentalized structure, possibly in response to an onslaught of new negative knowledge. In this case, self-esteem may drop as the structure becomes more compartmentalized. In other words, integrative organization may stabilize self-esteem in the short-term, but because this type of organization may itself be unstable, it may be associated with self-esteem instability in the long run.

Evaluative integration may also have implications for the certainty of self-beliefs (cf. Campbell, 1990). In an integrated structure, information about one characteristic or behavior may be linked to information about the self that is nearly opposite. For example, an individual with integrative organization may report, "I'm shy with strangers, but outgoing with my friends." Two possible implications of this make sense. On one hand, complex integrative thoughts may make it difficult to be certain about how to generate a summary description of the self: Am I mostly shy or mostly outgoing? Alternatively, the evaluatively integrative thinker may be quite certain of her self-perceptions, in all of their complexity. In the aforestated example, the integrative thinker may be quite certain that she is shy and, at the same time, quite certain that she is outgoing. Thus, the relationship between integrative organization and the stability of self-esteem and the certainty of self-beliefs is an intriguing area for further research.

ORIGINS OF EVALUATIVE ORGANIZATION

Up to this point, self-concept organization has been presented as a relatively stable feature of a person that exists prior to self-relevant events and influences affective reactions to them and implications for self-esteem. However, the correlational data presented here cannot rule out the possibility that the direction of causality is reversed, namely, that a person's affective state or level of self-esteem influences the organization of the self. In this section, I consider the possible origins of evaluative organization. Although self-concept organization may be the consequence of either affective or cognitive processes, perhaps the most interesting explanation is a motivational one. Different individuals may develop different types of organization because each type of organization serves a specific goal.

COGNITIVE ORIGINS

Individual differences in evaluative organization may correspond to the tendency to use an evaluative dimension as a basis for differentiating items of self-knowledge. In compartmentalized organization, the evaluative dimension (i.e., whether a piece of information is positive or negative) appears to be used as the basis of cognitive categorization. An evaluative basis for categorization may be either explicit (e.g., when a person generates self-aspects such as "good student" or "bad student") or implicit (e.g., "me as a creative scientist" or "me before exams"). In contrast, the integrative type of organization likely uses nonevaluative dimensions as the basis for categorization, such as situational or temporal contexts (e.g., "me at work" or "me in the future").

People may also differ in their initial tendency to make evaluative judgments about self-relevant information. In other words, some individuals may be especially prone to ask themselves, "Is this a positive (good) feature of myself?" or "Is this negative feedback I am hearing?" Again, such judgments may be either explicit or implicit and may reflect underlying differences in sensitivity to the positive or negative valence of self-relevant information (cf. Patterson & Newman, 1993). Presumably, people who are prone to evaluate incoming information are more likely to use an evaluative dimension as the basis for categorization.

AFFECTIVE ORIGINS

Affective states may influence self-organization in at least two ways. On one hand, an affective state may link similarly valenced items of information in memory via spreading activation (Bower, 1981). The more intense the affect, the stronger should be the associative links between items of the same valence. These strong associations should encourage a compartmentalized structure. Thus, individuals who are prone to experience certain affective states may develop cognitive self-structures that are consistent with those states.

Alternatively, intense affective states may increase the salience of the affective valence of information as a basis for categorization. Affectively laden information may feel especially similar to or different from the current affective state, and these feelings may be used as information in making judgments of similarity among items of self-knowledge (cf. Schwarz & Bless, 1991).

MOTIVATIONAL ORIGINS

The affective and cognitive origins described above suggest that self-organization depends on affective or cognitive processes over which the individual may have little control. According to these perspectives, an individual who is predisposed to evaluate information or (alternatively) one who frequently experiences extreme affect will be prone to a certain type of organization as an unintended result. However, a motivational perspective suggests that people may develop a particular type of organization because it is in some way adaptive or functional. In this view, each of the organizational structures described here—positive-compartmentalized, evaluatively integrative, and negative-compartmentalized—may be adaptive under a specific set of conditions, serving a specific goal. Individuals may develop preferences for particular types of organization that satisfy particular goals. Moreover, as needs change, organization may change to meet those needs. In this section, I speculate about the goals that may be served by each type of organization, and I outline preliminary evidence that is consistent with this interpretation.

Positive-compartmentalized organization may serve the goal of minimizing access to negative self-knowledge. This type of organization may be most effective when an individual has many important positive items of self-knowledge and negatives are not activated frequently. By compartmentalizing negatives into separate self-aspects (rather than integrating them with the more important positives), access to negatives may be even more easily avoided. Moreover, these negative self-aspect categories may come to be perceived as very low in importance, without jeopardizing access to any desirable features of the self.

The other two types of organization—evaluative integration and negative compartmentalization—may be adaptive for individuals who have many important, negative items of self-knowledge. For these individuals, attempts to avoid accessing negatives may be unrealistic. Evaluatively integrative organization may serve the goal of minimizing the impact of items of negative self-knowledge when access to this information cannot be avoided. Accessible negative thoughts bring to mind the positive self-beliefs to which they are linked, thereby mitigating the impact of the negative thoughts.

Although negative-compartmentalized organization is correlated with negative affect and low self-esteem in both the listing and paragraph tasks (Showers, 1992a) and the self-descriptive sorting task (Showers, 1992b), subsequent studies are suggesting ways in which compartmentalized organization can sometimes be advantageous even for individuals whose negative compartments are relatively important. Ironically, on one hand, negative compartmentalization may contribute to depression and low self-esteem by flooding the individual with negative information from purely negative self-aspects; on the other hand, the presence of some positive compartments, even though they are not ordinarily perceived to be important, may facilitate recovery from depressed mood when the self is threatened. The threatened individual may be able to fall back on those positive compartments to bolster weakened self-esteem. Kling and Showers (1994) examined the process of recovery from a negative mood in individuals who had completed the self-concept sorting task 1 week before. In one condition of this study, subjects were exposed to a sad mood induction and then performed a series of easy numerical tasks while rating their feelings at 5-minute intervals. It appears that success on the easy numerical tasks may have activated the pure positive self-aspects of individuals with compartmentalized organization. Both positive- and negative-compartmentalized individuals recovered more quickly from the sad mood than did those with evaluatively integrative organization. Presumably, both positive-and negative-compartmentalized individuals were able to access their pure positive self-aspects, regardless of their perceived importance, to aid in the process of mood recovery.

A similar idea has been suggested by Pelham (1991) in his analysis of the most positive self-views of individuals at different levels of depression. The most positive self-view of his severely depressed group was on average at least as positive as the most positive self-view of the nondepressed group. Pelham (1993) speculated that depressed persons may react to their misery by becoming especially invested in their most positive self-beliefs, thereby facilitating their own recovery from depression.

CONCLUSIONS

Recent literature on self-esteem has emphasized the importance of organizational features of the self-concept, in addition to the content and accessibility of specific self-beliefs. This chapter describes evaluative compartmentalization and evaluative integration as two types of self-organization that reflect both the individual's way of thinking about positive and negative characteristics of the self and the underlying category structure for self-knowledge. My initial studies link these types of organization to current self-esteem and mood (Showers, 1992a,b). For individuals with important positive self-aspects, compartmentalized organization is associated with higher self-esteem and less depressed mood than is integrative organization. For individuals with important negative self-aspects, the reverse is true. A process model is proposed in which self-organization is viewed as a cognitive vulnerability factor that influences affective reactions to stressful events, with concomitant implications for mood and self-esteem. Data from a study of the effects of relocation on older women are consistent with this model (Showers & Ryff, 1993).

Preferences for evaluatively compartmentalized vs. integrative organization may have implications for the stability of mood and self-esteem. For the most part, positive-compartmentalized organization should stabilize high self-esteem by limiting access to negative self-beliefs. However, compartmentalized individuals may also be vulnerable to trauma that alters the perceived importance of pure positive and negative self-aspects. Integrative organization should moderate the impact of self-relevant events, but this type of organization may be difficult to sustain in the face of severe stress. When negative self-aspects are highly important, negative compartmentalization may be associated with stable low self-esteem.

The origins of compartmentalized vs. integrative organization may lie in cognitive, affective, or motivational processes. Perhaps most interesting is the possibility that each type of organization has specific advantages and costs, and so an individual may develop a particular type of organization that serves a particular goal. Such goals include minimizing access to negative self-beliefs, minimizing the impact of unavoidable negative beliefs, and recovering from negative moods.

To summarize, a focus on organizational features of the self sheds light on the processes by which self-esteem arises, is maintained, or may change. In its turn, self-esteem may play a causal role, influencing and feeding back on organizational processes. Thus, self-concept organization is not necessarily a rigid, stable cognitive structure; rather, the organization of the self may be the manifestation of cognitive and affective processes that are quite flexible and even strategic in nature. An examination of the ways in which the organization of the self changes in response to mood, self-esteem, or situational factors should enhance our understanding of the goal-oriented functioning of the self-concept, as well as the origins and dynamics of self-esteem.

ACKNOWLEDGMENTS. Preparation of this chapter was supported by National Institute of Mental Health fellowship MH10058. Thanks to Michael Kernis, Kristen Kling, and Suzanne Reinke for their comments and suggestions.

REFERENCES

Alloy, L. B., & Abramson, L. Y. (1988). Depressive realism: Four theoretical perspectives. In L. B. Alloy (Ed.), *Cognitive processes in depression*. New York: Guilford Press.
Alloy, L. B., Hartlage, S., Metalsky, G., & Abramson, L. Y. (1989). The depression proneness

inventory: A brief, face-valid scale of vulnerability to depressive reactions in response to stress. Manuscript in preparation.

Bargh, J. A., & Pratto, F. (1986). Individual construct accessibility and perceptual selection. *Journal of Experimental Social Psychology, 22,* 293–311.

Bargh, J. A., & Tota, M. E. (1988). Context-dependent automatic processing in depression: Accessibility of negative constructs with regard to self but not others. *Journal of Personality and Social Psychology, 54,* 925–939.

Beck, A. T. (1976). *Cognitive therapy and the emotional disorders.* New York: International Universities Press.

Bower, G. H. (1981). Mood and memory. *American Psychologist, 36,* 129–148.

Campbell, J. D. (1990). Self-esteem and clarity of the self-concept. *Journal of Personality and Social Psychology, 59,* 538–549.

Everitt, B. S. (1977). *The analysis of contingency tables.* London: Chapman & Hall.

Fitts, W. H. (1964). *Tennessee self-concept scale: Test booklet.* Nashville: Counselor Recordings and Tests, Department of Mental Health.

Hammen, C., Marks, T., Mayol, A., & de Mayo, R. (1985). Depressive self-schemas, life stress, and vulnerability to depression. *Journal of Abnormal Psychology, 94,* 308–319.

Higgins, E. T., & Bargh, J. A. (1987). Social cognition and social perception. *Annual Review of Psychology, 38,* 369–425.

Higgins, E. T., & King, G. (1981). Accessibility of social constructs: Information-processing consequences of individual and contextual variability. In N. Cantor & J. F. Kihlstrom (Eds.), *Personality, cognition, and social interaction* (pp. 69–121). Hillsdale, NJ: Erlbaum Associates.

Higgins, E. T., Van Hook, E., & Dorfman, D. (1988). Do self-attributes form a cognitive structure? *Social Cognition, 6,* 177–206.

Hoge, D. R., & McCarthy, J. D. (1984). Influence of individual and group identity salience in the global self-esteem of youth. *Journal of Personality and Social Psychology, 47,* 403–414.

Kernis, M. H. (1993). The roles of stability and level of self-esteem in psychological functioning. In R. F. Baumeister (Ed.), *Self-esteem: The puzzle of low self-regard* (pp. 167–182). New York: Plenum Press.

Kernis, M. H., Brockner, J., & Frankel, B. S. (1989). Self-esteem and reactions to failure: The mediating role of overgeneralization. *Journal of Personality and Social Psychology, 57,* 707–714.

Kernis, M. H., Grannemann, B. D., & Mathis, L. C. (1991). Stability of self-esteem as a moderator of the relationship between level of self-esteem and depression. *Journal of Personality and Social Psychology, 61,* 80–84.

Kling, K. C., & Showers, C. (1994). Self-concept mediates mood recovery. Paper presented at the annual meeting of the Midwestern Psychological Association, Chicago, May 5–7.

Linville, P. W. (1985). Self-complexity and affective extremity: Don't put all of your eggs in one cognitive basket. *Social Cognition, 3,* 94–120.

Linville, P. W. (1987). Self-complexity as a cognitive buffer against stress-related illness and depression. *Journal of Personality and Social Psychology, 52,* 663–676.

Markus, H. (1977). Self-schemata and processing information about the self. *Journal of Personality and Social Psychology, 35,* 63–78.

Murphy, M. D. (1979). Measurement of category clustering in free recall. In C. R. Puff (Ed.), *Memory organization and structure.* New York: Academic Press.

Patterson, C. M., & Newman, J. P. (1993). Reflectivity and learning from aversive events: Toward a psychological mechanism for the syndromes of disinhibition. *Psychological Review, 100,* 716–736.

Pelham, B. W. (1991). On the benefits of misery: Self-serving bias in the depressive self-concept. *Journal of Personality and Social Psychology, 61,* 670–681.

Pelham, B. W. (1993). On the highly positive thoughts of the highly depressed. In R. F. Baumeister (Ed.), *Self-esteem: The puzzle of low self-regard* (pp. 183–199). New York: Plenum Press.

Pelham, B. W., & Swann, W. B., Jr. (1989). From self-conceptions to self-worth: On the sources and structure of global self-esteem. *Journal of Personality and Social Psychology, 57,* 672–680.

Radloff, L. (1977). The CES-D scale: A self-report depression scale for research in the general population. *Applied Psychological Measurement, 1,* 385–401.

Rosenberg, M. (1965). *Society and the adolescent self-image.* Princeton, NJ: Princeton University Press.

Ryff, C. D. (1989). Happiness is everything, or is it? Explorations on the meaning of psychological well-being. *Journal of Personality and Social Psychology, 57,* 1069–1081.

Ryff, C. D., & Essex, M. J. (1992). The interpretation of life experience and well-being: The sample case of relocation. *Psychology and Aging, 7,* 507–517.

Schwarz, N., & Bless, H. (1991). Happy and mindless, but sad and smart? The impact of affective states on analytic reasoning. In J. Forgas (Ed.), *Emotion and social judgment.* Oxford: Pergamon Press.

Segal, Z. V. (1988). Appraisal of the self-schema construct in cognitive models of depression. *Psychological Bulletin, 103,* 147–162.

Showers, C. (1992a). Evaluatively integrative thinking about characteristics of the self. *Personality and Social Psychology Bulletin, 18,* 719–729.

Showers, C. (1992b). Compartmentalization of positive and negative self-knowledge: Keeping bad apples out of the bunch. *Journal of Personality and Social Psychology, 62,* 1036–1049.

Showers, C., & Ryff, C. D. (1993). Self-differentiation and well-being in a life transition. Paper presented at the annual meeting of the American Psychological Association, Toronto, August 20–24.

Spielman, L. A., & Bargh, J. A. (1990). Does the depressive self-schema really exist? In C. D. McCann & N. S. Endler (Eds.), *Depression: New directions in theory, research, and practice.* Toronto: Wall & Emerson.

Watson, D., Clark, L. A., & Tellegen, A. (1988). Development and validation of brief measures of positive and negative affect: The PANAS scales. *Journal of Personality and Social Psychology, 54,* 1063–1070.

PART II

INTERPERSONAL/CONTEXTUAL CONCERNS

CHAPTER 6

INTERPERSONAL FUNCTIONS OF THE SELF-ESTEEM MOTIVE

THE SELF-ESTEEM SYSTEM AS A SOCIOMETER

MARK R. LEARY AND DEBORAH L. DOWNS

INTRODUCTION

In a discipline with few universally accepted principles, the proposition that people are motivated to maintain and enhance their self-esteem has achieved the rare status of an axiom. The notion that people want to think highly of themselves, behave in ways that promote self-esteem, and become distressed when their needs for self-esteem are unmet can be found in the writings of classic personality theorists (Adler, 1930; Allport, 1937; Horney, 1937; Rogers, 1959), contemporary social psychologists (Greenberg, Pyszczynski, & Solomon, 1986; Greenwald, 1980; Greenwald & Breckler, 1985; Steele, 1988; Taylor & Brown, 1988; Tesser, 1988), and clinicians (Bednar, Wells, & Peterson, 1989). The self-esteem motive has been invoked as an explanation for a wide variety of behaviors, including prejudice (Katz, 1960), self-serving attributions (Blaine & Crocker, 1993;

MARK R. LEARY • Department of Psychology, Wake Forest University, Winston-Salem, North Carolina 27109.   DEBORAH L. DOWNS • Department of Psychology, Ohio State University, Columbus, Ohio 43210.

Efficacy, Agency, and Self-Esteem, edited by Michael H. Kernis. Plenum Press, New York, 1995.

Snyder, Stephan, & Rosenfield, 1978), reactions to evaluations (S. C. Jones, 1973), self-handicapping (E. E. Jones & Berglas, 1978), responses to counterattitudinal behavior (Steele, 1988), and self-presentation (Schlenker, 1980). Furthermore, low self-esteem has been linked to problems such as depression, alcohol abuse, suicide, and eating disorders, and high self-esteem has been implicated in good mental health (e.g., Baumeister, 1991; Bednar et al., 1989; Taylor & Brown, 1988). If previous theorists and researchers are correct in their claims, the need to protect and enhance one's self-esteem constitutes an exceptionally pervasive and important motive.

Despite widespread attention to behaviors that result from the self-esteem motive, behavioral researchers have not adequately addressed the most basic questions about it, specifically, questions about its source and function. Why should people want to evaluate themselves positively? Why do they need to maintain, if not enhance, their self-esteem? Why is lowered self-esteem associated with negative affect? Why do people tend to behave in ways that protect and enhance their self-esteem, sometimes to the point of doing things that are detrimental to their well-being? Our goal in this chapter is to offer a conceptualization of the self-esteem motive that stresses its role in the maintenance of interpersonal relationships.

DEFINITIONAL ISSUES

To begin, we must clarify what we mean by self-esteem and by self-esteem motivation. Rosenberg (1965) and others have compared self-esteem to an attitude, specifically an attitude toward the self. Like all attitudes, self-esteem has both cognitive and affective components. The cognitive component refers to the person's beliefs about his or her worth, as exemplified by a statement such as "I am a good person" or "I am not worthwhile."

Of course, people are not dispassionate about their self-judgments. Self-evaluations are often accompanied by strong affect, a point first addressed by early theorists such as James (1890) and Cooley (1902). High self-esteem involves positive affect, whereas low self-esteem involves negative affect. Thus, the term "self-esteem" is not synonymous with self-beliefs or self-evaluations. Self-esteem includes an essential affective quality that simple cognitions about the self may not. In fact, Brown (1993) suggested that self-esteem is fundamentally based in affective processes—specifically, positive vs. negative feelings about oneself. The importance of affect in the self-esteem system will become obvious as we proceed.

Traditionally, researchers interested in self-esteem have focused on the individual's characteristic level of dispositional or *trait self-esteem*.

Thousands of studies show that persons scoring low vs. high in trait self-esteem differ in a myriad of ways (for reviews, see Baumeister, 1993).[1] Although each person can be characterized as having an overall or typical level of trait self-esteem, self-esteem also fluctuates over situations and time. The term *state self-esteem* refers to the quality of a person's self-feelings in a particular situation at a particular time (Heatherton & Polivy, 1991).

However, researchers interested in the self-esteem *motive* have not made a similar distinction between trait and state self-esteem. For purposes of this chapter, we assume (on the basis of no empirical data whatsoever) that people are motivated to preserve both their state and their trait self-esteem. That is, people want to feel good about themselves in the present moment as well as to maintain positive self-feelings over time.

EXPLANATIONS OF SELF-ESTEEM MOTIVATION

As noted above, self-esteem motivation has been implicated in a wide range of human behavior. A motive as pervasive and potent as the self-esteem motive must serve a very important function, yet relatively little attention has been given either to the function of the self-esteem motive or to its phylogenetic or developmental origins. However, three basic hypotheses regarding the function of self-esteem can be gleaned from the literature.

SELF-ESTEEM PROMOTES POSITIVE AFFECT

The first is that people seek to bolster their self-esteem because high self-esteem is associated with positive affect, whereas low self-esteem is associated with negative affect. In light of this proposition, people may seek self-esteem simply to experience positive emotions or to avoid negative emotions.

In support of this view, research shows that low self-esteem is undoubtedly associated with more negative emotions than high self-esteem. Compared to people with high self-esteem, those with relatively low self-esteem tend to experience virtually every negative emotion more intensely. Relative to highs, low self-esteem people tend to be more anxious,

---

[1]Although we often refer loosely to "low" vs. "high" self-esteem, these terms must be considered as relative only. Many people who score "low" on measures of self-esteem rate themselves in an average, neutral, or noncommittal fashion, rather than negatively (Baumeister, Tice, & Hutton, 1989).

depressed, jealous, and lonely (Cutrona, 1982; Goswick & Jones, 1981; Kanfer & Zeiss, 1983; Leary, 1983; Lewinsohn, Mischel, Chaplin, & Barton, 1980; Taylor & Brown, 1988; White, 1981). Furthermore, changes in state self-esteem are reliably associated with changes in affect (Spivey, 1990; Terdal & Leary, 1991), and people engage in self-esteem enhancement to regulate their mood (Baumgardner, Kaufman, & Levy, 1989).

However, this is not a fully adequate explanation of the motive itself because it begs the question of *why* self-esteem is associated with positive affect. Several possibilities have been suggested. One is that an inherent function of the self is to maximize the person's pleasure/pain ratio and to facilitate the maintenance of self-esteem (Epstein, 1973; Greenwald, 1980; Steele, 1988). Another explanation is that negative discrepancies between one's real and ideal selves lead naturally to low self-esteem and unpleasant affect, especially anxiety (Rogers, 1959). However, it is unclear why people should have developed a psychological mechanism that sustains their subjective sense of personal worth or why such a mechanism should be tied to affect.

In a recent discussion of this question, Greenberg et al. (1986) suggested that high self-esteem serves as a buffer against the existential anxiety people experience when they contemplate their own fragility and mortality. Their terror management theory posits that people maintain self-esteem by living according to the values that are prescribed by their culture, thereby giving them a sense of worth in an organized, just, and meaningful world. Living in ways that maintain self-esteem gives people a sense of safety and security both in their everyday lives and in the afterlife (because living according to cultural and moral values may lead to symbolic, if not literal, immortality). In three studies, Greenberg et al. (1992) showed that increasing subjects' self-esteem reduced their self-reported anxiety and physiological arousal in response to threatening stimuli, including videotaped depictions of death. Although their findings support the link between self-esteem and affect, it remains to be demonstrated that terror management is the exclusive function of the self-esteem system.

SELF-ESTEEM PROMOTES GOAL ACHIEVEMENT

A second explanation of the functional value of the self-esteem motive is that high self-esteem motivates people to pursue their goals and to persevere in the face of obstacles and set-backs. Bandura (1977) suggested that the sense of efficacy that accompanies high self-esteem enhances people's willingness to strive toward desired goals as well as to persist on difficult tasks. Similarly, Greenwald (1980) explained the beneffectance bias (i.e., the self-serving attributional bias) in terms of its effects on behavioral perseverance and, thus, survival.

Consistent with this line of reasoning, persons with high self-esteem perform better after an initial failure than persons with low self-esteem and are more likely to persevere in the face of obstacles (e.g., Perez, 1973; Schalon, 1968; Shrauger & Sorman, 1977). People who feel worthy, able, and competent are more likely to achieve their goals than those who feel worthless, impotent, and incompetent.

However, research shows that high self-esteem is not always functional in promoting task achievement. People with high self-esteem may demonstrate nonproductive persistence on insoluble tasks (McFarlin, Baumeister, & Blascovich, 1984), thereby undermining their effectiveness. They may also take excessive and unrealistic risks when their self-esteem is threatened. Excessively high self-esteem is associated with setting unrealistically high goals and making unrealistically positive claims about oneself (Baumeister, Heatherton, & Tice, 1993). It seems to us that a goal-achievement explanation of the self-esteem motive would predict that people should have a motive for *accurate* self-evaluations, whether those evaluations are positive or negative. People are most likely to be successful and efficacious if they evaluate themselves accurately, but recent evidence suggests that people are more strongly oriented toward self-enhancement than toward assessing themselves accurately (Sedikides, 1993). Thus, although a motive to maintain high self-esteem can spur people's accomplishments on occasion, we wonder whether this explanation alone is sufficient to account for such a powerful and pervasive motive.

SELF-ESTEEM IS ASSOCIATED WITH DOMINANCE

A third explanation of the self-esteem motive suggests that self-esteem is associated with dominance over other people. One variation on this theme was offered by Tedeschi and Norman (1985). They proposed that self-esteem feelings indicate to an individual that he or she has influence over others. In their view, people strive for self-esteem because it is "a generalized reinforcer which is associated in an indirect way with the facilitation of social influence and the attainment of rewards" (p. 310).

Barkow (1980) offered a similar analysis of self-esteem rooted in evolutionary theory. Ethologists assume that our prehominid ancestors lived in small groups that were structured in a dominance hierarchy resembling that found among nonhuman primates today. To the extent that being dominant in one's social group is associated with an increased access to mates, the tendency to monitor and increase one's relative social standing would confer adaptive benefits. Thus, as human beings developed the capacity for self-relevant thought, they may have developed psychological mechanisms for evaluating and enhancing their relative dominance. Barkow proposed that to the extent that self-esteem is associated with the deference of other people, the tendency to strive for self-esteem may serve to promote dominance.

Although we concur that a motive as potent and universal as the self-esteem motive must have conferred a reproductive advantage, we question whether it did so by promoting dominance. As we will see, self-esteem is more closely associated with social acceptance than with dominance and control. Furthermore, people are likely to suffer decreases rather than increases in self-esteem when they exert power over others in an underhanded, manipulative, or deceptive fashion. Self-esteem seems to be more strongly tied to behaving in socially desirable ways than to exerting influence per se (Greenberg et al., 1986).

SELF-ESTEEM AND SOCIAL EXCLUSION

In our view, none of these explanations fully accounts for the potency or pervasiveness of the self-esteem motive or explains why the self-esteem motive seems to be more or less innate. In the following discussion, we offer a novel perspective on self-esteem that may offer an answer to remaining questions about it.

THE FUNCTION OF SELF-ESTEEM

We propose that rather than reflecting a free-standing motive, or serving to promote achievement or dominance, self-esteem is involved in the maintenance of interpersonal relations. Human beings appear to possess a fundamental motive to avoid exclusion from important social groups (Baumeister & Leary, in press; Baumeister & Tice, 1990; Leary, 1990). Because humans in a natural state are unlikely to survive in isolation, strong pressures have evolved that promote gregariousness and social bonding (Ainsworth, 1989; Barash, 1977; Hogan, Jones, & Cheek, 1985; James, 1890). Put simply, people have an innate "need to belong." Indeed, a great deal of human behavior can be conceptualized as attempts to foster social ties and to minimize the possibility of falling into disfavor with others who are psychologically important (Baumeister & Leary, in press).

The successful maintenance of social bonds requires a system for monitoring others' reactions and one's inclusionary status. To the extent that one's inclusion can be jeopardized in a moment by behavioral indiscretions, people must have a ready way of assessing their standing in others' eyes. In our view, state self-esteem is the cornerstone of this system, functioning as a *sociometer* that (1) monitors the social environment for cues indicating disapproval, rejection, or exclusion and (2) alerts the individual via negative affective reactions when such cues are detected.[2]

To be effective in avoiding rejection and exclusion, such a system must monitor the social environment more or less continuously, yet not require attentional resources that are needed for other ongoing tasks. Consistent with this provision, the self-esteem system seems to operate at a relatively nonconscious or preattentive level, thereby allowing conscious processing of other information (e.g., Schneider & Shiffrin, 1977). This modus operandi explains why people are rarely aware of consciously monitoring their social environments, yet become quickly attuned to indications that others think negatively of them. Whereas in one moment the person has no self-relevant thoughts or feelings, in the next he or she may suddenly suffer a loss of self-esteem, accompanied by negative affect and a shift of conscious attention to the threat to the ego.

THE SELF-ESTEEM MOTIVE

To take the sociometer model of self-esteem a step further, we assert that people are motivated to behave in ways that maintain their self-esteem because behaviors that maintain self-esteem tend to be ones that decrease the likelihood that they will be ignored, avoided, or rejected by other people. Viewed in this manner, behaviors that protect or enhance self-esteem do not originate from a free-standing motive to maintain self-esteem, but rather from the motive to avoid social exclusion.

Although space does not allow a comprehensive review of the relevant literature, we contend that most behaviors that have been attributed to the need to maintain self-esteem may be parsimoniously explained in terms of the motive to avoid social exclusion. For example, self-serving attributions [which have often been explained as ways to protect self-esteem (D. T. Miller, 1976)] help to reduce the likelihood of social disapproval or rejection following failure (Schlenker, 1980). Similarly, people increase their efforts to obtain approval following failure or rejection not simply to boost self-esteem (e.g., Apsler, 1975; Walster, 1965), but to enhance others' acceptance of them. The finding that people are more troubled by upward social comparisons on personally relevant dimensions than on dimensions that are unimportant to them may reflect the fact that people have more to lose when others surpass them in ways that are

[2]The term "sociometer" is pronounced soci-OM-eter (not socio-METER).

relevant to their includability rather than because they have a need to preserve self-esteem per se (cf. Morse & Gergen, 1970; Tesser 1988). Finally, the effects of "mortality-salience" manipulations on self-esteem and anxiety may occur because death connotes ultimate excludability rather than because self-esteem buffers fears of death per se (cf. Greenberg et al., 1986, 1992). In brief, most reactions to self-esteem threats appear to occur under conditions in which one's inclusionary status in important groups or relationships is in jeopardy.

This is not to say that the self-esteem motive is elicited only in social situations. People may behave in ways that maintain their self-esteem even when they are alone because, to assist the person in avoiding exclusion, the sociometer must function in private to deter behaviors that have the potential to negatively affect one's interpersonal relationships. Furthermore, over time, the self-esteem motive can become functionally autonomous as self-esteem becomes a "generalized reinforcer" (Tedeschi & Norman, 1985). Because increases in self-esteem accompany acceptance and inclusion, and because acceptance and inclusion are associated with positive affective states, people may sometimes behave in ways that maintain self-esteem even in the absence of explicit interpersonal implications. Even so, their behaviors tend to be ones that, if known by others, would increase others' acceptance and inclusion of them.

EVIDENCE FOR THE SOCIOMETER HYPOTHESIS

Available evidence provides indirect yet consistent support for the sociometer hypothesis. Below we describe findings that support central predictions derived from this perspective: (1) Events that threaten self-esteem are those that, if known by others, would increase the likelihood of exclusion; (2) exclusion and rejection lower state self-esteem; (3) trait self-esteem is associated with a generalized expectancy of rejection; and (4) rejection motivates approval-seeking behaviors.

ESTEEM-DEFLATING EVENTS ARE THOSE THAT UNDERMINE INCLUSION

If one examines the sorts of events that are most likely to damage self-esteem, they are precisely those events that are likely to result in social exclusion. Put differently, what have been viewed previously as threats to self-esteem are, at a more basic level, events that make the possibility of exclusion or rejection salient.

Terdal and Leary (1990) presented 150 undergraduates with a list of behaviors that varied in social desirability, such as "I cheated on a final exam," "I donated blood," and "I saved a drowning child." Subjects were asked to indicate on 5-point scales how they thought others would react toward them if they performed each behavior (response options ranged from "Many other people would reject or avoid me" to "many other people would accept or include me"). Later, subjects were asked how they would *personally* feel if they performed each behavior on four 7-point bipolar scales (good–bad, proud–ashamed, valuable–worthless, happy–dejected). Ratings on these adjectives were summed to provide an index of self-esteem feelings resulting from each behavior.

The canonical correlation between subjects' ratings of others' reactions and their own feelings of resultant self-esteem across all situations was 0.70. That is, expectations of the degree to which one's behavior would result in social inclusion or exclusion correlated highly with the impact of those behaviors on feelings about oneself. On an item-by-item basis, the correlations between expectations of social inclusion–exclusion and resultant self-esteem across the situations ranged from 0.14 to 0.47.

Interestingly, subjects showed considerable agreement regarding the relative orderings of how others would respond to the situations. Kendall's coefficient of concordance for ratings of inclusion–exclusion was 0.79. This result suggests that people within a social milieu share beliefs about the effects of certain behaviors on social exclusion.

SOCIAL EXCLUSION LOWERS STATE SELF-ESTEEM

Perceptions of social exclusion lead to sometimes dramatic changes in state self-esteem. Spivey [1990 (Experiment 1)] asked subjects how they would feel about themselves in hypothetical social situations. In all cases, subjects indicated that they would feel worse about themselves after exclusion than after inclusion. Furthermore, when subjects' ratings of felt exclusion were partialed out, the relationship between rejection and self-esteem disappeared.

In another study (Tambor & Leary, 1993), subjects were asked to recall the last instance in which they experienced certain social emotions. Correlations between how excluded subjects felt in each situation and state self-esteem ranged from −0.68 to −0.92. Thus, perceived exclusion accounted for a very large portion of the variance in state self-esteem.

Terdal and Leary (1991) examined effects of real exclusion on self-esteem in a laboratory experiment. Subjects were assigned to work as part of a group (i.e., included) or to work alone (i.e., excluded) and were told that this assignment was based either on the preferences of the other participants or on a random procedure. Subjects then rated themselves on adjectives drawn from the McFarland and Ross (1982) low and high self-esteem factors (e.g., good, proud, valuable). Results showed that inclusion or exclusion greatly affected subjects' feelings about themselves, but only if inclusion or exclusion was due to acceptance or rejection by the group. In another experiment, Downs (1993) also showed that rejection by another person lowered subjects' self-evaluations, even if the rejection was based on only minimal information about the subject and the subject remained anonymous.

LOW TRAIT SELF-ESTEEM IS ASSOCIATED
WITH PERCEIVED EXCLUSION

If self-esteem is a sociometer that monitors social exclusion. people who characteristically feel included and accepted should have higher trait self-esteem than those who usually feel rejected. Consistent with this proposition, peer acceptance appears to be crucial for the maintenance of positive self-esteem among adolescents (Eskilson, Wiley, Muehlbauer, & Dodder, 1986), and parental rejection has been shown to be a major contributor to low self-esteem (Bhatti, Derezotes, Kim, & Specht, 1989; Coopersmith, 1967). Furthermore, Spivey [1990 (Experiment 3)] found that scores on the Rosenberg (1965) Self-Esteem Inventory correlated 0.55 with the degree to which people think others include them and seek them out.

Trait self-esteem is also strongly related to the degree to which people think they behave consistently with the values of the culture or subculture with which they identify. One of the surest ways to increase one's social acceptance is to conform to the norms of one's primary social groups (Schachter, 1951). For example, self-esteem is related to the degree to which one successfully measures up to cultural standards for gender-appropriate behavior (Josephs, Markus, & Tafarodi, 1992) and to cultural values regarding morality (Greenberg et al., 1986). Trait self-esteem also correlates highly with interpersonal skills, which presumably facilitate acceptance (Riggio, Throckmorton, & DePaola, 1990).

THREATS TO SELF-ESTEEM MOTIVATE APPROVAL-SEEKING

A fourth source of support for the sociometer model involves the fact that threats to self-esteem increase the desire to obtain social approval. This observation alone provides support for the model, because it suggests that events that threaten self-esteem have something to do with potential decrements in social inclusion.

In addition, esteem-deflating events motivate behaviors that promote social approval and acceptance (Apsler, 1975) and increase our attraction to people who accept us (Walster, 1965). Although this effect has been interpreted in terms of a desire to restore our fallen self-esteem, it is as parsimoniously explained in terms of an increased motive to be included.

INCLUSION FACILITATION OR EXCLUSION AVOIDANCE?

In describing the self-esteem system as a sociometer, we have purposefully emphasized its function in avoiding exclusion rather than in enhancing inclusion. We offer three reasons for thinking that the self-esteem system responds primarily to exclusion rather than inclusion (assuming that such a distinction is not merely semantic). First, evolutionary pressures are more likely to lead to systems that respond to deprivation states than to systems that respond to less than total satiation. To use a physical analogy, we are more motivated to eliminate hunger than we are motivated to be full (i.e., hunger must reach a certain threshold before eliciting cognitions, emotions, and motives relevant to eating). Because people quite naturally form social bonds with one another and because most interpersonal encounters are characterized by neutral civility or acceptance, people have no need for a system that continuously monitors degrees of inclusion. Rather, they need only a system that responds when the potential for rejection or exclusion reaches some critical threshold. From the standpoint of survival and the propagation of one's genes, a motive to avoid exclusion would be more important than a motive that pushed the person toward wholesale inclusion.

A second, closely related point is that people may suffer losses of self-esteem even when they do not specifically wish to be included by those who have rejected them. Although a person may have no motive to be included or accepted by anonymous supermarket checkout clerk, the person may nonetheless suffer a momentary loss of self-esteem if he or she perceives, for whatever reason, that he or she was rejected by the clerk.

Third, research suggests that exclusion or rejection is more likely to lower self-esteem than inclusion or acceptance is to raise it. In the experiment described above, Terdal and Leary (1991) found that although subjects felt no better about themselves when the group included them than when they were included randomly, subjects who thought they were excluded on the basis of the group's preferences rated themselves significantly more negatively than those who thought they had been randomly excluded. Personalized acceptance had no effect on self-esteem, but personalized rejection caused self-esteem to plummet. Similarly, Downs (1993) obtained subjects' self-ratings during pretesting, then provided them with either accepting, rejecting, or no feedback, ostensibly from another subject. Subjects who received accepting or no feedback showed no change in self-ratings from pretesting to the experimental session, but those who received rejecting feedback showed a significant decrease in self-esteem.

SELF-ESTEEM AND AFFECT

As we noted above, decreases in self-esteem are invariably accompanied by negative affect. The sociometer model sheds light on the importance of affect in the self-esteem system (Brown, 1993). Most motivational and drive systems involve hedonic consequences that alert the individual to undesired state changes, that motivate behaviors that restore the desired state, and that, if removed, serve as negative reinforcement for goal attainment. To return to our analogy, feelings of hunger alert us that we should seek food and motivate us to eat, and the abatement of hunger pangs reinforces us for having done so.

In a similar way, negative affect alerts people to threats to their inclusionary status and motivates remedial behaviors. Furthermore, inclusion-facilitating behaviors alleviate dysphoria, thereby reinforcing actions that decrease the likelihood of exclusion. Baumeister and Tice (1990) proposed that the anxiety people experience when confronted with social exclusion serves such a function, and R. S. Miller and Leary (1992) suggested that feelings of embarrassment serve a similar role in the maintenance of interpersonal relationships. The role of affect in exclusion–avoidance explains why negative affectivity often includes "a sense of rejection" (Watson & Clark, 1984, p. 465). Precisely speaking, people do not suffer negative emotions *because* their self-esteem is damaged. Rather, decreased self-esteem and negative affect are co-effects of the sociometer system that monitors social exclusion.

As Brown (1993) suggested, these kinds of affective reactions may be central to self-esteem. From the sociometer perspective, the reason is clear. Theorists have suggested that the affective system is a relatively primitive system (compared to the cognitive system) that allows rapid and gross discriminations of events that pose an immediate threat to the individual (Izard, Kagan, & Zajonc, 1984; Zajonc, 1980, 1984). Like other affectively based systems, the sociometer/self-esteem system responds quickly to cues that connote disapproval or rejection with minimum cognitive analysis. This phenomenon may explain why people sometimes "feel bad" when they are demeaned, ignored, or rejected by people who are, rationally speaking, of absolutely no import to them. As James (1890, p. 328) observed, "The noteworthy thing about the desire to be 'recognized' by others is that its strength has so little to do with the worth of the recognition computed in sensational or rational terms." On detecting cues that imply rejection, people automatically experience negative affect and lowered self-esteem. A person who has behaved (or, perhaps, is about to behave) in ways that will jeopardize his or her social connections needs to be alerted *immediately* when the potential for disapproval, rejection, or ostracism exists. However, on rationally assessing the situation, people sometimes consciously opt to disregard the other person's reaction rather than to react to the threat.

SELF-ESTEEM MOTIVES OF LOW AND
HIGH SELF-ESTEEM PEOPLE

Much attention has been devoted to the question of whether people with chararacteristically low and high trait self-esteem differ in self-esteem motivation. Some have suggested, for example, that because people desire to verify their existing self-concepts, low self-esteem people are not motivated to enhance their self-esteem in the same way as high self-esteem people (see S. C. Jones, 1973; Swann, Griffin, Predmore, & Gaines, 1987). However, little evidence exists to directly show that low self-esteem people are not motivated to maintain or enhance their self-esteem. In fact, people with low self-esteem seem to be as bothered by negative feedback as highs (Swann et al., 1987) and prefer feedback about their positive rather than negative self-views (Swann, Pelham, & Krull, 1989).

Data do show, however, that low and high self-esteem people differ in how they respond to threats to their self-esteem. Rather than reflecting differences in self-esteem motivation, these differences may reflect differences in people's confidence that they are or are not likely to be accepted. To the extent that high self-esteem people are more likely to feel that others accept and include them than are low self-esteem people (Spivey, 1990), they may react differently to threats to inclusion. For example, the fact that high self-esteem people are affected less by evaluative feedback than are low self-esteem people (Brockner, 1983) may reflect the fact that a single incident that connotes potential rejection is less bothersome to people who perceive their inclusion needs to be met. Similarly, Seta and Seta (1992) suggested that low self-esteem people sometimes favor failing groups because they assume that their status in a failing group will be higher than their status in a successful group. Put differently, low self-esteem people may think that their inclusion in an unsuccessful group is less tenuous than their inclusion in a successful group. For low self-esteem people, social inclusion may be more important than success.

Furthermore, people who already feel accepted and who generally expect others to include them need not worry as much about rejection. Thus, they can take social risks to maximize their successes. In contrast, people who generally question their ability to be included—those with low self-esteem—may worry more about being excluded and focus more on remedying perceived deficiencies to avoid exclusion than on enhancing their chances of success. This conceptualization is consistent with previous theory and research on the motivations and interpersonal behavior of low and high self-esteem people (e.g., Baumeister & Tice, 1985; Baumeister, Tice, & Hutton, 1989).[3] In essence, high self-esteem people play offensively and low self-esteem people play defensively.

One difficulty in interpreting the research on differences in trait self-esteem is that people who obtain low vs. high scores on standard measures of self-esteem differ in many ways. They hold different beliefs about themselves, experience different patterns of self-relevant feelings, differ in their assumptions regarding the degree to which others are likely to accept vs. reject them, present different impressions of themselves to others, and differ in their motivation to promote success vs. avoid failure. When cognitive, affective, or behavioral differences between low and high self-esteem people are observed, it is difficult to know why the differences occurred, because the role of each of these processes in the effect is unclear. Much would be gained from distinguishing among these various facets of self-esteem.[4]

---

[3]Baumeister et al. (1989) convincingly argued that measures of trait self-esteem assess not only people's beliefs and feelings about themselves, but also their styles of self-presentation. Thus, low and high self-esteem people differ not only in their self-views, but also in the interpersonal strategies they use to convey impressions of themselves to others. Our sociometer model is perfectly consistent with their interpretation of self-esteem scores, although we add that low and high self-esteem people use different styles of self-presentation because of differential motivations and strategies vis-à-vis social exclusion.

[4]If we may be allowed a notion even more speculative than others we offer in this chapter, we suggest that the sociometer model provides two interrelated reasons that so few people have truly low self-esteem and that those with truly low self-esteem tend to be psychologically disturbed (Baumeister et al., 1989). First, from the perspective of the model, true low trait self-esteem would result from receiving consistently rejecting feedback. However, not only are most interpersonal relations characterized by neutrality or polite civility, but also the need to belong is so strong that people generally do not jeopardize their connections with everyone they know. Furthermore, even people with highly undesirable characteristics can typically find others who accept and include them. Thus, at worst, most normal people receive some mixture of positive and negative feedback. Second, from a sociobiological standpoint, people with truly low self-esteem were less "evolutionarily fit" than highs. Early humans who had no inclination to develop and maintain supportive social relationships (and thus to maintain self-esteem) were ostracized, banished, or killed.

DOMAINS OF SELF-ESTEEM

Although we often speak of self-esteem as a global construct, a person's self-esteem may differ across various domains or dimensions (Fleming & Courtney, 1984; Heatherton & Polivy, 1991; Pelham & Swann, 1989; Savin-Williams & Demo, 1983). For example, a person who has high self-esteem regarding his or her intellectual ability may have low self-esteem in athletics, or vice versa. Likewise, self-esteem motivation differs across domains. The person described above may work hard to maintain intellectual self-esteem, but care not a whit for his or her athletic self-esteem. Furthermore, he or she may be distressed by evidence indicating deficient intellect, but pay no attention whatsoever to what others might consider to be threats to athletic self-esteem.

The sociometer model easily explains these differences in how people respond to events that reflect on various domains of self-esteem. The meaning or importance that people attach to particular self-views influences the effects of those self-views on their self-esteem (Marsh, 1993; Pelham & Swann, 1989). James (1890, p. 310) noted that "our self-feeling . . . depends entirely on what we back ourselves to be and do." From our perspective, the importance of various domains of self-esteem depends on the degree to which the person perceives that his or her social relationships depend on each. People can follow many routes to social acceptance. Only when people have staked their connections to others on certain aspects of themselves should their self-esteem be affected by events that reflect on those aspects.

This reasoning explains why self-esteem motivation and self-esteem threats are often situation- and audience-specific. If the self-esteem motive served only to affirm an inner, subjective sense of self-worth, a threat to an important aspect of self should result in lowered self-esteem and in negative affect irrespective of who else might be around. Yet this is certainly not the case. A boy may not worry about his physique in front of his mother, yet suffer an acute loss of self-esteem when he undresses for gym class. Along these lines, Baldwin and Holmes (1987) showed that simply imagining different "audiences" affected subjects' self-evaluations.

This consideration also explains why a threat to self-esteem on one dimension often triggers compensatory efforts to enhance self-esteem in other domains and, often, before different audiences. A person who has suffered a loss of self-esteem by behaving in some undesirable fashion is understandably motivated to reduce feelings of disapproval or rejection. If possible, people may try to restore their relationship with those who were directly involved in the esteem-threatening event. However, if that is not an option, people may compensate by behaving in esteem-promoting ways to people who were not privy to the initial esteem threat (Apsler, 1975; Steele, 1975). From the standpoint of the sociometer hypothesis, this compensatory behavior comes about because decrements in self-esteem and affect that occur when one is excluded by one person can be reduced by being accepted by others (Baumeister & Leary, in press). This analysis also offers an explanation for the fact that members of stigmatized groups have self-esteem that is as high as that of members of nonstigmatized groups (cf. Crocker & Major, 1989). As long as a person's basic needs for inclusion and belonging are being met, the rejecting reactions of others have little long-term effect on trait self-esteem.

WHEN THE SOCIOMETER MALFUNCTIONS

When functioning optimally as a sociometer, the self-esteem system alerts the individual (via a drop in feelings of self-esteem and the accompanying negative affect) when behavior threatens to undermine his or her inclusionary status and may motivate actions that reduce the risk of exclusion. A functional sociometer should optimize a person's outcomes over time by promoting behavior that facilitates inclusion and fosters positive self-relevant affect. However, the system sometimes "malfunctions."

Most commonly, the sociometer is improperly calibrated such that it is either hypersensitive or hyposensitive to rejection cues. Sometimes, the sociometer registers "low," detecting disapproval, rejection, and exclusion where none, in fact, exists. People who are excessively sensitive to slights, criticism, rejection, and other ego threats may be disposed to interpret others' reactions as more rejecting and as less supportive than they really are (Lakey & Cassady, 1990). A history of rejection may lead to an improperly calibrated sociometer, chronically low self-esteem, and negative affectivity (Coopersmith, 1967). On the other hand, some people have a sociometer that registers too "high." Such people think others regard them more favorably and accept them more enthusiastically than is, in fact, the case. A narcissist would represent the extreme case of a person whose sociometer is calibrated too high. As described by Millon (1981, p. 158), narcissistic people "overvalue their personal worth . . . and expect others will not only recognize but cater to the high esteem in which [they] hold themselves."

Other people's sociometers simply get "stuck" like a faulty fuel gauge. When the sociometer becomes generally unresponsive to cues that connote rejection, people experience no changes in self-esteem or self-esteem motivation as cues connoting rejection and acceptance change. Some people seem unable to assess the effects of their behavior on others' reactions and, as a result, often mismanage their interactions with others. Similar interpersonal difficulties may occur when people intentionally "disable" their sociometers through alcohol consumption, drug use, and other escapist activities (Baumeister, 1991).

Some people's sociometers are unstable or unreliable. When they are, changes in self-esteem and self-esteem motivation are only loosely contingent on changes in the social environment. Some people display sweeping changes in their self-esteem and self-esteem motive that, from an outsider's perspective, appear to be overreactions to how they are being treated by other people (Bednar et al., 1989). For example, people with unstable self-esteem (who show considerable fluctuations in state-based self-esteem feelings over time) are particularly sensitive to feedback from other people (Kernis, Cornell, Sun, Berry, & Harlow, 1993); perhaps such persons have an unstable or overly reactive sociometer. The developmental antecedents of unstable self-esteem are poorly understood, but the sociometer model suggests that they may involve a history of highly inconsistent treatment by other people vis-à-vis acceptance and rejection.

On occasion, people's efforts to maintain self-esteem result in behaviors that are dysfunctional or dangerous to themselves or others (Baumeister, 1991; Mecca, Smesler, & Vasconcellos, 1989). For example, people may conform to antisocial group norms to avoid exclusion and maintain their self-esteem. Strictly speaking, such behaviors do not usually result from a malfunction in the sociometer itself. People's assumptions that engaging in certain dysfunctional behaviors will result in greater social acceptance are sometimes quite correct. Rather, the difficulty is that, as we've seen, the sociometer may respond preconsciously and automatically. If the person does not then engage in an adequate conscious and rational assessment of the consequences of engaging in such behaviors, he or she may try to maintain self-esteem even at a personal cost.

CONCLUSIONS

The universality and potency of the self-esteem motive suggests that it must serve an extremely important function for human beings. In our view, this function involves the maintenance of interpersonal relations. From an evolutionary perspective, no social motive is more essential for survival and reproduction than the maintenance of one's connections with other people. Thus, we propose that the self-esteem system evolved as a sociometer that allowed preconscious monitoring of the social environment for cues connoting disapproval and rejection, and that motivated behavior needed to enhance acceptance and inclusion by people who were psychologically important to the individual. Whatever role self-esteem may play in minimizing anxiety about death (Greenberg et al., 1986), affirming one's subjective sense of worth or adequacy (Steele, 1988), spurring movement toward one's ideal self (Rogers, 1959), monitoring one's power relations (Barkow, 1980; Tedeschi & Norman, 1985), or promoting task accomplishment (Greenwald, 1980), an affective–motivational process with the properties of the self-esteem system may have evolved because of its effect on the maintenance of interpersonal relationships. We acknowledge that, by necessity, our presentation of the sociometer hypothesis has been as much a theoretical sketch as a fully developed and substantiated model and that we have not addressed many important implications of and potential objections to our perspective. Nonetheless, we hope that our ideas spur further investigations into the source, function, and consequences of the self-esteem motive.

REFERENCES

Adler, A. (1930). *Understanding human nature.* New York: Greenberg.
Ainsworth, M. D. S. (1989). Attachments beyond infancy. *American Psychologist, 44,* 709–716.
Allport, G. W. (1937). *Personality: A psychological interpretation.* New York: Holt.
Apsler, R. (1975). Effects of embarrassment on behavior toward others. *Journal of Personality and Social Psychology, 32,* 145–153.
Baldwin, M. W., & Holmes, J. G. (1987). Salient private audiences and awareness of self. *Journal of Personality and Social Psychology, 52,* 1087–1098.
Bandura, A. (1977). Self-efficacy: Toward a unifying theory of behavioral change. *Psychological Review, 84,* 191–215.
Barash, D. P. (1977). *Sociobiology and behavior.* New York: Elsevier.
Barkow, J. (1980). Prestige and self-esteem: A biosocial interpretation. In D. R. Omark, F. F. Strayer, & D. G. Freedman (Eds.), *Dominance relations* (pp. 319–332). New York: Garland.
Baumeister, R. F. (1991). *Escaping the self.* New York: Basic Books.
Baumeister, R. F. (Ed.) (1993). *Self-esteem: The puzzle of low self-regard.* New York: Plenum. Press.
Baumeister, R. F., & Leary, M. R. (in press). The need to belong: Desire for interpersonal attachments as a fundamental human motivation. *Psychological Bulletin.*
Baumeister, R. F., & Tice, D. M. (1985). Self-esteem and responses to success and failure: Subsequent performance and intrinsic motivation. *Journal of Personality, 53,* 450–467.
Baumeister, R. F., & Tice. D. M. (1990). Anxiety and social exclusion. *Journal of Social and Clinical Psychology, 9,* 165–195.
Baumeister, R. F., Tice, D. M., & Hutton, D. G. (1989). Self-presentational motivations and personality differences in self-esteem. *Journal of Personality, 57,* 547–579.
Baumeister, R. F., Heatherton, T. F., & Tice, D. M. (1993). When ego threats lead to self-regulation failure: The negative consequences of high self-esteem. *Journal of Personality and Social Psychology, 64,* 141–156.

Baumgardner, A. H., Kaufman, C. M., & Levy, P. E. (1989). Regulating affect interpersonally: When low esteem leads to greater enhancement. *Journal of Personality and Social Psychology, 56,* 907–921.

Bednar, R. L., Wells, M. G., & Peterson, S. R. (1989). *Self-esteem: Paradoxes and innovations in clinical theory and practice.* Washington, DC: American Psychological Association.

Bhatti, B., Derezotes, D., Kim, S., & Specht, H. (1989). The association between child maltreatment and self-esteem. In A. M. Mecca, N. J. Smelser, & J. Vasconcellos (Eds.), *The social importance of self-esteem* (pp. 24–71). Berkeley: University of California Press.

Blaine, B., & Crocker, J. (1993). Self-esteem and self-serving biases in reactions to positive and negative events: An integrative review. In R. F. Baumeister (Ed.), *Self-esteem: The puzzle of low self-regard* (pp. 55–85). New York: Plenum Press.

Brockner, J. (1983). Low self-esteem and behavioral plasticity: Some implications. In L. Wheeler (Ed.), *Review of personality and social psychology,* Vol. 4 (pp. 237–271). Beverly Hills: Sage.

Brown, J. D.(1993). Self-esteem and self-evaluations: Feeling is believing. In J. Suls (Ed.), *Psychological perspectives on the self,* Vol 4. Hillsdale, NJ: Erlbaum Associates.

Cooley, C. H. (1902). *Human nature and the social order.* New York: Scribner.

Coopersmith, S. (1967). *The antecedents of self-esteem.* San Francisco: W. H. Freeman.

Crocker, J., & Major, B. (1989). Social stigma and self-esteem: The self-protective properties of stigma. *Psychological Review, 96,* 608–630.

Cutrona, C. E. (1982). Transition to college: Loneliness and the process of social adjustment: In L. A. Peplau & D. Perlman (Eds.), *Loneliness: A sourcebook of current theory, research, and therapy* (pp. 291–309). New York: John Wiley.

Downs, D. L. (1993). *Self-presentation in response to social exclusion: Social compensation or internalization?* Unpublished master's thesis. Winston-Salem, NC: Wake Forest University.

Epstein, S. (1973). The self-concept revisited: Or a theory of a theory. *American Psychologist, 28,* 404–416.

Eskilson, A., Wiley, M. G., Muehlbauer, G., & Dodder, L. (1986). Parental pressure, self-esteem, and adolescent reported deviance: Bending the twig too far. *Adolescence. 21,* 501–515.

Fleming, J. S., & Courtney, B. E. (1984). The dimensionality of self-esteem. II. Hierarchical facet model for revised measurement scales. *Journal of Personality and Social Psychology, 46,* 404–421.

Goswick, R. A., & Jones, W. H. (1981). Loneliness, self-concept, and adjustment. *Journal of Psychology, 107,* 237–240.

Greenberg, J., Pyszczynski, T., & Solomon, S. (1986). The causes and consequences of a need for self-esteem: A terror management theory. In R. F. Baumeister (Ed.), *Public self and private self* (pp. 189–207). New York: Springer-Verlag.

Greenberg, J., Solomon, S., Pyszczynski, T., Rosenblatt, A., Burling, J., Lyon, D., Simon, L., & Pinel, E. (1992). Why do people need self-esteem? Converging evidence that self-esteem serves an anxiety-buffering function. *Journal of Personality and Social Psychology, 63,* 913–922.

Greenwald, A. G. (1980). The totalitarian ego: Fabrication and revision of personal history. *American Psychologist, 35,* 603–613.

Greenwald, A. G., & Breckler, S. (1985). To whom is the self presented? In B. R. Schlenker (Ed.), *The self and social life* (pp. 126–145). New York: McGraw-Hill.

Heatherton, T. F., & Polivy, J. (1991). Development and validation of a scale for measuring state self-esteem. *Journal of Personality and Social Psychology, 60,* 895–910.

Hogan, R., Jones, W. H., & Cheek, J. M. (1985). Socioanalytic theory: An alternative to armadillo psychology. In B. R. Schlenker (Ed.), *The self and social life* (pp. 175–198). New York: McGraw-Hill.

Horney, K. (1937). *The neurotic personality of our time.* New York: W. W. Norton.

Izard, C. E., Kagan, J., & Zajonc, R. B. (Eds.) (1984). *Emotions, cognition, and behavior.* New York: Cambridge University Press.

James, W. (1890). *Principles of psychology.* New York: Dover.

Jones, E. E., & Berglas, S. (1978). Control of attributions about the self through self-handicapping strategies: The appeal of alcohol and the role of underachievement. *Personality and Social Psychology Bulletin, 4,* 200–206.

Jones, S. C. (1973). Self-and interpersonal evaluations: Esteem theories versus consistency theories. *Psychological Bulletin, 79,* 185–199.

Josephs, R. A., Markus, H. R., & Tafarodi, R. W. (1992). Gender and self-esteem. *Journal of Personality and Social Psychology, 63,* 391–402.

Kanfer, R., & Zeiss, A. M. (1983). Depression, interpersonal standard setting, and judgments of self-efficacy. *Journal of Abnormal Psychology, 92,* 319–329.

Katz, D. (1960). The functional approach to the study of attitudes. *Public Opinion Quarterly, 24,* 163–204.

Kernis, M. H., Cornell, D. P., Sun, C., Berry, A., & Harlow, T. (1993). There's more to self-esteem than whether it is high or low: The importance of stability of self-esteem. *Journal of Personality and Social Psychology, 65,* 1190–1204.

Lakey, B., & Cassady, P. B. (1990). Cognitive processes in perceived social support. *Journal of Personality and Social Psychology, 59,* 337–343.

Leary, M. R. (1983). *Understanding social anxiety: Social, personality and clinical perspectives.* Beverly Hills: Sage.

Leary, M. R. (1990). Responses to social exclusion: Social anxiety, jealousy, loneliness, depression, and low self-esteem. *Journal of Social and Clinical Psychology, 9,* 221–229.

Lewinsohn, P. M., Mischel, W., Chaplin, W., & Barton, R. (1980). Social competence and depression: The role of illusory self-perceptions. *Journal of Abnormal Psychology, 89,* 203–212.

Marsh, H. W. (1993). Relations between global and specific domains of self: The importance of individual importance, certainty, and ideals. *Journal of Personality and Social Psychology, 65,* 975–992.

McFarland, C., & Ross, M. (1982). Impact of causal attributions on affective reactions to success and failure. *Journal of Personality and Social Psychology, 43,* 937–946.

McFarlin, D. B., Baumeister, R. F., & Blascovich, J. (1984). On knowing when to quit: Task failure, self-esteem, advice, and nonproductive persistence. *Journal of Personality, 52,* 138–155.

Mecca, A. M., Smelser, N. J., & Vasconcellos, J. (Eds.) (1989). *The social importance of self-esteem.* Berkeley: University of California Press.

Miller, D. T. (1976). Ego involvement and attributions for success and failure. *Journal of Personality and Social Psychology, 34,* 901–906.

Miller, R. S., & Leary, M. R. (1992). Social sources and interactive functions of emotion: The case of embarrassment. In M. S. Clark (Ed.), *Emotion and social behavior* (pp. 202–221). Newbury Park, CA: Sage.

Millon, T. (1981). *Disorders of personality: DSM-III: Axis II.* New York: John Wiley.

Morse, S. J., & Gergen, K. J. (1970). Social comparison, self-consistency, and the concept of self. *Journal of Personality and Social Psychology, 16,* 149–158.

Pelham, B. W., & Swann, W. B., Jr. (1989). From self-conceptions to self-worth: On the sources and structure of global self-esteem. *Journal of Personality and Social Psychology, 57,* 672–680.

Perez, R. C. (1973). The effect of experimentally-induced failure, self-esteem, and sex on cognitive differentiation. *Journal of Abnormal Psychology, 81,* 74–79.

Riggio, R. E., Throckmorton, B., & DePaola, S. (1990). Social skills and self-esteem. *Personality and Individual Differences, 11,* 799–804.

Rogers, C. (1959). A theory of therapy, personality, and interpersonal relationships, as developed in the client-centered framework. In S. Koch (Ed.), *Psychology: A study of a science,* Vol. 3 (pp. 184–256). New York: McGraw-Hill.

Rosenberg, M. (1965). *Society and the adolescent self-image.* Princeton, NJ: Princeton University Press.

Savin-Williams, R. C., & Demo, D. H. (1983). Situational and transituational determinants of adolescent self-feelings. *Journal of Personality and Social Psychology, 44,* 824–833.

Schachter, S. (1951). Deviation, rejection, and communication. *Journal of Abnormal and Social Psychology, 46,* 190–207.

Schalon, C. L. (1968). Effect of self-esteem upon performance following failure stress. *Journal of Consulting and Clinical Psychology, 32,* 497.

Schlenker, B. R. (1980). *Impression management: The self-concept, social identity, and interpersonal relations.* Monterey, CA: Brooks/Cole.

Schneider, W., & Shiffrin, R. M. (1977). Controlled and automatic human information processing. I. Detection, search, and attention. *Psychological Review, 84,* 1–66.

Sedikides, C. (1993). Assessment, enhancement, and verification determinants of the self-evaluation process. *Journal of Personality and Social Psychology, 65,* 317–338.

Seta, C. E., & Seta, J. J. (1992). Observers and participants in an intergroup setting. *Journal of Personality and Social Psychology, 63,* 629–643.

Shrauger, J. S., & Sorman, P. B. (1977). Self-evaluations, initial success and failure, and improvement as determinants of persistence. *Journal of Consulting and Clinical Psychology, 45,* 784–795.

Snyder, M. L., Stephan, W. G., & Rosenfield, D. (1978). Attributional egotism. In J. H. Harvey, W. Ickes, & R. F. Kidd (Eds.), *New directions in attribution research,* Vol. 2 (pp. 91–117). Hillsdale, NJ: Erlbaum Associates.

Spivey, E. (1990). *Social exclusion as a common factor in social anxiety, loneliness, jealousy, and social depression: Testing an integrative model.* Unpublished master's thesis. Winston-Salem, NC: Wake Forest University.

Steele, C. (1975). Name-calling and compliance. *Journal of Personality and Social Psychology, 31,* 361–369.

Steele, C. M. (1988). The psychology of self-affirmation: Sustaining the integrity of the self. In L. Berkowitz (Ed.), *Advances in experimental social psychology,* Vol. 21 (pp. 261–302). San Diego: Academic Press.

Swann, W. B., Jr., Griffin, J. J., Jr., Predmore, S. C., & Gaines, B. (1987). The cognitive–affective crossfire: When self-consistency confronts self-enhancement. *Journal of Personality and Social Psychology, 52,* 881–889.

Swann, W. B., Jr., Pelham, B. W., & Krull, D. S. (1989). Agreeable fancy or disagreeable truth? Reconciling self-enhancement and self-verification. *Journal of Personality and Social Psychology, 57,* 782–791.

Tambor, E. S., & Leary, M. R. (1993). *Perceived exclusion as a common factor in social anxiety, loneliness, jealousy, depression, and low self-esteem.* Unpublished manuscript. Winston-Salem, NC: Wake Forest University.

Taylor, S. E., & Brown, J. D. (1988). Illusion and well-being: A social psychological perspective on mental health. *Psychological Bulletin, 103,* 193–210.

Tedeschi, J. T., & Norman, N. (1985). Social power, self-presentation, and the self. In B. R. Schlenker (Ed.), *The self and social life* (pp. 293–322). New York: McGraw-Hill.

Terdal, S., & Leary, M. R. (1990). *Self-esteem and perceived social exclusion*. Paper presented at the meeting of the Southeastern Psychological Association, Atlanta.

Terdal, S., & Leary, M. R. (1991). *Social exclusion, self-esteem, and dysphoria*. Paper presented at the meeting of the Southeastern Psychological Association, New Orleans.

Tesser, A. (1988). Toward a self-evaluation maintenance model of social behavior. In L. Berkowitz (Ed.), *Advances in experimental social psychology*, Vol. 21 (pp. 181–227). San Diego: Academic Press.

Walster, E. (1965). The effect of self-esteem on romantic liking. *Journal of Personality and Social Psychology, 1,* 184–197.

Watson, D., & Clark, L. A. (1984). Negative affectivity: The disposition to experience aversive emotional states. *Psychological Bulletin, 96,* 465–490.

White, G. L. (1981). Some correlates of romantic jealousy. *Journal of Personality, 49,* 129–147.

Zajonc, R. B. (1980). Feeling and thinking: Preferences need no inferences. *American Psychologist, 35,* 151–175.

Zajonc, R. B. (1984). On the primacy of affect. *American Psychologist, 39,* 117–123.

CHAPTER 7

SELF-ESTEEM AND THE EXTENDED SELF-EVALUATION MAINTENANCE MODEL

THE SELF IN SOCIAL CONTEXT

STEVEN R. H. BEACH AND ABRAHAM TESSER

INTRODUCTION

The self may be viewed as a collection of symbols created within a social framework, a collection that has some inherent fluidity (cf. Baumeister, 1991; Wicklund & Gollwitzer, 1982). The fluidity of the self may be seen as following from its ability to assimilate symbols from the social environment and add to the self-definition as required by social feedback, as well as from its ability to adjust and perhaps delete symbols as they become unworkable. Of particular importance for global self-esteem is the subset of self-symbols pertaining to "important things I do well," i.e., the performance domain of the self (James, 1890; Rosenberg, 1979) (but for a discussion of possible cross-cultural differences, see also Markus & Kitayama, 1991). Importantly, the performance domain of the self may undergo adjustment in relation to the performance of close others through a series of

STEVEN R. H. BEACH AND ABRAHAM TESSER • Department of Psychology and Institute for Behavioral Research, University of Georgia, Athens, Georgia 30602.

Efficacy, Agency, and Self-Esteem, edited by Michael H. Kernis. Plenum Press, New York, 1995.

processes described by the self-evaluation maintenance (SEM) model (Tesser, 1988). SEM processes can therefore be seen as being directly involved in the manipulation of the fundamental building blocks of global self-esteem, particularly as it relates to changes in self-definition.

As recently reported by Steele, Spencer, and Lynch (1993) and Tesser and Cornell (1991), there apparently are ways, however, in which global self-esteem may affect the use of SEM processes. Specifically, there appears to be a mechanism linked to global self-esteem by which the self-protective processes described in the SEM model can be disengaged. This disengagement can be accomplished, for example, by allowing persons to affirm positively evaluated aspects of the self or to engage in a self-enhancing behavior along an unrelated dimension. This diversion of attention from a threatening area to an area of solidly positive self-evaluation appears to eliminate the need for other self-protective strategies. This circumstance suggests that persons with stable positive global self-esteem may have greater resources for dealing with self-evaluation threats and may more easily deactivate SEM processes than those with lower or less stable, global self-esteem (Steele et al., 1993). Perhaps surprisingly, it does not appear that the greater resources of those with high self-esteem result in their showing a distinctly different pattern of response to most situations. Even persons with relatively high self-esteem may find a specific aspect of their self-definition under challenge and use SEM processes to bring the self back into internal coherence (J. D. Brown & Gallagher, 1992). Likewise, even someone with relatively low self-esteem may harbor pretensions of positive performance in a few areas, and should one of these areas come under assault, this challenge would be expected to occasion the use of SEM processes (cf. Pelham, 1993). Accordingly, both high and low self-esteem persons may be expected to engage in SEM processes when the conditions are right, and in the laboratory both high and low self-esteem persons do engage in self-evaluation maintenance (Tesser, 1988). Accordingly, SEM processes may be viewed as being relatively robust with regard to level of global self-esteem.

A recent elaboration of the SEM model (Beach & Tesser, 1993) focuses on the operation of SEM processes within close relationships. This focus is important in the context of this discussion because the integrity of dyadic relationships may have striking effects on an individual's sense of well-being as well as on global self-evaluation (Beach, Smith, & Fincham, 1994). Indeed, it seems likely that close others may play a disproportionately large role in the evaluative processes that determine whether the self that an individual has constructed is esteemed or devalued (Becker, 1979; G. W. Brown, Bifulco, Veiel, & Andrews, 1990b; G. W. Brown, Bifulco, & Andrews, 1990a). Accordingly, the functioning of SEM processes in the context of close relationships may have important indirect effects on global self-evaluation in terms both of effects on changes in self-definition and of effects on the functioning of the marital dyad. It is these various potential indirect effects of SEM processes on global self-esteem that will be the primary focus of attention in this chapter. We will highlight particularly those processes that have the potential to create a self that is more or less likely to be esteemed, and those processes that create an environment of close others who are more likely to be esteeming or devaluing, but we assume that it is the social environment (or an internalized representation of the social environment), not SEM processes per se, that more directly influence level of self-esteem.

We take as our starting point the SEM model, its extension to dyadic interaction, and recent evidence supporting the model. We then turn to consideration of likely effects over time on global self-esteem.

THE SELF-EVALUATION MAINTENANCE MODEL

THE ORIGINAL SEM MODEL

The SEM model (Tesser, 1988) identifies two antagonistic processes central to the maintenance of a positive self-evaluation: reflection and comparison. The comparison process either leads to adjustments to avoid the threat to one's self-evaluation that might result from comparison to the outstanding accomplishments of a close other (cf. Suls & Wills, 1991; Wills, 1981) or serves to bolster self-evaluation through comparison with the poor performance of another (Gibbons, 1986; Taylor, Wood, & Lichtman, 1983; Wood & Taylor, 1991). Examples of negative comparison are quite common, as when one spouse feels threatened because the other spouse is seen as smarter or more verbal, or because the other spouse makes more money. The SEM model predicts that persons will tend to avoid situations that threaten self-evaluation but be attracted to situations that bolster self-evaluation.

The reflection process can be seen as the mirror image of the comparison process. In this process, self-evaluation is bolstered by the outstanding accomplishments of a close other (cf. Cialdini, Borden, Thorne, Walker, Freeman, & Sloan, 1976) and threatened by the poor performance of another. Examples of the positive side of this process are frequent, as when one spouse takes pride in the other's accomplishments at work or in the community (as when one partner basks in the reflected glory of a partner's fame, attractiveness, or standing in the community).

What determines when spouses bask in reflected glory rather than wither under negative comparison? According to the SEM model, the relative balance of comparison and reflection processes is determined by the *relevance* of the performance dimension involved. That is, although the self may recognize good performance on a variety of dimensions, the self aspires to be "good at" only a few such dimensions. Those dimensions that a spouse finds "self-defining" or *relevant* prompt comparison. Those dimensions that a spouse finds to be not "important" or *relevant* prompt reflection. Thus, it is facilitative to self-evaluation maintenance to outperform a close other on a dimension high in self-relevance, but facilitative to be outperformed by a close other if the dimension is low in self-relevance.

In sum, it can be seen that the SEM model has three basic parameters, closeness, relevance (importance), and performance, and these parameters are all assumed to interact with each other. The interaction of these parameters is predicted to be important in determining which types of situations spouses will seek out and which they will avoid as well as which will produce relatively positive affect and which more negative affect. It is assumed that these processes will often operate outside awareness (cf. Pilkington, Tesser, & Stephens, 1991; Pleban & Tesser, 1981; Tesser & Collins, 1988; Tesser & Paulhus, 1983; Tesser, Millar, & Moore, 1988).

THE EXTENDED SEM MODEL

Early research supported the original SEM model for interactions involving strangers, acquaintances, and friends (e.g.,Tesser, 1988; Tesser et al, 1988). In that research, however, the SEM model had no component that weighted the person's investment in the relationship with the other. That is, if the person was given an opportunity for positive comparison with another, no effort was made to take into account the person's reaction to the fact that his or her partner might well be suffering from negative comparison or conversely basking in reflected glory. The literature on close relationships suggests that this assumption is untenable once the model is extended to marriages (Kelley & Thibaut, 1978).

Spouses in committed relationships show a communal orientation to each others' needs, leading them to keep track of, and respond sympathetically to, each other's needs (Clark, 1984; Clark, Mills, & Powell, 1986; Mills & Clark, 1982). This suggests the potential in close relationships for a partner to feel less positively about an outcome that enhances his or her own self-evaluation if it would simultaneously threaten the partner's self-evaluation. While the emotion experienced would not necessarily be the same as the partner's, it would be expected to be similarly valenced. In addition, to the extent that spouses are sympathetic to each other's SEM needs they would be expected to behave in ways that benefit the partner (cf. Eisenberg & Miller, 1987). To the extent that the partner is likely to suffer negative comparison as a result of one's performance in a given area, to that extent should one's affective reaction tend to be less positive and the attractiveness of the situation tend to be decreased. Conversely, to the extent that the partner is basking in reflected glory as a result of one's good performance, to that extent should the positive reaction to the situation tend to be augmented and the attractiveness of the situation tend to be increased.

In line with these findings about close relationships, the SEM model can be expanded to propose that partners in committed relationships respond sympathetically to their spouse's outcomes, as well as directly to their own outcomes. An extended SEM model predicts that spouses placed in SEM situations will react with affect that reflects both the valence of the affect predicted for them *and* the valence of the affect predicted for their partners. The extended model therefore predicts that in many cases a spouse's benefit from positive comparison or reflection may be offset by the knowledge that the partner is suffering negative comparison or failing to benefit from positive reflection. Alternately, a spouse benefiting from positive comparison might have positive reactions intensified by the knowledge that the partner is benefiting from basking in reflected glory. In all cases, the results of SEM processes become less positive and more negative, the model suggests that closeness may be reduced in order to reduce the intensity of the negative process. Also, the presence of spouse relevance as a parameter in the model highlights the potential for situations to arise in which the emotions predicted for the self are either effectively congruent or effectively incongruent with the emotions predicted for the partner. In congruent SEM conditions (e.g., where the actor's performance benefits both self and partner), the actor will not show ambivalent affective responses, but may show an intensification of the predicted affect. In conflict situations (e.g., where actor's performance benefits self but injures partner or vice versa), however, the actor will show more ambivalent affective responses. This ambivalence suggests the potential for especially strong emotional activation in the latter situations.

COMBINING THE ORIGINAL AND THE
EXTENDED SEM MODELS

In essence, the original SEM model posited that there are two basic categories of performance-based evaluations: one category for those areas that are important to one's own self-definition and another category for those areas that are not important to one's self-definition. The extended model posits that spouses also recognize that some areas are important to their partner's self-definition while others are not. The resulting state of affairs for spouses in committed relationships is represented by the Venn diagram in Fig. 1.

Four qualitatively different categories emerge within the dyad: (1) those areas that are important only to the first partner and not to the other, (2) those areas that are important only to the second partner and not to the first, (3) those areas that are important to both partners, and (4) those areas that are important to neither. If the goal is to maximize outcomes for both persons in the relationship (cf. Kelley & Thibaut, 1978), then spouses should behave differently for areas that fall in each of these four categories. In particular, the joint outcome for the spouses is maximized if the first partner typically is the expert or does best in area A and the second partner typically is the expert or does best in area B. For areas C and D, relative performance makes less difference vis-à-vis maximum couple benefit, one

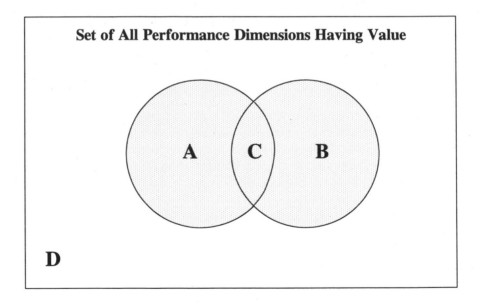

A - Highly important to Partner A but not Partner B

B - Highly important to Partner B but not Partner A

C - Highly important to both Partners

D - Not important to either Partner

FIGURE 1. Venn diagram of four categories of couple importance.

might suspect that other considerations would play a larger role in the way couples divide expertise or relative performance for these areas.

STRATEGIES FOR STAYING CLOSE

Given the pressures explicated above, it seems clear that maintaining relationship closeness in the context of rather similar performance-oriented self-definitions should be difficult. Yet, with the breakdown of traditional, enforced division of responsibilities along gender lines, there is increasing opportunity for couples to confront this situation. Indeed, since similarity is known to be a primary factor in attraction and marriage (O'Leary & Smith, 1991), it is likely that persons with overlapping relevance will often form romantic relationships. Clark and Bennett (1992) provide a cogent examination of this problem and the various ways that persons may adjust their self-definitions or their joint behavior to manage these potential difficulties. In particular, they highlight several possible strategies of interest. First, couples might choose to pursue different domains within the same field. This can be seen as simply drawing finer distinctions between areas within the field than others might. To the extent that the couple can come to view themselves as pursuing excellence within distinct areas of performance, they should be able to gain the benefits of reflection and avoid the pitfalls of negative comparison, even if the distinctions are not readily apparent or comprehensible to others. Alternatively, Clark and Bennett note that a couple could make comparison impossible by doing everything jointly so that no issue of relative performance could arise. They give the example of two professors of similar rank in the same field who might decide to co-author all their papers.

Clark and Bennett (1992) also discuss the potential relationship and emotional benefits of maximizing one's opportunities for reflection in the partner's achievements. For example, if one's partner is an artist, one might benefit from displaying his or her art work prominently in one's office. An important point is that Clark and Bennett note the potential value of complementarity in the performance domain for partners in close relationships.

EXTENDING THE SEM MODEL TO CLOSE RELATIONSHIPS: EMPIRICAL SUPPORT

AFFECTIVE OUTCROPPINGS

A previous generation of studies has revealed predictable changes in affect based on the original SEM model (Tesser, 1991). A more recent series of studies has tested the predictions of the extended SEM model with regard to affective reactions of persons in close relationships. In the first investigation of this sort (Beach & Tesser, 1994), 224 members of marital dyads completed a measure of recalled affect for the marital situations based on the Positive and Negative Affect Scales (PANAS) (Watson, Clark, & Tellegen, 1988). Subjects were asked to think about tasks and activities representing each of eight conditions highlighted by the extended SEM model. These conditions are defined by crossing high and low self-relevance with high and low partner-relevance with whether self outperforms partner or partner outperforms self. Positive affect terms were summed and negative affect terms were subtracted to form a total "pleasantness" score. The effect of the eight potential SEM configurations on pleasantness of mood was examined via a 2 (gender, male or female) × 2 (Self-Relevance, high or low) × 2 (Spouse-Relevance, high or low), × 2 (relative performance, outperform partner or partner outperforms) repeated-measures analysis of variance (ANOVA).

The two interaction effects predicted by the SEM model and its extension were found to be significant. The significant Self-Relevance × Performance interaction reflected the relatively greater pleasantness of being outperformed by rather than outperforming one's partner at a task that was low in Self-Relevance, while the opposite was true for tasks high in Self-Relevance. That is, the crossover pattern predicted by the SEM model was obtained. Similarly, the Spouse-Relevance × Performance interaction reflected the relatively greater pleasantness of being outperformed by one's partner when the task was high in Spouse-Relevance rather than low in Spouse-Relevance, while the opposite was true for outperforming the partner. Thus, the crossover pattern predicted by the extended SEM model was also obtained.

A second investigation of affective outcroppings was conducted by Mendolia, Beach, and Tesser (1993). In this study, 53 married couples were interviewed over the phone and asked to describe personal experiences that conformed to the eight types of situations defined by the extended SEM model. Then, after describing the situation in some detail, each subject indicated on a 7-point scale the degree to which he or she felt negative affect (distressed, nervous, hostile) and the degree to which he or she felt positive affect (active, elated, enthusiastic). Repeated-measures ANOVAs (Self-Relevance by Partner-Relevance by Performance by Gender) were conducted separately for positive and negative affect. For both positive and negative affect, the central predictions of the extended SEM model were obtained. That is, for positive affect, there was a significant interaction of both Self-Relevance × Performance and Partner-Relevance × Performance. Similarly, for negative affect, the predicted two-way interactions were significant. That is, both the interaction of Self-Relevance × Performance and the interaction of Partner-Relevance × Performance were significant. In all cases, when the pattern of means was plotted, it was found to conform to the pattern predicted by the extended SEM model. Thus, the predictions of the extended SEM model with regard to affective outcroppings of SEM processes seem robust across somewhat different self-report strategies.

Of course, the two studies reported above used *recalled* experiences. Use of recalled experiences has the advantages of eliciting real-world stimuli with real-world importance to spouses, but it also allows for the possibility of distorted recall and considerable variability across couples in the type of experiences elicited. Accordingly, one might wonder whether the impact of experimenter-manipulated feedback would also support the predictions of the extended SEM model. In a test of manipulated feedback, 36 married couples were asked to report affect following activities in which they interacted with the computer and received feedback about their performance relative to the partner (Mendolia, Beach, Tesser, Wakefield, & Wright, 1992). Subjects were given a list of 30 topic areas and asked to pick two areas that reflected each of the following situations: topic important to both, topic important to husband but not to wife, topic important to wife but not to husband, topic important to neither. One of the topics in each area was selected at random to serve as the area in which the subject was "outperformed," while the other topic was used to provide feedback that the subject had outperformed the other spouse. All subjects participated in all eight conditions. Affect was assessed after the task by providing subjects with their answers and the feedback and then asking them how they felt when they received the feedback. Affect terms were taken from the PANAS. As predicted, and as when recalled affect for personally significant events was used, negative affect was a function of the interaction of Self-Relevance × Performance and also a function of the interaction of Spouse-Relevance × Performance. In both cases, the shape of the interaction conformed to the predictions of the SEM model and the extended SEM model.

Taken together, the studies offer rather strong support for the extended model's prediction that SEM effects on emotional outcroppings will be apparent in the context of close relationships and that the sympathetic response of each partner to the other's SEM needs will influence the valence of their emotional reaction as well. To the extent that these emotional reactions color an individual's self-evaluation (e.g., Schwartz & Clore, 1988), there may be some direct effect on self-esteem of these SEM processes. We suspect, however, that the greater effect is indirect. That is, we suspect that the greater effect comes through the influence these emotional reactions may exert on the types of behaviors each spouse chooses to engage in, the areas in which they attempt to do their best vs. those in which they attempt to let the partner do better, the way they divide power in the relationship, and the way they may ultimately come to redefine themselves. It is these issues to which we turn next. First, we examine the issue of SEM influences on shared, enjoyable couple activities. To the extent that couples structure their interactions in accordance with self and partner SEM needs, these processes can be seen to have important implications for couple cohesion and couple closeness.

SHARED ACTIVITIES AND THE EXTENDED SEM MODEL

In one of the studies described above (Beach & Tesser, 1994), subjects were also assessed as to frequency of various types of activities. For each type of situation, the frequency with which this type of situation occurred was assessed by questions of the following format: "Please think about the various tasks and activities that you think are (are not) very important to your spouse. How often would you say that you do better than your spouse (your spouse does better than you) on tasks or activities which are important (not very important) to you but not very important (important) to your spouse?" In each case, spouses indicated whether the situations occurred often, frequently, rarely, or never. A 2 (Gender, male or female) × 2 (Self-Relevance, high or low) × 2 (Spouse-Relevance, high or low) × 2 (Relative Performance, outperform partner or partner outperforms) repeated-measures ANOVA was conducted. For both husbands and wives, the two types of tasks reported to be least frequent were (1) tasks high in Self-Relevance, low in Spouse-Relevance, with the spouse performing better, and (2) tasks low in Self-Relevance, high in Spouse-Relevance, with self performing better. These are the situations predicted by the SEM model to have the least benefit for self-evaluation maintenance and greatest potential threat for the couple. Also, both the Self-Relevance × Performance interaction and the Spouse-Relevance × Performance interaction were significant. Again, these are the interaction effects predicted by the SEM model and the extended SEM model. The Self-Relevance × Performance interaction reflected the greater reported frequency of being outperformed by rather than outperforming one's partner at a task that was low in Self-Relevance, while the opposite was true for tasks high in Self-Relevance. This is, of course, the pattern predicted by the SEM model. The Spouse-Relevance × Performance interaction reflected the relatively greater reported frequency of being outperformed by rather than outperforming one's spouse when the task was high in Spouse-Relevance, while the opposite was true when Spouse-Relevance was low. Again, this is the pattern predicted by the extended SEM model.

The results strongly support the view that the behavior of spouses, or at least their recollections of that behavior, are influenced by their own and their partner's SEM needs. Thus, over time, there is pressure for spouses to conform their performances so that each spouse is outperformed in the areas that are best for relationship maintenance, rather than potentially destabilizing to the relationship. Clearly, over time, this pressure must begin to influence the way an individual views the self. However, one might suspect that the way decision-making power in the relationship is divided might influence one's view of the self even more strongly. This issue was addressed in a recent study by Beach and Tesser (1993), and it is to this issue that we turn next.

DISTRIBUTION OF POWER AND THE EXTENDED SEM MODEL

Beach and Tesser (1993) assessed 90 married couples with regard to 24 decision-making areas based on the powergram of Stuart (1981). For each of these 24 decision-making areas, each spouse was asked to indicate: (1) whether the couple agreed for the most part in this area of decision making, (2) whether decisions in this area were made primarily by the self or by the partner, (3) whether making decisions in this area was important or not to the self, and (4) whether making decisions in this area was important or not to the partner. Responses were analyzed in a 2^5 repeated-measures ANOVA with marital satisfaction as a between-couples factor and four within-couple factors (decision-making power × self-importance of the area × partner-importance of the area × gender). As predicted, a significant three-way interaction of power × self-importance × satisfaction was found. According to the SEM model, this effect should be the result of satisfied couples experiencing greater reflection and comparison benefits than do dissatisfied couples. Thus, within satisfied couples, both husbands and wives should report a higher percentage of agreements when power is high and self-importance is high (i.e., category A or C in Fig. 1) or when power is low and self-importance is low (i.e., category B or D in Fig. 1), but this effect should be attenuated for dissatisfied spouses. In fact, this is exactly the pattern that was obtained.

Second, also as predicted, there was a significant interaction of power × *partner*-importance × satisfaction. According to the extended SEM model, this interaction should be the result of more satisfied couples affording greater reflection and comparison benefits to their partners than do dissatisfied couples. Thus, within satisfied couples, both husbands and wives should report higher agreement when power is high and partner-importance is low (category A or D) or when power is low and partner-importance is high (category B or C), but this effect should be attenuated for dissatisfied spouses. Again, the obtained pattern of means was in the predicted direction.

Interestingly, a significant three-way interaction of gender × power × partner-importance indicated that wives conferred greater SEM benefits on their partners in terms of reflection and positive comparison opportunities than did husbands. While this was not a predicted effect, to the extent that it is replicated in future work, it suggests that women more than men may be at risk of "losing themselves" due to pressures to help their partner maintain a positive self-evaluation. Accordingly, it represents a potentially very important gender difference in the way concern for the partner's self-evaluation maintenance needs may affect global self-esteem.

The decision-making data are consistent with the view that couples negotiate a distribution of decision-making power that supports both partners' SEM needs. Given the central nature of decision-making control for one's general sense of control in one's life, this would appear to reflect another example of the way in which SEM processes may come to subtly shape a person's view of himself or herself over time. However, perhaps the most powerful relationship variable influencing a person's self-view and general sense of well-being is the extent to which he or she is getting along with the partner (Beach et al., 1994). Accordingly, SEM effects on the extent to which problems are addressed in a more or less conflictual way may be of considerable potential importance for understanding self-esteem (G. W. Brown et al., 1990b).

COMMUNICATION FOLLOWING SEM CHALLENGE

In an investigation of the potential effect of SEM processes on couples' attempts to resolve problems, 129 couples were given feedback designed to produce either positive reflection (R+) for one partner and positive comparison (C+) for the other, negative comparison (C−) for one partner and positive comparison (C+) for the other, or negative comparison for one partner (C−) and negative reflection for the other (R−). In all conditions, subjects selected topic areas from a list of 30 topics and then engaged in a Trivial Pursuit–type task, ostensibly competing against the partner. All interactions were done via the computer, and feedback regarding relative performance was provided via the computer. Following the computer interaction, couples were asked to engage in a 10-minute problem-solving interaction. The interactions were subsequently content-analyzed using the MICS-IV (Weiss, 1992).

The content codes were combined into three categories that were both theoretically related to SEM processes and potentially consequential for dyadic functioning. One category was formed by combining behaviors reflective of dominance by one partner or the other. Behaviors combined included command, interrupt, comply, and noncomply. A second category was formed by combining the high intensity negative behaviors labeled "blaming" in the MICS. This category included codes such as put-down, criticism, and negative mind-reading. A third category included lower-level negative behaviors such as disapprove, give an excuse, and disagree. In all cases, it was hypothesized that as the SEM effects for the couple became more negative, the behavior following the manipulation would become increasingly negative. Accordingly, it was predicted that we would find a linear trend across the three groups for each of these negative behavior codes, with each being least frequent for couples in which neither partner felt threatened (R+/C+), becoming more frequent for couples in which one partner experienced a negative outcome (C+/C-), and more negative still for couples in which both partners experienced a negative SEM outcome (C-/R-).

As predicted, the effect of condition was significant in the predicted direction for the three sets of negative behavior, and there was a very strong linear trend across the three conditions. That is, negative comparison tended to produce more negative behavior across a variety of indices than did positive-reflection experiences, and if the partner was experiencing negative reflection, this experience resulted in still more negative behavior. Accordingly, these preliminary results indicate that SEM manipulations may produce changes in communication behavior of the sort typically associated with dysfunctional relationships. More specifically, following a negative-comparison experience, spouses are more likely to be negative and more likely to try to dominate their partners. Presumably, these behaviors could have serious repercussions for the relationship if continued over a long enough period of time. Thus, it may be that some instances of undermining or failure to provide self-esteem support to the partner may be the direct result of SEM strategies. If so, SEM effects could have a very large indirect effect on the self-esteem of partners.

JEALOUSY AND ENVY

SEM processes may also be relevant to understanding important dyadic transactions such as partner envy and jealousy (Tesser, 1990; Tesser & Collins, 1988). As has been highlighted by Salovey and Rothman (1991), there is considerable overlap between the relationship processes highlighted by the SEM model and those discussed as reactions to envy. For example, the envious individual may distort beliefs about relative performance (cf. Salovey & Rodin, 1988), or reduce closeness (cf. Salovey & Rodin, 1984), or change what is self-defining or seen as important. But these are precisely the domains that the SEM model also highlights. Accordingly, the SEM model may provide guidance in understanding better the potentially intractable problems associated with jealousy and envy in marital relationships.

Recent work (Beach, Mendolia, & Tesser, 1991) highlights the negative effects of perceived partner envy regarding those areas in which one takes greatest pride. In a sample of 230 married persons, it was found that persons who perceived their partner as being more envious and less proud in an area of personal importance were less happy with their relationships, more likely to have thoughts of leaving the relationship, and saw their relationships as less cohesive, less intimate, and less supportive of their self-esteem. As can be seen in Table 1, pride and envy ascribed to the partner, rather than one's self-reported pride and envy, were related to quality of the relationship. Thus, the extent to which the partner is suffering negative comparison or basking in reflected glory may have important implications for overall dyadic functioning.

IMPLICATIONS FOR SELF-ESTEEM

Pressure To Change Self-Definition

As we have seen in the review of the recently accumulated empirical evidence, self-evaluation maintenance processes place considerable pres-

TABLE 1. Regression of Pride and Envy on Intimacy
for Males and Females

Variables	Males	Females
Partner Pride	2.23^c	0.967^c
	(0.359)	(0.281)
Partner envy	-0.913^b	-0.825^c
	(0.397)	(0.235)
Pride in partner	0.568	0.224
	(0.628)	(0.582)
Envy of partner	-0.022	-0.036
	(0.388)	(0.241)
Adjusted R^2	0.337^c	0.250^c

[a]Unstandardized regression weights (standard errors in parentheses).
[b,c]Probability: $^b p < 0.05$; $^c p < 0.001$.

sure on couples to define relatively unique areas of competence and expertise within the dyad (see also Campbell, 1980; Clark & Petaki, 1994). By doing so, they maximize their joint benefit in the relationship and make closeness more sustainable even as each of them outperforms the other in their respective areas of expertise and competence. However, as they enter into deeper relationship with each other, this process clearly puts pressure on one or both partners to modify or redefine the areas in which they claim competence. For example, a person who had previously seen himself or herself as a good cook, might come under pressure to relinquish this area to a partner who also entered the relationship defining cooking as an area of expertise. Over time, the couple is likely either to jointly conclude that one partner is "the cook" or to divide the cooking domain into subareas so each can claim greater expertise within some subset of the cooking domain. Presumably, the pressure to continue refining each partner's self-definition within the relationship would come from the generalized negative feelings and discomfort that result from each partner's continuing to define cooking in general as a domain of personal relevance.

Allowing the Self to Be Outperformed by the Partner

A second process that could indirectly affect global self-esteem is pressure to allow the partner to display competence in an area of self-relevance. The data reviewed above suggest that females more than males may be inclined to allow the partner to display superior performance in areas that are perceived to be important to him (Beach & Tesser, 1993). Specifically, there is likely to be some pressure in relationships to allow the partner to outperform the self if the area is of importance to the partner. To the extent that the partner is able to perform outstandingly in the area, this need not pose any particular problem. However, if the area is one in which the self has typically done well, perhaps as well as or even better than the partner, then there may be pressure to sabotage one's own performance in order to allow the partner to perform better. Likewise, there is reason to expect, as well, some level of covert sabotage by the partner to help ensure that the performance is poor enough to be nonthreatening (cf. Tesser & Smith, 1980). In either case, a series of suboptimal performances could lead to a changed sense of competence in a given area. Concurrently decreasing the relevance of the area should prevent at least some of the immediate negative consequences for self-esteem. However, even if the change in perceived self-competence did not translate into immediate changes in global self-esteem, it seems likely that these changes would constrain the complexity of potential future selves (Niedenthal, Setterlund,

& Wherry, 1992) and so again make the self more vulnerable to subsequent challenges.

Another factor that might influence global self-esteem is the chronicity of being outperformed across a range of potentially valued areas. To the extent that one partner is almost always the "better-performing" spouse in the areas most esteemed at a societal level, that partner would seem to be put in the position of having many areas with which to support a high self-esteem. As noted by Baumeister (1991), this dynamic may be in place in many marital relationships due to the pattern of slightly older men marrying somewhat younger women. Although the average age difference between husbands and wives is only 2 years, this difference may be sufficient to create differential earning potential early in marriage, create a pattern of deference with regard to decision making in important areas, and support a performance differential in favor of husbands across many areas. Accordingly, it may be that being chronically outperformed in areas esteemed at a societal level is more common for wives than for husbands. From an SEM perspective, this circumstance need not lead to any immediate decrement in self-esteem or any immediate experience of negative mood, since it should be possible in many cases to make these areas less central to self-definition. However, to the extent that areas that are esteemed at the societal level have been systematically excluded from one's self-definition, the individual should be left with relatively little basis for high self-esteem. Accordingly, it may be that common patterns of marriage set the stage for higher self-esteem in men than in women.

NARROWING OR DELETING AREAS FROM ONE'S SELF-DEFINITION

So, what might happen to each person's self-definition and beliefs about areas of "expertise" as relationships deepen? One possibility is that one of the partners may experience a narrowing of the areas in which he or she claims expertise. To continue the earlier example, one person may entirely abandon "cooking" as an area of personal relevance and expertise. This relinquishment need not have any immediate implications for global self-evaluation, but it may make the foundation of that global self-evaluation somewhat more narrow, leaving the individual more vulnerable to subsequent challenges (Linville, 1985, 1987). Alternatively, each person may experience only evolution in self-definition. Rather than only one being a good cook, one may now be a good "gourmet" cook, while the other becomes an expert at vegetarian cuisine. In this way, neither experiences a diminished number of areas of claimed expertise, but both make some adjustments for the sake of the relationship and to maximize positive experiences within the relationship. It is possible that this sort of development might create long-term self-esteem benefits if specialized expertise is developed in areas that attract favorable external reactions. Indeed, this dynamic could lead spouses who enter relationships with overlapping areas of relevance to perform with particularly high competence (e.g., Bryson, Bryson, Licht, & Licht, 1976).

ADDING AREAS TO ONE'S SELF-DEFINITION

Another process that may occur in relationships involves pressure from the partner to take on new self-definitions. A common example arises in the domain of parenting. Consider, for example, the couple in which one partner has a strong desire for children while the other does not. It is likely that the partner who wishes to have children will anticipate not only desired roles for the self, but also roles in which the partner would be expected to be the expert. Should the couple become parents, there will be considerable pressure for the previously uncommitted parent to adopt these new areas of expertise. As in the previous examples, this pressure could result in an expansion of self-definition in a way that is ultimately self-esteem-enhancing, or it could mean adopting as self-defining some areas in which performance is likely to be seen as suboptimal. In the latter case, there might well be an erosion of self-esteem, particularly if there is little opportunity to escape the performance demands of the role.

Alternatively, one may adopt new roles that are simultaneously both self-esteem-enhancing in some respects and problematic in other respects. This possibility is discussed by Baumeister (1991) in his description of factors related to felt need to escape the self. Specifically, it is possible that the adoption of new roles expands the self and creates new potential for the self to be evaluated positively but at the same time creates anxiety about meeting the demands of the roles. This need not result in low self-esteem, but as Baumeister points out, it might place the individual at increased risk to engage in problematic escapist behavior designed to relieve the burden of a self grown too large.

In sum, close relationships should provide a context in which the self-definition can be either enriched or impoverished. The pressure to change self-definition, change relative performance, or adopt new self-definitions should not be directly related to global self-esteem in the short term, but these processes might well shape the constituent elements of global self-esteem, and so become related to global self-esteem over the longer term or in interaction with other factors. Finally, these processes may lead to escapist tendencies as spouses attempt to maintain a positive self-evaluation in areas that do not come naturally but that may have assumed some considerable importance.

INDIRECT PRESSURE ON SELF-ESTEEM FROM SEM
PROCESSES IN CLOSE RELATIONSHIPS

EFFECTS OF RELATIONSHIP DISSOLUTION

Dissolution of the relationship is self-esteem-threatening for many individuals. At times, the reason may be that the individual has defined relationship maintenance as an area of personal expertise, and so dissolution of the relationship is a direct threat to self-evaluation. At other times, relationship difficulties may first affect mood (cf. Beach et al., 1994) and affect global judgments of self-esteem through the effect on mood (cf. Schwartz & Clore, 1988). In either case, to the extent that SEM processes set the stage for relationship problems or dissolution, there could be a considerable indirect effect on global self-esteem.

Can SEM processes set the stage for relationship difficulties for which the cause is not immediately clear or propel a couple toward relationship dissolution? Evidence reviewed above would suggest that such an effect is possible. In particular, a relatively greater proportion of negative-comparison experiences are related to decreased satisfaction in relationships (Beach & Tesser, 1993), and experimentally induced negative-comparison experiences increase the level of negative communication and domineering behavior displayed in subsequent interactions (Beach et al. 1993). At the same time, it seems unlikely that partners would be able typically to identify the source of their negative behavior as the self-evaluation threat (cf. Tesser, 1988). This failure of identification allows the behavior to be misattributed to the partner or the self. Accordingly, self-blame and depression as well as partner blame and a cycle of destructive interactions seem available in the aftermath of SEM-induced negativity. To the extent that an individual has accepted personal responsibility for relationship maintenance, he or she might be more prone to respond to relationship disturbance with loss of self-esteem and depression.

From an SEM perspective, if an individual saw relationship maintenance as an area of great self-relevance, then he or she would tend to be constrained with regard to the display of closeness-reducing behavior. Specifically, in the context of negative comparison with the spouse, such an individual would have a diminished ability to utilize distancing as a defensive strategy. To the extent that there are gender differences, then, for women one might see a relatively greater effect of negative comparison on dysphoric mood and loss of self-esteem. On the other hand, to the extent that the partner is seen as responsible for relationship closeness, relatively little constraint against using distance should be experienced. Accordingly, for men, one might expect a greater effect of negative comparison on negative behavior toward the partner and less effect on dysphoric mood state.

HELP-GIVING

A related process of potential relevance to self-esteem is comprised of partner responses to the other's attempts to provide help or direct esteem support. Help-giving is clearly amenable to an SEM analysis, and the implications for marital relationships are not always intuitive. An interesting analysis of responses to help has been provided by Nadler & Fisher (1986), and many of the implications drawn seem pertinent for understanding spousal reactions to help-giving in the marital dyad. The Nadler and Fisher analyses suggest that help-giving can be construed as a high-level performance, while receiving help can be construed as being outperformed. Thus, receiving help from the spouse should produce more negative affective reactions if the help is perceived to be on a highly self-relevant dimension than if it is on a dimension that is not self-relevant. However, as noted by Nadler and Fisher (1986), greater effort toward self-help may be stimulated by a threatening than by a nonthreatening situation if the person perceives the goal to be potentially controllable. If aid from the partner is threatening and redoubled effort provides a means of reducing the need for this aid, then spouses may be motivated to intensify their efforts to achieve. This phenomenon provides another possible mechanism for high achievement in dual professional dyads (Bryson et al., 1976). Of course, should the partner be perceived as providing aid in an area that is not self-relevant, there should be no discomfort and so no motivation to intensify effort. Likewise, if the partner receiving aid does not see any way of achieving the goal without aid, threatening aid is likely to result only in more negative affect but no greater effort. Accordingly, if Nadler and Fisher's analysis is correct, spouses may provide both maximally useful and maximally destructive aid to a spouse in difficulty.

The foregoing analysis suggests that spousal efforts to help a partner may often succeed for reasons other than those suspected by the helpful partner. In particular, the most helpful partner may succeed precisely because the partner found it so uncomfortable to receive the aid. Conversely, the least helpful partner may fail by providing exactly the same advice or help for a partner who finds it uncomfortable, but does not see how to exert any control over their situation. In both cases, negative comparison is engendered by the help-giving behavior, but in the first case, it provides a facilitative motivation, while in the second, it provides only a painful emotional condition. One suspects that in this latter case, the spousal help could erode global self-esteem over time, while in the former case, it might enhance global self-esteem over time.

ARE SOME PEOPLE MORE EXTREME IN THE MANEUVERS THEY USE TO PROTECT SELF-EVALUATION?

An important issue in the application of the extended SEM model to marital dyads is whether or not some sorts of persons may use self-protective strategies more, or more intensely, than others. Recent work by Tesser & Cornell (1991) and by Steele et al. (1993) suggests that under some circumstances, some people may be in a position to turn off self-protective strategies. In particular, Steele et al. (1993) argue that high self-esteem persons may more commonly be able to call upon their positive self-view to affirm themselves or remind themselves of other areas of positive performance and so be less in need of other self-protective behavior after having faced a self-evaluation challenge. In the context of dyadic behavior, one might suspect that the use of self-affirmation by high self-esteem spouses would occur primarily when self-protective strategies in a given area were constrained either by informational factors or by an unacceptably high cost of engaging in self-protective strategies. The first type of constraint would be exemplified by a situation in which someone is outperformed by his or her spouse but has little opportunity to dismiss the feedback as false or interpret the dimension as irrelevant to the self An example of the second type of constraint would be the recognition that acting on the urge to distance from the partner would result in discomfort and negative effects for the partner that are unacceptable. If correct, this analysis suggests that high self-esteem spouses may be better able to cope with the negative feelings engendered by negative comparison without engaging SEM processes.

In a related theoretical development, Tesser and Cornell (1991) found that it was indeed possible to shut off SEM processes by allowing persons to self-affirm or engage in other "self" processes. This finding suggests that there may be a confluence of self-processes through some shared mechanism or final common pathway that would allow persons to exit the SEM system under special circumstances. Interestingly, however, there is little evidence that level of self-esteem per se typically moderates SEM effects (Tesser, 1988). Accordingly, the hypothesis that global self-esteem moderates SEM effects is not well supported at present.

An alternative framework offered by Kernis (e.g., Kernis, Cornell, Sun, Berry, & Harlow, 1993) suggests that a possible reason for the failure of global self-esteem to moderate SEM effects is that it confounds level with stability of self-esteem. Indeed, it is possible that it is stability of self-esteem rather than level of self-esteem that more adequately captures the intensity of an individual's response to self-esteem threat. According to this analysis, it may be productive to examine stability of self-esteem as a moderator of SEM effects.

THE SELF IN EVOLUTIONARY CONTEXT: FUTURE ISSUES AND DIRECTIONS

The integration of the literatures on global self-esteem and self-protective processes is clearly timely and, with the advent of this book, is well under way. One framework to guide such an integration is provided by an evolutionary perspective. It seems likely that this framework may provide plausible accounts not only of the evolution of global self-esteem, but also of self-protective processes. For example, one might speculate that in our evolutionary past, self-esteem functioned as a proxy for dominance, which in turn conferred reproductive advantage in the small-group setting that was the predominant social form for most of human evolutionary history (Barkow, 1980). An alternative suggestion is that self-esteem helps regulate adaptive social behavior (Baumeister & Leary, 1993) (see also Chapter 6). Central to this proposal is the idea that global self-esteem serves as a sociometer that can guide persons to behave in ways that limit the likelihood of their being rejected by the social groups to which they belong. In this way, global self-esteem may function to guide the selection of interpersonal strategies, with high self-esteem persons choosing riskier and more direct approaches and lower self-esteem persons choosing more indirect strategies that carry less potential for immediate social rejection (but for potential for longer-term rejection, see Joiner, Alfano, & Metalsky, 1993). Again, in the context of small stable groupings that presumably characterized "society" for much of human evolutionary history and that continue to constitute the primary form of human social grouping (Mann, 1980), such a mechanism might be maximally adaptive (Mann, 1980).

A plausible evolutionary account of the processes described by the SEM model may also be possible. Further, to the extent that it intersects with evolutionary accounts already provided for global self-esteem, an evolutionary account may facilitate our understanding of the ways in which the two systems interact. To begin, we propose that a well-functioning self-evaluation maintenance mechanism should facilitate an individual's functioning in the small-group environment. Specifically, SEM processes might be seen as helping the individual create a self capable of functioning well within the small group. SEM processes, on average, should lead to the gradual sculpting of a self that is focused on enhancing performance in precisely those domains in which a unique contribution to the group is most likely to be realized, as well as a self capable of appreciating the unique contribution of other group members.

Indeed, one might anticipate considerable adaptive advantage for the group and the individual if group members were motivated to maximize their ability to fill important roles within the group. That is, by focusing each person's energy on further refining and developing those abilities most valued and most needed by the primary social group in order to avoid negative comparison, SEM processes would tend to propel the individual to greater status within the group and so, presumably, to greater reproductive success. Likewise, by basking in the reflected glory of group members who are successfully filling important roles, the individual would tend to affiliate more closely with valued group members and so obtain the potentially important benefits conferred by such others. A mechanism shaped by such contingencies would motivate persons to become proficient in areas that are both currently *unoccupied* or underoccupied and highly *valued* by others in the individual's primary group. This would also seem to be advantageous to the group on average, since it ensures interest in assuming roles important for the group, but minimizes the need for intragroup aggression in maintaining role divisions.

Important for a smoothly functioning mechanism designed to maximize group efficiency, cohesion, and specialization is a mechanism that allows changes in the relevance of roles. That is, it would be important to allow for change in the roles at which the individual is motivated to be best and those roles at which the individual is pleased to see others excel. Importantly, since SEM processes allow efficient readjustment of roles even if the roles designated as important are in relative flux, SEM processes would seem maximally adaptive when social roles are at least somewhat specialized, but are subject to potential change over time. However, given the normal process of growth and social transition over the human life cycle, such a pattern seems likely across many human contexts. In addition, as social groupings grow in size, SEM processes can be seen as continuing to provide potentially substantial adaptive benefits. Indeed, so long as increased specialization within an accepted social framework continues to be highly rewarded, one can view SEM processes as continuing to confer a selective advantage to individuals on average.

These considerations would lead one to integrate the literatures on self-evaluation maintenance and global self-esteem in terms of the interplay between two systems designed to regulate behavior in small primary groups. The first system (the global self-esteem system) would be viewed as providing global sociometric feedback guiding one to adopt a more or less defensive posture in interactions with other group members or orienting one to the danger of social exclusion (see Chapter 6). The second system would be viewed as harmonizing the behavior of the members of the group in such a way that the greater good of the group (however defined by group consensus) is maximized by increasing the unique contribution of each individual to the greater good. Thus, adopting an evolutionary framework might help generate hypotheses about interconnections between SEM processes and global self-esteem and the ways each mechanism might come to affect the other.

SUMMARY

The past five years have seen the expansion of the self-evaluation maintenance model to the dyadic context. This expansion has occasioned the theoretical developments and empirical tests reviewed above. It now appears that in addition to protecting their own self-evaluation, persons are motivated to protect, their partners' self-evaluation, although this motive may be stronger on average for women than for men. In addition, it seems clear that SEM processes can influence a variety of nontrivial interactions in marriage that have the potential to influence each marital partner's global sense of well-being and global self-esteem.

There are a number of potential avenues by which SEM processes could produce shifts in self-conception or closeness to others and thereby indirectly influence global self-esteem. Of the areas identified above, those with the greatest potential to influence self-esteem result in the adoption of self-limiting or self-defeating self-definitions, and those processes may lead to the dissolution or disruption of harmonious marital relations. However, it is clear that many of the potential effects of SEM processes on the enhancement or erosion of global self-esteem are likely to be indirect and nonintuitive. Accordingly, it may be useful to study more closely the way in which various common marital conditions bring SEM processes into play. In addition, it may be particularly fruitful to investigate the effect of concern for the partner's self-evaluation maintenance needs, which may bias some persons to develop lower self-esteem over time, preclude them from developing a more positive global self-view, or leave them more vulnerable to negative life events.

The success of the extended SEM model in accounting for the emotional and behavioral reactions of partners in close relationships to potentially competitive situations suggests that SEM processes may be central in understanding the dynamics of close relationships and the way in which these dynamics are ultimately translated into global self-esteem. In addition, the potential of stability of self-esteem to moderate the intensity of SEM processes and the viability of an evolutionary perspective for better understanding both SEM processes and the nature of global self-esteem point to a period of fruitful interchange between the literature on global self-esteem and the literature on SEM processes. It is to be hoped that the resulting dialogue will enrich both.

REFERENCES

Barkow, J. (1980). Prestige and self-esteem: A biosocial interpretation. In D. R. Omark, F. F. Stayer, D. G. Freedman (Eds.), *Dominance relations* (pp. 319–332). New York: Garland.

Baumeister, R. F. (1991). *Escaping the self.* New York: Basic Books.

Baumeister, R. F., & Leary, M. R. (1993). The need to belong as a fundamental human motivation (in review).

Beach, S. R. H., Tesser, A. (1993). Decision making power and marital satisfaction: A self-evaluation maintenance perspective. *Journal of Social and Clinical Psychology 12*, 471–494.

Beach, S. R. H., & Tesser, A. (1994). *So what do the two of you like doing together? The effects of self-evaluation maintenance in marriage.* Unpublished manuscript.

Beach, S. R. H., Mendolia, M., & Tesser, A. (1991). Self-esteem maintenance and relationship closeness. Paper presented at the 25th Annual Meeting of the Association for the Advancement of Behavior Therapy, New York, November 1991.

Beach, S. R. H., Smith, D. A., & Fincham, F. D. (1994). Marital interventions for depression: Empirical foundation and future prospects. *Applied and Preventive Psychology, 3*, 233–250.

Beach, S. R. H., Tesser, A., Mendolia, M., Anderson, P., Crelia,R., & Whitaker, D. (1994). *Social comparison and intimate interaction: Is envy an influence in romantic relationships?* (in review).

Becker, J. (1979). Vulnerable self-esteem as a predisposing factor in depressive disorders. In R. A. Depue (Eds.), *The psychobiology of the depressive disorders: Implications for the effects of stress* (pp. 317–334). New York: Academic Press.

Brown, G. W., Bifulco, A., & Andrews, B. (1990a). Self-esteem and depression. IV. Effects on course and recovery. *Social Psychiatry and Psychiatric Epidemiology, 25*, 244–249.

Brown, G. W., Bifulco, A., Veiel, H. O. F., & Andrews, B. (1990b). Self-esteem and depression. II. Social correlates of self-esteem. *Social Psychiatry and Psychiatric Epidemiology, 25*, 225–234.

Brown, J. D., & Gallagher, F. M. (1992). Coming to terms with failure: Private self-enhancement and public self-effacement. *Journal of Experimental Social Psychology, 28*, 3–22.

Bryson, R. B., Bryson, J. B., Licht, M. H., & Licht, B. G. (1976). The professional pair: Husband and wife psychologists. *American Psychologist, 31*, 47–53.

Campbell, J. (1980). Complementarity and attraction: A reconceptualization in terms of dyadic behavior. *Representative Research in Social Psychology, 11*, 74–95.

Cialdini, R. B., Borden, R. J., Thorne, A., Walker, M. R., Freeman, S., & Sloan, L. R. (1976). Basking in reflected glory: Three (football) field studies. *Journal of Personality and Social Psychology, 34*, 366–375.

Clark, M. S. (1984). Record keeping in two types of relationships. *Journal of Personality and Social Psychology 47*, 549–557.

Clark, M. S., Bennett, M. E. (1992). Research on relationships: Implications for mental health.

In D. N. Ruble, P. R. Costanzo, & M. E. Oliveri (Eds.), *The Social Psychology of mental health.* New York: Guilford Press.

Clark, M. S., & Pataki, S. P. (1994). Interpersonal processes influencing attraction and relationships. In A. Tesser (Ed.), *Advanced social psychology* (pp. 283–331). New York: McGraw-Hill.

Clark, M. S., Mills, J., & Powell, M. C. (1986). Keeping track of needs in communal and exchange relationships. *Journal of Personality and Social Psychology, 51,* 333–338.

Eisenberg, N., & Miller, P. (1987). The relation of empathy to prosocial and related behaviors. *Psychological Bulletin, 101,* 91–119.

Gibbons, F. X. (1986). Social comparison and depression: Company's effect on misery. *Journal of Personality and Social Psychology, 51,* 1–9.

James, W. (1890). *Principles of Psychology,* Vol. 1. New York: Henry Holt.

Joiner, T. E., Alfano, M. S., & Metalsky, G. I. (1993). Caught in the crossfire: Depression, self-consistency, self-enhancement, and the response of others. *Journal of Social and Clinical Psychology, 12,* 113–134.

Kelley, H. H., & Thibaut, J. W. (1978). *Interpersonal relations: A theory of interdependence.* New York: John Wiley.

Kernis, M. H., Cornell, D. P., Sun, C., Berry, A., & Harlow, T. (1993). There's more to self-esteem than whether it is high or low: The importance of stability of self-esteem. *Journal of Personality and Social Psychology, 65,* 1190–1204.

Linville, P. (1985). Self-complexity and affective extremity: Don't put all of your eggs in one cognitive basket. *Social Cognition, 3,* 94–120.

Linville P. 1987 . Self-complexity as a cognitive buffer against stress-related illness and depression. *Journal of Social and Personality Psychology, 52,* 663–676.

Mann, L. (1980). Cross-cultural studies of small groups. In H. Triandis & Brislin (Eds.), Handbook of cross-cultural psychology, Vol. 5, Social psychology pp. 155–209). Boston: Allyn & Bacon.

Markus, H., & Kitayama, S. (1991). Culture and self: Implications for cognition, emotion, and motivation. *Psychological Review, 98,* 224–253.

Mendolia, M., Beach, S. R. H ., & Tesser, A. (1993). *Affective reactions to one's own and ne's spouse's self-evaluation maintenance needs: Implications for marital interaction* (in review).

Mendolia, M., Beach, S. R. H., Tesser, A., Wakefield, R., & Wright, K. R. (1992). A self-evaluation maintenance perspective on marital interaction. Paper presented at the 26th Annual Convention of the Association for the Advancement of Behavior Therapy. Boston, November 1992.

Nadler, A., & Fisher, J. D. (1986). The role of threat to self-esteem and perceived control in recipient reaction to help: Theory development and empirical validation. In L. Berkowitz (Ed.), *Advances in experimental social psychology,* Vol. 19 (pp. 81–121). Orlando, FL: Academic Press.

Niedenthal, P. M., Setterlund, M. B., & Wherry, M. B. (1992). Possible self-complexity and affective reactions to goal-relevant evaluation. *Journal of Personality and Social Psychology, 63,* 17–29.

O'Leary, K. D., & Smith, D. A. (1992). Marital interaction. *Annual Review of Psychology, 42,* 191–212.

Pelham, B. (1991). On the benefits of misery: Self-serving biases in the depressive self-concept. *Journal of Personality and Social Psychology, 61,* 670–681.

Pilkington, C. J., Tesser, A., & Stephens, D. (1991). Complementarily in romantic relationships: A self-evaluation maintenance perspective. *Journal of Social and Personal Relationships, 8,* 481–504.

Pleban, R., & Tesser, A. (1981). The effects of relevance and quality of another's performance on interpersonal closeness. *Social Psychology Quarterly, 44*, 278–285.

Rosenberg, M. (1979). *Conceiving the Self.* New York: Basic Books.

Salovey, P., & Rodin, J. (1984). Some antecedents and consequences of social comparison jealousy. *Journal of Personality and Social Psychology, 47*, 780–792.

Salovey, P., & Rodin, J. (1988). Coping with envy and jealousy. *Journal of Social and Clinical Psychology, 7*, 15–33.

Salovey, P., & Rothman, A. (1991). Envy and jealousy: Self and society. In P. Salovey (Ed.), *The psychology of jealousy and envy* (pp. 271–286). New York: Guilford Press.

Schwartz, N., & Clore, G. L. (1983). Mood, misattribution, and judgements of well-being: Informative and directive functions of affective states. *Journal of Personality and Social Psychology, 45*, 513–523.

Steele, C. M., Spencer, S. J., & Lynch, M. (1993). Self-image resilience and dissonance: The role of affirmational resources. *Journal of Personality and Social Psychology, 64*, 885–896.

Stuart, R. B. (1980). *Helping couples change.* New York: Guilford Press.

Taylor S. E., Wood, J. V., & Lichtman, R. R. (1983). It could be worse: Selective evaluation as a response to victimization. *Journal of Social Issues, 39*, 19–40.

Tesser, A. (1988). Toward a self-evaluation maintenance model of social behavior. In L. Berkowitz (Ed.), *Advances in Experimental Social Psychology, 21*, 181–227.

Tesser, A. (1990). Smith & Ellsworth's appraisal model of emotion: A replication, extension, & test. *Personality and Social Psychology Bulletin, 16*, 210–223.

Tesser, A. (1991). Emotion in social comparison and reflection processes. In J. Suls & T. A. Wills (Eds.), *Social comparison: Contemporary theory and research* (pp. 117–148). Hillsdale, NJ: Erlbaum Associates.

Tesser, A., & Collins, J. E. (1988). Emotion in social reflection and comparison situations: Intuitive, systematic, and exploratory approaches. *Journal of Personality and Social Psychology, 55*, 695–709.

Tesser, A., & Cornell, D. (1991). On the confluence of self processes. *Journal of Experimental Social Psychology, 27*, 501–526.Tesser, A., & Paulhus, D. (1983). The definition of self: Private and public self-evaluation maintenance strategies. *Journal of Personality and Social Psychology, 44*, 672–682.

Tesser, A., Smith, J. (1980). Some effects of friendship and task relevance on helping: You don't always help the one you like. *Journal of Experimental Social Psychology, 16*, 582–590.

Tesser, A., Millar, M., & Moore, J. (1988). Some affective consequences of social comparison and reflection processes: The pain and pleasure of being close. *Journal of Personality and Social Psychology, 54*, 49–61.

Watson, D., Clark, L. A., & Tellegen, A. (1988). Development and validation of brief measures of positive and negative affect: The PANAS scales. *Journal of Personality and Social Psychology, 54*, 1063–1070.

Weiss, R. L. (1992). MICS-IV marital interaction coding system: Training and reference manual for coders. Unpublished manual. Available from: Oregon Marital Studies Program, Department of Psychology, Straub Hall, University of Oregon, Eugene, OR 97403.

Wicklund, R. A. & Gollwitzer, P. M. (1982). *Symbolic self-completion.* Hillsdale, NJ: Erlbaum Associates.

Wills, T. A. (1981). Downward comparison principles in social psychology. *Psychological Bulletin, 90*, 245–271.

Wood, J. V., & Taylor, K. L. (1991). Serving self-relevant goals through social comparison. In J. Suls & T. A. Wills (Eds.), Social comparison: Contemporary theory and research (pp. 23–49). Hillsdale, NJ: Erlbaum Associates.

CHAPTER 8

OVERCOMING A LACK OF SELF-ASSURANCE IN AN ACHIEVEMENT DOMAIN

CREATING AGENCY IN DAILY LIFE

ROBERT E. HARLOW AND NANCY CANTOR

INTRODUCTION

Murray (1938) suggested that the study of personality can be enriched by an understanding of individuals' goal-directed behavior and their views of the world in relation to their important goals. Current cognitive perspectives in personality have in part taken up this agenda by considering the behavior of individuals as they work toward advancing their important life tasks, in light of knowledge about themselves, about others, and about the task at hand (Cantor, 1990). Knowledge about the self in general—for example, one's attributes and interests—informs individuals' selection of which tasks to pursue (Markus, 1983). Self-views of competence at a task determine how individuals are going to work toward making progress on

ROBERT E. HARLOW AND NANCY CANTOR • Department of Psychology, Princeton University, Princeton, New Jersey 08544.

Efficacy, Agency, and Self-Esteem, edited by Michael H. Kernis. Plenum Press, New York, 1995.

those tasks and how they respond to task-relevant challenges (Bandura, 1982; Niedenthal, Setterlund, & Wherry, 1992). This interaction of self-knowledge and life-task pursuit is not unidirectional, because task-relevant behavior may in turn generate knowledge that is assimilated into existing self-concepts, and this dynamic relationship sometimes affords self-concept change (Bandura, 1982; Bem, 1972).

Individuals pursue many life tasks at one time, some easy and some hard, some common and others highly idiosyncratic. There are a multitude of ways available for pursuing the same life task, and this variety becomes apparent when we examine the behavior of several different individuals that is directed toward the pursuit of highly similar tasks (Rotter, Chance, & Phares, 1972). One does not have to look too far to find such instances of shared goals. For example, individuals living within a given socio-cultural environment, such as college students living in a dormitory, con-sensually endorse certain life tasks as being relevant to their daily lives (e.g., doing well academically), even as they vary widely in their feelings of competence to make progress on these goals (Cantor, Norem, Nieden-thal, Langston, & Brower, 1987). We refer to these goals as *life tasks*, in part to acknowledge that individuals have taken on a task that others share and made it their own.

SELF-DOUBT AND LIFE-TASK PURSUIT

Self-knowledge, and in particular how one thinks about one's competence to work on a task, is a critical component in considering how *individuals* address these common life tasks. Perceived-competence images largely direct how an individual will appraise, or "see," a life task (Cantor & Fleeson, in press). For example, individuals who are uncertain of their competencies will approach the task with some trepidation, while more confident individuals will find the task less challenging (e.g., Langston & Cantor, 1989). Different task appraisals (across individuals working on the same life task, or even within an individual across that individual's life tasks) are associated with different ways of approaching and working on the task. These life-task *strategies* are functionally coherent patterns of cognition and action that address the challenges that individuals them-selves see as inherent in those tasks. They include components of thought, effort, feeling, and action that reflect task-specific needs as seen by in-dividuals.

Individuals need to feel competent if they are going to exercise com-petence (Markus, Cross, & Wurf, 1990). However, individuals do not al-ways feel competent in even those tasks that they see as most important, and in this case they must somehow mobilize their efforts in order to gain this feeling of competence if they are to advance their efforts on the task. Consider the life task "making new friends," a task that confronts many young adults as they move away from their families. While some may find this task easy and enjoyable, others may doubt their abilities to maintain a smooth interaction and therefore experience stress or anxiety at the thought of going out to meet new people. If ignored, this stress has the potential to interfere with task pursuit (Bandura, 1982; Cantor & Harlow, in press; Sarason, 1975). Although withdrawal from the task may be one potential consequence of self-doubt (e.g., Bandura, Adams, & Beyer, 1977; Schunk, 1981), task outcomes may be so important that such withdrawal is neither desirable nor feasible. In these cases, individuals must employ strategies that are directed both toward alleviating or minimizing stress or anxiety and toward more instrumental life-task work.

One such strategy is academic defensive pessimism. Academic defensive pessimists recognize past successes, but this recognition of past success does not prevent them from experiencing renewed doubt as they face upcoming challenges. This self-doubt is associated with anxiety that has the potential to impair their performance (Norem & Cantor, 1986a). Defensive pessimists prevent this performance impairment by directly confronting that anxiety before the task—imagining possible worst-case outcomes that they then work hard to avoid. In doing so, they convert their anxiety into motivation and are able to perform as well as their counterparts whose strategies involve consideration of more optimistic possibilities (Norem & Cantor, 1986b). This conversion of anxiety into motivation creates agency in daily life-task pursuits where self-defeat might otherwise be expected. The importance of defensive pessimists' strategic efforts to their success was demonstrated by Norem and Cantor (1986a), who found that when defensive pessimists were *encouraged* that things would go well on an upcoming task, this encouragement interfered with their strategy of confronting their anxieties, and they performed worse than when left to their own pessimistic strategy (see also Norem & Illingworth, 1993).

While the strategies that individuals use to overcome self-doubt account for only a small portion of the strategies that they may use for pursuing important tasks, these strategies best reveal individuals' capacities for creating agency in their daily lives, because such strategies represent individuals' efforts to *take control* of a task where we might otherwise expect self-defeat (e.g., Bandura, 1982; Schunk, 1981). In this chapter, we discuss self-concerns among a group of individuals who felt generally positive about their academic abilities but found academic setbacks to be extremely troubling. We call them *outcome-focused* because of their tendency to be excessively swayed by academic outcomes and because of their concern that good outcomes would be difficult to achieve (Harlow & Cantor, 1994). Despite their outcome focus, they persevered in their task pursuits, yet not without a careful eye on task-relevant outcomes. When academic outcomes were bad, inducing a sense of self-doubt, these individuals responded in highly patterned (and, we argue, strategic) ways directed at obtaining reassurance and thereby preventing immobilization. Below, we describe in detail the behaviors, eliciting conditions, and contexts associated with their strategy. We also examine the costs associated with this strategy and others that are used to overcome self-doubt. We illustrate how outcome-focused individuals' strategic reassurance-seeking aided them in their task-pursuit efforts and consider what task pursuit might be like without such a strategy. In doing so, we give particular attention to the short-term and long-term fluctuations in self-doubt that prompt and may be prompted by their strategic efforts.

A strategy analysis is a process analysis of task pursuit. The environment in which tasks are pursued is not static: Changes occur in the environment as challenges are faced, performance unfolds, and feedback is received, all within a context of one's self-concerns, which set the agenda for pursuing the task. Individuals regulate task pursuit in light of these changing conditions. In other words, strategies delineate conditions of life-task pursuit; the relevant behaviors are performed in specific places, with specific people, and at specific times. Therefore, in investigating life-task pursuit, it is necessary to map its patterning in response to these conditions. The data we refer to below are from our examinations of the life tasks and strategies of a group of women in a residential undergraduate sorority over the course of a semester (Cantor, Norem, Langston, Zirkel, Fleeson, & Cook-Flannagan, 1991; Harlow & Cantor, 1994). This investigation included experience-sampling data collected over a 15-day period that allowed us to track patterns of life-task pursuit within specific *situational* contexts, *interpersonal* contexts, and *temporal* contexts (i.e., in response to certain *events* or task conditions). In short, the academic task-pursuit patterns that outcome-focused women displayed in this experience-sampling data indicate a dynamic strategy for overcoming their academic self-doubts that were induced by negative academic outcomes.

Such an analysis requires an understanding of the temporal dynamics of self-competence, because competence images may be on the line at different stages of task pursuit—and at different times for different individuals (e.g., Blaine & Crocker, 1993; cf. Kernis, Granneman, & Barclay, 1989). Individuals' idiosyncratic competence concerns emerge at difficult times in task pursuit, as illustrated, for example, in the anticipatory concerns of a defensive pessimist or the postoutcome concerns of outcome-focused individuals. Therefore, individuals' protective and motivating efforts also have a patterned temporal signature that must be captured in a strategy analysis.

ACADEMIC SELF-DOUBTS AND TASK APPRAISALS

Whereas individuals living within a common environment, such as the college sorority studied here, may share some common life tasks, they typically differ a great deal in their views of what it is like for them to pursue the same task. We believe that these views of *self-at-the-task* largely determine how individuals appraise the task itself and their choice of strategies for task pursuit. In this way, features of the self-concept become played out in task-relevant contexts. When a person believes that he or she can do the task but that it will be very stressful and difficult, then task pursuit most likely will necessitate the use of a strategy that protects the self from the repercussions of negative outcomes. Some self-protective strategies may be directed toward alleviating anxiety beforehand in order to motivate effort on the task, as is the case for defensive pessimists; in other instances, strategic behavior may be in the service of ensuring an excuse for poor performance, as is the case with self-handicappers. Outcome-focused women in the sorority sample devised their strategy more around obtaining reassurance following negative task-relevant outcomes. What these various forms of self-protective strategies share is their ability to protect the competence images that promote task involvement, even in the face of these self-doubts. In contrast, when a basically negative view of one's own abilities bolsters such self-doubts, then a more helpless strategy of withdrawal often surfaces (e.g., Schunk, 1981).

A sense of self-doubt alongside a desire to actively pursue academics is clear in the self-views and task-pursuit strategy of the women in our sorority sample with an outcome focus in academics. In this study (Harlow & Cantor, 1994), we used a cluster analysis technique (see Borgen & Barnett, 1987) to characterize subjects' appraisals of the life task "getting good grades; doing well academically" across 15 meaning dimensions representing various aspects of challenge, difficulty, and rewardingness. On the basis of this analysis, we identified a group of subjects whom we call outcome-focused ($N = 23$). In contrast to the other women in the sample ($N = 29$), these subjects expressed an intense concern with attaining good academic outcomes and avoiding bad ones, along with a belief that doing so would be difficult (yet potentially rewarding) to accomplish in this important life domain (Cantor & Harlow, 1992; Harlow & Cantor, 1994).

Because task appraisals follow from individuals' self-at-task images, we examined self-concept data to see whether the individuals' lack of assurance about the task was reflected in their conceptions of their own task-relevant ability. This examination was informed by experience sampling (e.g., Campbell, Chew, & Scratchley, 1991) and laboratory studies (Ryan, Koestner, & Deci, 1991; Trope & Ben-Yair, 1982) that suggest that an outcome orientation or outcome focus is associated with self-uncertainty. Consistent with this past work, we found that outcome-focused subjects in this sample were uncertain about their competencies in the academic domain. They were less likely than other subjects to endorse such items as "I am certain of my intelligence," "I am certain of my abilities," and "I believe my performance will reflect my intelligence."

Despite their self-uncertainty, outcome-focused subjects did not feel more negative than other subjects about their academic abilities. At the outset of the study, we asked subjects to list characteristics that described their actual selves in academic situations, and then to rate the positivity of those attributes. There was no difference between the outcome-focused and other women in terms of this positivity. Taken together, this mix of positivity and uncertainty suggested a general sense of competence, but one that was somewhat tenuous (cf. Higgins & Snyder, 1986), that could be easily threatened by negative academic outcomes and therefore require reassurances. Other investigations suggest that individuals possessing self-uncertainty are highly reactive to environmental events. Further, these individuals both are wary of task outcomes and engage in vigorous task pursuit efforts aimed at obtaining further diagnostic information and eradicating uncertainty when these outcomes are negative (e.g., Strube, 1987; Trope & Ben-Yair, 1982; cf. Campbell, et al., 1991). In other words, self-doubt can be accomplished by task pursuit—and even motivate it—under the right circumstances.

REASSURANCE-SEEKING: A STRATEGIC RESPONSE TO SELF-DOUBT

Self-doubts, such as those reflected in the outcome-focused subjects' academic task appraisals and self-views, present a motivated individual with a tough dilemma. That is, how does one maintain the confidence necessary to persevere on this important task when one is bound to be confronted with setbacks that might undermine confidence? The conditions that shake that confidence most will differ from person to person, but the dilemma is a basic one. For the outcome-focused women, the conditions that most likely threaten self-confidence at the task are precisely the occurrence of the negative academic outcomes that they most fear. Contrast these individuals with defensive pessimists, for whom the threat comes first *and is confronted* before the actual challenge, and who are less thrown by outcomes (Norem & Cantor, 1986b). Nonetheless, the need for a strategy to overcome self-doubt is common across these and other cases.

Certainly, most college students find it desirable to achieve good academic outcomes and avoid bad ones. Outcome-focused individuals are distinguished by their being *excessively* swayed by these outcomes, and by their belief that such achievement of good outcomes and avoidance of bad ones will be difficult to accomplish, which lends a sense of precariousness to their otherwise positive self-at-task image. Their uncertainty and concern with outcomes may be especially troublesome for them when they are confronted with academic setbacks. Ryan et al. (1991), for example, examined free-choice activities of ego-involved individuals working on a novel activity ostensibly related to cognitive ability. Ego involvement engenders a concern with outcomes, and when ego-involved subjects received an ambiguous assessment of their performance on the novel activity, they pursued that activity during a subsequent free-choice period. This pursuit was not an enjoyable, intrinsically motivated one, however, but a pressured one, leading Ryan and his colleagues to conclude that it was in the service of obtaining further performance feedback. Furthermore, this pressured pursuit precluded partaking in other activities that might have been more enjoyable.

Analogously, we found that our outcome-focused women, like "ego-involved" individuals in the study of Ryan et al. (1991), were unlikely to set academic concerns aside following academic setbacks. More specifically, we found that following these setbacks, they continued their task pursuits in order to gain reassurances about their academic work. We describe their efforts in detail below, but first point out that given their outcome focus, academic setbacks could be especially emotionally distressing (e.g., Dweck & Leggett, 1988) and likely to give rise to feelings of tension and pressure (e.g., Deci & Ryan, 1985). Further, given their self-uncertainty, reassurance might have been difficult for them to obtain on their own, and therefore seeking out others' opinions about the implications of the academic crisis in question may be especially beneficial for them. The literature on social support suggests that discussion with others in one's social network can aid in providing just such reassurance or in clarifying the meaning and implications of negative events (e.g., Thoits, 1986). This behavior, therefore, is complementary to their own self-uncertainty. One might have expected a more extensive concern with academics following academic crises—one that cut across all temporal and situational contexts. However, consistent with experimental work on individuals' efforts to eradicate uncertainty and our prior work suggesting that individuals' task efforts are directed toward alleviating self-concerns, we found a more directed, patterned, strategic reassurance-seeking.

In carrying out the study, we examined subjects' daily life-task pursuit over a 15-day observation period (for detailed coverage of the method, see Cantor et al., 1991). Subjects wore alarm watches that sounded at five randomly chosen times during the course of each day. When their alarms sounded, they completed experience-sampling reports on which they indicated what they were doing and whom they were with, the kind of situation they were in (e.g., in class or relaxing with others), and their emotional state. These reports allowed us to later reconstruct their typical activities, and these reconstructions were supplemented further by nightly diary reports of these sampled events, in which subjects provided such information as what tasks were relevant to the activities in which they were engaged at the time their alarms sounded. Also in these diaries, subjects chronicled especially positive and especially negative events in their lives. These events were categorized as relevant to one of seven life domains important to college students, including the academic domain. In conjunction with task-pursuit data, these reports allowed us to determine the extent to which task pursuit varied as a function of task-relevant events, providing a fairly complete picture of task-pursuit efforts and task-relevant events.

As suggested above, we had expected that the task pursuit of outcome-focused women would be strategically patterned to meet their specific task needs, which would include reassurance-seeking following negative academic events. We had reasoned that such reassurance-seeking would be associated with a specific *situational context*, one that is amenable to reassurance-seeking; namely, we expected that outcome-focused women, more than other individuals, would address academic concerns in the company of friends. Their reassurance-seeking would also occur within a specific *temporal context*, in that it would be especially likely following unfavorable academic outcomes. Finally, it would involve an *interpersonal context* as well, such that following unfavorable outcomes, outcome-focused individuals would surround themselves with those individuals who are best able to provide encouragement.

As expected, we (Harlow & Cantor, 1994) found several examples of enhanced task pursuit following the negative academic outcomes that outcome-focused individuals reported in their diaries. All these examples took the form of a "social pursuit" of academics. For example, we observed that on days following negative academic events, the academic life task was more relevant for outcome-focused individuals in social and leisure time activities with their friends than it was on other days. This extra pursuit did not extend to nonsocial situations, such as relaxing alone (where one might have expected to see them ruminating over negative outcomes) (cf. Nolen-Hoeksema, 1987). General academic conditions as well were related to the social pursuit of academics. For example, an index of how well things were going in class (mood in the classroom) was strongly negatively associated with the tendency to address academic concerns in situations where they were socializing, such as parties (suggesting that when things were not going well in class, they were more likely to address academic concerns in the company of friends). None of these forms of social pursuit was characteristic of non-outcome-focused subjects.

If reassurance-seeking was the goal of social pursuit, then outcome-focused individuals should have surrounded themselves with others who they felt could best provide such reassurance when it was necessary (e.g., when things were not going well academically). As part of this study, subjects had listed the people who were close to them socially and also indicated the capacity in which they tended to interact with those people. Subjects indicated, among other things, the individuals in their network who encouraged them and in whom they confided. We cross-referenced these data with their reports of whom they were with on the experience-sampling records they completed in the "beeper" portion of the study and uncovered the expected interpersonal dimension to outcome-focused women's social pursuit of academics. Specifically, when things were not going well in class (as indicated by an index of positive affect in the situation "in class"), outcome-focused women spent a greater percentage of their social time with individuals whom they saw as encouraging and in whom they could confide. There was a strong relation between positive affect in class and the percentage of social situations in which an individual was present who either shared confidences or provided encouragement (Harlow & Cantor, 1994). This patterning, and the literature on the functions of social interaction following negative events (Cohen & Wills, 1985; Thoits, 1986), suggest that their social pursuit was in the service of obtaining reassurance.

Interestingly, non-outcome-focused women displayed the opposite pattern. That is, when things *were* going well in class, they were *more* likely to seek the company of those who were encouraging and in whom they could confide, suggesting that they tended to "mark" positive events (Langston, 1990). In other words, these women were able to capitalize on their good academic times by being with confidants with whom they could share their successes, whereas the outcome-focused women spent relatively more of their time with confidants sharing their disappointments and anxieties.

Outcome-focused individuals' extra academic effort following academic setbacks was not an all-out assault that crossed contextual, inter-personal, and temporal contexts. As opposed to a general pattern of ru-mination, which might be somewhat debilitating, or a stress-engendering preoccupation with working at the task whenever and wherever possible, as is the case with the "Type A" strategy (e.g., Price, 1982), outcome-focused individuals directed their task-pursuit efforts toward alleviating the emotional distress and uncertainty associated with an outcome focus (i.e., obtaining reassurance of their academic abilities).

Their turning to others for reassurance was well suited to their self-views and task appraisals: Given the importance of task outcomes, aca-demic setbacks are especially troubling and require assurances that these setbacks can be overcome; given outcome-focused individuals' self-un-certainty and external orientation, such reassurance is best obtained from others (cf. Rosenberg, 1976). In seeking reassurance, outcome-focused subjects seemed intent on finding others who were more self-assured academically—namely, non-outcome-focused women. As part of the study, outcome-focused women reported which sorority members provided encouragement to them, and their reports suggested this selec-tivity. Only 13% of the sorority members from whom outcome-focused women reported getting encouragement were other outcome-focused women. Of the other sorority members from whom non-outcome-focused women reported receiving encouragement, 45% were outcome-focused, a figure that more closely matches the proportion of outcome-focused to non-outcome-focused women in the sample. [This difference between the two groups is significant, $F(1,32) = 10.94$, $p < 0.005$.] In other words, when seeking encouragement, outcome-focused women were more likely to look toward non-outcome-focused women.

BENEFITS OF STRATEGIC
REASSURANCE-SEEKING

An informal examination of subjects' diary reports of negative events and their reactions to them suggests that reassurance-seeking can facilitate life-task pursuit and prevent withdrawal from academic pursuits for these individuals, who might otherwise be immobilized by their self-uncertainty (cf. Rosenberg, 1976). It's easy to imagine that faced with an academic setback, an individual who is already uncertain about his or her ability to stay on top of academics could fall quickly into a nonproductive brooding over the event and dread returning to task efforts. Such brooding or rumination can easily be debilitating and further exacerbate self-doubt (Hixon & Swann, 1993; Nolen-Hoeksema, 1987; Showers, 1988). Subjects' diary reports suggest that consistent with the social support literature, reassurance-seeking can curtail this potential immobilization.

For example, one outcome-focused subject reported that one evening she was overwhelmed with obligations and felt too exhausted to study and at this point felt stressed and uncertain about her academic pursuits. At the library, she met up with a friend and "talked with him to relieve stress." As a result, she "felt more relaxed and able to study." This is especially interesting because one might think that distraction from academics—not a continuation of academic pursuits—would be the best way to alleviate negative affect (e.g., Nolen-Hoeksema, 1987). The potential that addressing academic concerns in social contexts has for relieving stress becomes clear when we contrast the impact of academic setbacks when social-pursuit opportunities are available at one point but not another. One outcome-focused subject, for example, reported that she received a bad grade on an exam and, following this event, did not seek solace from friends, but went home and slept. Not surprisingly, she reported that afterward she felt "the same—I hate getting bad grades." This report is typical when reactions to academic setbacks did not include seeking reassurances. If such negative feelings are left untempered, they can lead to diminished motivation for the task in the long run. Contrast this diary report with that same subject's report 5 days earlier, in which she reported feeling stressed and depressed on receiving a 68 on her Spanish class midterm exam. After Spanish class, however, she went to the library and saw some friends, and after talking with them she reported that she "realized that I'm not the only one who occasionally does poorly." She further reported feeling *better* after this, and this is important because such relief from stress is the key to preventing withdrawal or immobilization (Bandura, 1982; Sarason, 1975). We would suspect, following Thoits (1986), that obtaining reassurance is equally effective for non-outcome-focused women. However, these benefits are especially likely to be relevant for outcome-focused women, who seek reassurance more often and without it would have to find another way to prevent immobilization.

Further evidence of the benefits of the strategy come from participation and performance data. For example, outcome-focused women report academic performance that is on par with their non-outcome-focused counterparts. Their actual participation level is no different, in terms of the percentage of time they spend in academic situations such as class or studying (both groups spend an average of 36% of their time in these situations), nor are their grade point averages different. Both groups also reported similar levels of satisfaction with their academic performance, as indicated by a three-item index in which they rated their satisfaction with their academic work, their desire for change (reversed), and how much their performance met their expectations. Again, these data (Harlow & Cantor, 1994) run counter to what we would expect from a group of individuals plagued with self-doubt if we did not know that their strategy for pursuing academics functioned in part to alleviate this doubt.

This performance is important in and of itself, and as a potential cornerstone for establishing self-assurance. Perhaps the most salutary aspect of pursuing academics socially is its potential to provide a lasting sense of reassurance that can reduce self-doubts. If reassurance can enable an individual to get through an academic setback and prevent withdrawal of effort, then the person can keep building self-assurance by working at the task. That individual may even be able to duplicate the behaviors of others from whom reassurance is sought and thus come to see the task as less intimidating (Markus et al., 1990). These reassurance-seeking efforts should be especially effective given that reassurance is sought from non-outcome-focused others, individuals who might be most able to persuade outcome-focused people to relax and to just "roll with the punches." It may be that selectivity in choosing encouragers and confidants is another critical facet of a relatively "successful" strategy of reassurance-seeking.

OVERCOMING OBSTACLES AND PAYING A COST

Clearly, the strategy can be beneficial, but like other strategies used to overcome self-doubt, there are unintended side effects of the strategic behavior. Given the heavy reliance on social interaction, it is not surprising that in this case the strategy has a negative impact on social life. Outcome-focused women reported lower levels of social life satisfaction than non-outcome-focused women, as indicated by a three-item self-report scale in which they rated how much their performance met their expectations, their general satisfaction, and their desire for change (reversed) (Harlow & Cantor, 1994). The costs of their strategy represent a "spillover" of academic concerns into the social domain, as social opportunities were used to address academic concerns. Relative to other kinds of social interaction, reassurance-seeking yields little *social* pleasure (cf. Coyne, 1976). One can easily imagine that a quick bite grabbed after a stressful exam could be a time to relax and unwind from that exam. However, for the individual who insists on talking about the exam and fretting over his performance, that meal will be an extension of an already unpleasant experience both for himself and for his interaction partner. These missed opportunities for social enjoyment can accumulate over time to have long-term effects. In fact, for outcome-focused women, social satisfaction was strongly negatively associated with the percentage of their social time spent with individuals whom they saw as encouraging and in whom they could confide (Harlow & Cantor, 1994). This association is especially important given that this encouragement-seeking was strongly associated with how well things were going in academics.

These costs in social enjoyment and satisfaction are ironic given that these outcome-focused women did not express self-doubts or concerns about the social life task, as they did about academics. In other words, insofar as their academic strategy impacts on their day-to-day satisfaction in their social pursuits, it does so in the context of a task that these women appraised as relatively easy and rewarding for them.

Over time, the strategy may exact greater cumulative costs in the social domain. Interaction partners are unlikely to be amenable to having their interactions repeatedly converted into "counseling sessions" (Coyne, 1976; Joiner, Alfano & Metalsky, 1992, 1993) and in the long term may work to avoid the outcome-focused individual, suggesting perhaps more serious costs of pursuing academics socially. In fact, outcome-focused women in the sorority study reported losing more friends over the course of a semester than did non-outcome-focused women. These women may increasingly feel unsatisfied in meeting their strategic needs (Fleming, Baum, Gisriel, & Gatchel, 1985) or in developing close friendships (for other illustrations of negative repercussions of reassurance-seeking, see also Joiner et al., 1992, 1993).

FANNING SELF-DOUBTS OR
BUILDING SELF-CONFIDENCE?

A social pursuit of academics can exact costs in social life, and there may be some serious implications for the "target" academic task as well. One potential cost is an exacerbation of self-doubt, especially if the strategy behaviors perpetuate or reinforce negative academic self-concepts. For example, strategic reassurance-seeking is likely to elicit nurturing behaviors from others that might just serve to verify that the outcome-focused recipients are indeed less than fully competent and in need of assistance (Swann, 1987; cf. Pelham, 1991). Furthermore, in order to obtain reassurance, outcome-focused individuals may have to present themselves to others as needing such encouragement (Benjamin, 1974; Jones & Pittman, 1982; Leary, 1957). Even though they may recognize their behavior as self-presentation, outcome-focused individuals may internalize the images they portray and as a consequence actually exacerbate their self-doubts (Jones, Rhodewalt, Berglas, & Skelton, 1981). Furthermore, insofar as outcome-focused individuals obtain a variety of opinions following academic setbacks, they may find these difficult to integrate and thereby exacerbate their own self-uncertainty (Rosenberg, 1976).

Self-competence images are in part influenced by the reactions of others to one's performance, and the content of the reassurance that one gets may itself be less than fully reassuring when it is consistently elicited in the context of a negative event. Unlike non-outcome-focused subjects in our sorority sample, who appear to mark their academic successes by obtaining encouragement when things are going well academically, out-come-focused women seek encouragement only following negative aca-demic events. Thus, they are setting up a negatively toned situation in which the sort of social support that outcome-focused individuals receive may be less effective for bolstering self-confidence. Friends would be more likely to hear only of academic failures but not successes and therefore develop views of that individual as incompetent, perhaps giving back cues that in subtle ways reinforce that person's self-view as incompetent. A large literature (e.g., Darley & Fazio, 1980; Snyder, Tanke, & Berscheid, 1977; Word, Zanna, & Cooper, 1974) suggests that others' expectations are powerful elicitors of behavior. Peers' opinions may come over time to influence competence images, even perceived academic competence (Cole, 1991). What began as self-*uncertainty* could become self-*negativity* over time, prompting outcome-focused individuals to shun academic pursuits (cf. Markus, 1983).

Converging evidence from analyses of other strategies indicates that there is a fine line between the self-enhancing and the self-defeating influences of reassurance. For example, defensive pessimists are likely to share their pessimistic predictions with others, but they are also debilitated when and if these partners respond with all-out encouragement (Norem & Cantor, 1986a). And, in a more strikingly negative example of this prob-lem, individuals with social anxiety who turn to others for guidance in a social interaction frequently ruminate afterward about being too reliant on others in the interaction (Langston & Cantor, 1989). This is true even when their other-directedness actually helps them to continue to participate in social events.

Inadvertently, therefore, those who strategically seek reassurance af-ter negative events turn others into props that can support their own self-doubts, at the same time as these others also help get them through these setbacks. By routinely seeking reassurance, and less frequently mark-ing positive events with friends, these individuals "solve" the dilemma of persevering in the face of obstacles but perhaps simultaneously increase their likelihood of facing new obstacles with increasing self-doubt. The more they depend on others in their social environment for reassurance, rather than for affirmation, the less self-reliant they will feel, the more their confidants may inadvertently feed their self-doubts, and the more their confidants may come to feel somewhat imposed on in the process.

Thus, the "solution" provided by strategic reassurance-seeking runs the risk of being too routine a facilitator for muddling through momentary crises (Nasby & Kihlstrom, 1986). Whereas this form of "social rumination" may be better than withdrawing into self-rumination (Nolen-Hoeksema, 1987), it is not an ideal way to resolve self-doubts because it is likely in the long run to deter individuals from striving to gain confidence in their own task pursuits if it is overused. Even in the short run, individuals may run through their available confidants at a rather high rate (Coyne, 1976; Harlow & Cantor, 1994). However, before we run the risk of sounding too pessimistic, let us reiterate our optimism that outcome-focused individuals can benefit from the strategy, but only if they do not mindlessly rely on the strategy without monitoring the costs as well as the benefits (Cantor & Harlow, 1994; Langer, 1980).

KEEPING COSTS DOWN

Although there clearly are costs associated with pursuing academic setbacks socially, judgments about the relative costliness of the strategy are not entirely straightforward. Before making judgments about the relative effectiveness and intelligence of the strategy, consider what task pursuit *for these individuals* might be like without the strategy—but with their self-doubt and the potential for immobilization still in place.

These individuals might find it difficult to reassure themselves following academic setbacks (at the very least, they feel that others who are non-outcome-focused are better able to provide reassurance). Therefore, although it is tempting to hypothesize how much better off outcome-focused individuals would be without their strategy, a more practical question to consider is how they might obtain the desired (and perhaps required) reassurances and at the same time keep strategy costs at a minimum. In this regard, we believe that *moderation* in strategy use is one solution (Cantor & Harlow, in press). Troubling academic events, unfortunately, are not rare occurrences, and if outcome-focused individuals seek reassurance in every case, then their social lives, and potentially their academic lives, will surely suffer. By contrast, as noted above, reassurance-seeking can be beneficial, and so it should be a reasonably good strategy in the face of genuinely problematic, but less frequent, setbacks.

Another fruitful direction would involve a redirection of the situational context for reassurance-seeking behavior. The most costly aspect of the strategy is the conversion of social situations to situations for academic task pursuit, because academic pursuits are probably to the majority of students relatively unenjoyable in the context of a typically enjoyable social event, such as a party (Cantor & Fleeson, 1993). Therefore, a more situationally appropriate social pursuit of academics may not be as costly (cf. Cantor & Fleeson, 1991). That is, confining social pursuit to situations that are already academic in nature can minimize social side effects while promoting perseverance at the task. To some extent, outcome-focused women do engage in this more contextually appropriate social pursuit. More than other women in the study, outcome-focused individuals studied with more people. When studying with others, outcome-focused subjects were less likely to endorse the statement "I wish I were doing something else" than when they were studying alone ($M_{with\ others}$ = 6.2, M_{alone} = 6.9, 7-point scale, t = 2.10, p < 0.05). Furthermore, they reported greater positive affect at these times than when they were studying alone. Studying with others, then, is a more enjoyable experience than studying alone, and more likely to be repeated. This finding is especially surprising when we might otherwise predict that these women would engage in behaviors that would increase the likelihood of their withdrawal from academic pursuits.

Contextually appropriate social pursuit may even be an important time for sharing and social bonding, as long as it remains confined to study sessions and fits the objectives of others in the situation (e.g., studying rather than relaxing). In that way, study groups provide a forum for addressing academics in the company of friends without necessarily sacrificing social life.

Additionally, changing the temporal context in which reassurance is sought could curtail potential negative repercussions of strategic reassurance-seeking for social life. Because competence images are shaped in part by the responses of others to one's task progress (Markus, et al., 1990), one underutilized route that outcome-focused individuals could take for bolstering their competence images is to seek encouragement following *success*. This orientation toward positive outcomes as opposed to negative ones can also increase intrinsic motivation for the task (e.g., Canavan-Gumpert, 1977), and within the context of social interaction, reassurance-seeking following positive outcomes is less likely to be emotionally dampening.

Although these forms of social pursuit of academics may have less negative impact on social life, they also may be less effective when a genuinely negative academic setback has occurred. Under some circumstances, outcome-focused individuals may be too upset or shaken to find a study group beneficial and therefore may need to turn to more purely social contexts for reassurance (Thane Pittman, personal communication).

(In this sample, the outcome-focused subjects who studied in groups tended to be experiencing more positive affect in class in general—suggesting that perhaps group studying was not being used as a response to setbacks.) Thus, again we return to the view that some moderation in use of the strategy, with a mixing of social studying on a regular basis, social marking of academic success, and reassurance-seeking in social settings on an infrequent basis, might prove effective and less costly over time.

LIFE TRANSITIONS AND SELF-CONCEPT REVISION

Depending on others for guidance and reassurance in the face of anxiety or self-doubt may be a hard habit to break. For example, in the case of outcome-focused individuals, even if they "work" to resist being excessively swayed by daily academic setbacks, it would probably take only a pat on the shoulder from one of their friends to reinforce their self-doubts. And insofar as these friends have become props for them, the friends may rather routinely play into their strategy. Of course, interpersonal and social contexts do change for individuals throughout their lives, and in these life transitions, individuals are less constrained by the built-up expectations of others (Kihlstrom & Cantor, 1989). Therefore, it is at these times that we can expect a maximum potential for change.

Somewhat discouragingly, however, if the transition is too stressful, a hasty retreat to old routines might ensue (Caspi & Moffitt, 1991; Wright & Mischel, 1987). In fact, we suspect that the outcome-focused women in this sample are particularly at risk for this retreat. They are highly sensitized to watch for and evaluate outcomes, and so they may "see" obstacles all too quickly in a new environment. Further, in the face of such setbacks, they will rather automatically turn to others for reassurance, thus reinstating their "old" contexts and perhaps indirectly reinforcing their old self-doubt. As always, it would take an act of "will" for them not to fall prey to their strategy. Nonetheless, they may indeed come to have that willpower if they persevere long enough at academics and come to be more concerned about their diminishing enjoyment of social life.

Life transitions are not common occurrences, and short of these, change may still be facilitated if the individual extends his or her domain of activity to include new individuals, who would be more willing to recognize an increasing sense of self-confidence (cf. Haemmerlie & Montgomery, 1982; Harter, 1993). For example, new contexts or smaller-scale interpersonal context changes can allow people to try out new behaviors that reinforce new self-conceptions. Even such small changes can be helpful. Conquering a few setbacks without the "help" of others, and identifying a few friends as people with whom to affirm positive happenings, may create some pockets of reinforcement for self-confidence rather than for self-doubts (cf. Swann, 1987). Such efforts require persistence, but then this discussion is all about persistence, and so we return to the ever-present need for individuals to persist in the face of obstacles—sometimes in the face of their selves.

Social-learning theorists have long valued guided mastery experiences, modeling, desensitization, and other clinical techniques that reduce stress at exactly those moments when activities become most threatening, and these procedures facilitate the implementation of behaviors that individuals once thought were not possible. These mastery behaviors prompt revision of beliefs about what the self is capable of accomplishing. The major dilemma for individuals experiencing self-doubt in their daily life-task pursuits is how to promote these new experiences when the anxiety emanating from self-doubt encourages them to withdraw. In daily life, where situations are not as structured as they are in clinical settings, promoting active task involvement is not so easy. However, carefully patterned strategic behavior may provide such structure, minimizing stress or anxiety at exactly those times that would otherwise be likely to bring about withdrawal. Insofar as self-protecting strategies, such as defensive pessimism or the strategic reassurance-seeking outlined above, are successful in fending off anxiety and promoting perseverance precisely when needed—at those moments when the individual feels most threatened—they may promote the task experiences necessary for self-concept revision and less troublesome task pursuit.

Of course, for outcome-focused individuals, a few successful task experiences may not be sufficient to lead directly or easily to self-concept revision, as a straight "self-perception" perspective might suggest. Uncertain individuals are not likely to attribute successes to themselves, and so the right combination of situational factors that allow for such attributions, and at the same time reduce affective distress, must be present. Even so, Haemmerlie and Montgomery (1982) have demonstrated that carefully structured success experiences can prompt attributions that bolster one's confidence—even when anxiety would be most expected to interfere with these attributions. A critical element of these mastery experiences is that they somehow alleviate anxiety, enabling individuals to direct their efforts to the task at hand (Arkin, Lake, & Baumgardner, 1986). If outcome-focused individuals can combine their reassurance-seeking—which can be effective in alleviating emotional distress—with some risk-taking, they may over time reduce their self-uncertainty and develop positive competence images. After seeing the potential of outcome-focused individuals to strategically pattern their behavior at specific times with specific individuals and within specific situations that can best serve these purposes, we cannot help arguing that these individuals (and others experiencing self-doubt) can potentially create agency in their own lives, even when they themselves might least expect it.

SELF-DOUBTS AND THE
DYNAMICS OF SELF-ESTEEM

As we noted at the outset, self-doubts about one's life-task pursuits take many specific forms, from the anxiety of defensive pessimists before a task to the self-uncertainty of outcome-focused individuals in the face of task setbacks. Nevertheless, regardless of the exact form, there are consistent implications of this self-doubt for task pursuit and task perseverance. Moreover, the life-task approach illustrated here (see also Cantor & Fleeson, in press) has implications for the conceptualization and measurement of some aspects of self-esteem (cf. Baumeister, 1993). Most particularly, this approach focuses on individuals' self-views of competence at their tasks rather than on their global sense of self-worth or self-regard (Swann, personal communication). Within this piece of the self-esteem puzzle, the life-task approach emphasizes three foci: a distinction between the positivity of competence images and the certainty with which those views are held (Campbell et al., 1991), the temporal dynamics of self views (Markus & Wurf, 1987), and the domain specificity of self-competence and self-assurance (Harter, 1990; Bandura, 1986). Here, we briefly consider these three foci in the context of the analysis of the strategic efforts of outcome-focused individuals in their academic and social pursuits.

First, as noted earlier, one of the most interesting aspects of many effective life-task strategies, such as the defensive pessimists' worst-case analysis or the outcome-focused individual's strategic reassurance-seeking, is that the strategies are used by individuals who generally acknowledge their past successes (e.g., defensive pessimists) and by those who have basically positive self-competence views and find the task itself reasonably rewarding to pursue (e.g., outcome-focused individuals). Nonetheless, these strategies are necessitated by their self-doubts, as those doubts create potentially debilitating anxiety in the face of task pursuit and uncertainty in the face of task setbacks. Therefore, in understanding strategic pursuits and in evaluating the efficacy of these responses, the context of self-doubt becomes a critical feature. What, for example, distinguishes self-doubt that creates anxiety about taking on each new task challenge from uncertainty about being able to persist in the face of negative task outcomes? Self-doubt is clearly a general construct covering a variety of specific exemplars, and we need to define in more detail self-doubt and self-certainty as features of self-esteem (e.g., Campbell et al., 1991).

Second, the life-task approach is quite consistent with the emphasis in the self-esteem literature on assessing the stability or instability or individuals' self-assurance or esteem (cf. Kernis et al., 1989). That is, whether one considers the fluctuations in anxiety, competence, and perceived control of defensive pessimists from before to after a task (Cantor & Norem, 1989; Norem & Cantor, 1990) or the reactivity and emotional distress of the outcome-focused individuals discussed here in the face of academic setbacks (Harlow & Cantor, 1994), the temporal ebb and flow of self-assurance is clear. In fact, a central feature of a life-task approach is its emphasis on the temporal patterning of individuals' strategic efforts to create agency in daily life (Cantor & Harlow, in press; see also Larsen, 1989). Strategic behavior is often linked to these ups and downs of self-assurance that occur in regular ways as individuals try to pursue their life tasks.

Therefore, although the general level of positivity of the competence images of defensive pessimists and outcome-focused individuals may often be reasonably high, their specific self-doubts are regularly triggered in particular task conditions (e.g., before a threatening task for a defensive pessimist, after a task setback for an outcome-focused individual). In turn, the triggering of these self-doubts is associated with heightened anxiety and emotional distress, with lowered self-efficacy and perceived control over the task, and sometimes even with a diminution of global feelings of self-worth or esteem (Cantor & Norem, 1989; Harlow & Cantor, 1994; Langston, 1990). These doubts are in turn met with self-regulatory efforts to alleviate these aversive effects and thereby overcome self-doubt, and these efforts are integral to individuals' strategies. Consequently, in our view, the key to their strategic behavior resides more in the fluctuating task-specific self-doubts or uncertainties than in their more stable but perhaps less critical global self-esteem (Heatherton & Polivy, 1991; Kernis, 1993).

Moreover, in addition to these microdynamics of the ebb and flow of self-assurance in daily life, we also need to continue to recognize the macroshifts in self-assurance that come from continued utilization of strategies (cf. Kernis, 1993). For example, as we described earlier, the outcome-focused women in our sample face a tough self-esteem dilemma: Their strategic reassurance-seeking is critical to their ability to overcome self-doubt and persist in the face of setbacks, yet this same reassurance-seeking may result in feedback from their "encouragers" that actually perpetuates or even exacerbates their self-doubts and uncertainties. Therefore, a central piece of the dynamics of self-assurance for these individuals—and for many people using other strategies—resides in their moderation over time of use of their preferred but costly strategy. The profile of self-esteem for these individuals must extend over time in order to monitor the potential slide from self-doubt to self-negativity or, more optimistically, to see the potential diminution of self-doubt in the face of persistence at their important life-task pursuits.

We take a similar, "bottom-up" perspective on the domain or task specificity of self-efficacy and self-esteem. Just as there are important temporal fluctuations in self-assurance that can have real implications for strategic behavior and that are easily missed if one assesses only global self-esteem, so too do individuals' self-doubts vary enormously across different life domains, from life task to life task (Harter, 1990). For example, one of the most interesting features of the outcome-focused women's task profile in our study was the presence of an outcome-focused orientation and self-uncertainty in the academic and not in the social life task (Harlow & Cantor, 1994). As a consequence of this specificity, we were able to identify real costs of their academic reassurance-seeking behavior for their social life satisfaction over time. Life-task pursuits are of course quite interdependent, and self-doubts in one task can have considerable repercussions for satisfaction in another (Cantor, Acker, & Cook-Flannagan, 1992; Emmons & King, 1988). To be able to identify these "ripple effects" for task satisfaction and personal well-being, it is essential to understand the full profile of an individual's self-perceived competence, over time and across life-task pursuits.

REFERENCES

Arkin, R. M., Lake, E. A., & Baumgardner, A. H. (1986). Shyness and self-presentation. In W. H. Jones, J. M. Cheek, & S. R. Briggs (Eds.), *Shyness: Perspectives on research and treatment* (pp. 189–203). New York: Plenum Press.

Bandura, A. (1982). The self and mechanisms of agency. In J. Suls (Ed.), *Psychological perspectives on the self* (pp. 3–39). Hillsdale, NJ: Erlbaum Associates.

Bandura, A. (1986). *Social foundations of thought and action: A social cognitive theory.* Englewood Cliffs, NJ: Prentice-Hall.

Bandura, A., Adams, N. E., & Beyer, J. (1977). Cognitive processes mediating behavioral change. *Journal of Personality and Social Psychology, 35,* 125–139.

Baumeister, R. F. (Ed.) (1993). *Self-esteem: The puzzle of low self-regard.* New York: Plenum Press.

Bem, D. J. (1972). Self-perception theory. In L. Berkowitz (Ed.), *Advances in experimental social psychology,* Vol. 6 (pp. 1–62). New York: Academic Press.

Benjamin, L. S. (1974). Structural analysis of social behavior. *Psychological Review, 81,* 392–425.

Blaine, B., & Crocker, J. (1993). Self-esteem and self-serving biases in reactions to positive and negative events. In R. F. Baumeister (Ed.), *Self-esteem: The puzzle of low self-regard* (pp. 55–85). New York: Plenum Press.

Borgen, F. H., & Barnett, D. C. (1987). Applying cluster analysis in counseling psychology research. *Journal of Counseling Psychology, 34*(4), 456–468.

Campbell, J., Chew, B., & Scratchley, L. S. (1991). Cognitive and emotional reactions to daily events: The effects of self-esteem and self-complexity. *Journal of Personality (Special Issue on Daily Events and Personality), 59*(3), 473–505.

Canavan-Gumpert, D. (1977). Generating reward and cost orientations through praise and criticism. *Journal of Personality and Social Psychology, 35,* 501–513.

Cantor, N. (1990). From thought to behavior. "Having" and "doing" in the study of personality and cognition. *American Psychologist, 45*(6), 735–750.

Cantor, N., & Fleeson, W. (1991). Life tasks and self-regulatory processes. In M. Maehr & P. Pintrich (Eds.), *Advances in motivation and achievement* (Vol. 7, pp. 327–369). Greenwich, CT: JAI Press.

Cantor, N., & Fleeson, W. (1993). Social intelligence and intelligent goal pursuit: A cognitive slice of motivation. *Nebraska symposium on motivation,* Vol. 41.

Cantor, N., & Harlow, R. E. (1992). Keeping "friends" and "grades" separate: The role of self-assurance in life task pursuits. Invited talk presented at the First Annual Conference on Agency, Self-Efficacy and Self-Esteem, University of Georgia, Athens.

Cantor, N., & Harlow, R. E. (1994). Social intelligence and personality: Flexible life task pursuit. In R. J. Sternberg & P. Ruzgis (Eds.), *Personality and intelligence* (pp. 137–168). New York: Cambridge University Press.

Cantor, N., & Harlow, R. E. (in press). Personality, strategic behavior and daily-life problem-solving. *Current Directions in Psychological Science.*

Cantor, N., & Norem, J. K. (1989). Defensive pessimism and stress and coping. *Social Cognition, 7,* 92–112.

Cantor, N., Norem, J. K., Niedenthal, P. M., Langston, C. A., & Brower, A. M. (1987). Life tasks, self-concept ideals, and cognitive strategies in a life transition. *Journal of Personality and Social Psychology, 53,* 1178–1191.

Cantor, N., Norem, J., Langston, C., Zirkel, S., Fleeson, W., & Cook-Flannagan, C. (1991). Life tasks and daily life experience. *Journal of Personality (Special Issue on Daily Events and Personality), 59*(3), 425–451.

Cantor, N., Acker, M., & Cook-Flannagan, C. (1992). Conflict and preoccupation in the intimacy life task. *Journal of Personality and Social Psychology, 63*(4), 644–655.

Caspi, A., & Moffitt, T. E. (1991). Individual differences are accentuated during periods of social change: The sample case of girls at puberty. *Journal of Personality and Social Psychology, 61,* 157–168.

Cohen, S., & Wills, T. A. (1985). Stress, social support, and the buffering hypothesis. *Psychological Bulletin, 85,* 310–357.

Cole, D. A. (1991). Change in self-perceived competence as a function of peer and teacher evaluation. *Development Psychology, 27,* 682–688.

Coyne, J. C. (1976). Depression and the response of others. *Journal of Abnormal Psychology, 85*(2), 186–193.

Darley, J. M., & Fazio, R. H. (1980). Expectancy confirmation processes arising in the social interaction sequence. *American Psychologist, 35,* 867–881.

Deci, E. L., & Ryan, R. M. (1985). *Intrinsic motivation and self-determination in human behavior.* New York: Plenum.

Dweck, C. S., & Leggett, E. L. (1988). A social–cognitive approach to motivation and personality. *Psychological Review, 95,* 256–273.

Emmons, R. A., & King, L. A. (1988). Conflict among personal strivings: Immediate and long-term implications for psychological and physical well-being. *Journal of Personality and Social Psychology, 54*(6), 1040–1048.

Fleming, R., Baum, A., Gisriel, M. M., & Gatchel, R. J. (1985). Mediating influences of social support on stress at Three Mile Island. In A. Monat & R. S. Lazarus (Eds.), *Stress and coping* (pp. 95–106). New York: Columbia University Press.

Haemmerlie, F. M., & Montgomery, R. L. (1982). Self-perception theory and unobtrusively biased interactions: A treatment for heterosocial anxiety. *Journal of Counseling Psychology, 29,* 362–370.

Harlow, R. E., & Cantor, N. (1994). The social pursuit of academics: Side-effects and spillover of strategic reassurance seeking. *Journal of Personality and Social Psychology, 66,* 386–397.

Harter, S. (1990). Adolescent self and identity development. In S. S. Feldman & G. R. Elliot (Eds.), *At the threshold: The developing adolescent* (pp. 352–387). Cambridge: Harvard University Press.

Harter, S. (1993). Causes and consequences of low self-esteem in children and adolescents. In R. F. Baumeister (Ed.), *Self-esteem: The puzzle of low self-regard* (pp. 87–116). New York: Plenum Press.

Heatherton, T. F., & Polivy, J. (1991). Development and validation of a scale for measuring state self-esteem. *Journal of Personality and Social Psychology, 60,* 895–910.

Higgins, R. L., & Snyder, C. R. (1986). The role of uncertain self-esteem in self-handicapping. *Journal of Personality and Social Psychology, 51,* 451–458.

Hixon, J. G., & Swann, W. B., Jr. (1993). When does introspection bear fruit? Self-reflection, self-insight and interpersonal choices. *Journal of Personality and Social Psychology, 64*(1), 35–43.

Joiner, T. E., Alfano, M. S., & Metalsky, G. I. (1992). When depression breeds contempt: Reassurance seeking, self-esteem, and rejection of depressed college students by their roommates. *Journal of Abnormal Psychology, 101*(1), 165–173.

Joiner, T. E., Jr., Alfano, M. S., & Metalsky, G. (1993). Caught in the crossfire: Depression, self-consistency, self-enhancement, and the response of others. *Journal of Social and Clinical Psychology, 12,* 113–134.

Jones, E. E., & Pittman, T. S. (1982). Toward a general theory of strategic self-presentation. In J. Suls (Ed.), *Psychological perspectives on the self* (pp. 231–262). Hillsdale, NJ: Erlbaum Associates.

Jones, E. E., Rhodewalt, F., Berglas, S., & Skelton, J. A. (1981). Effects of strategic self-presentation on subsequent self-esteem. *Journal of Personality and Social Psychology, 41,* 407–421.

Kernis, M. H. (1993). The roles of stability and level of self-esteem in psychological functioning. In R. F. Baumeister (Ed.), *Self-esteem: The puzzle of low self-regard* (pp. 167–182). New York: Plenum Press.

Kernis, M. H., Granneman, B. D., & Barclay, L. C. (1989). Stability and level of self-esteem as predictors of anger arousal and hostility. *Journal of Personality and Social Psychology, 56,* 1013–1023.

Kihlstrom, J. F., & Cantor, N. (1989). Social intelligence and personality: There's room for growth. In R. S. Wyer & T. K. Srull (Eds.), *Advances in social cognition,* Vol. 2 (pp. 197–214). Hillsdale, NJ: Erlbaum Associates.

Langer, E. J. (1980). The illusion of incompetence. In L. C. Perlmuter & R. A. Monty (Eds.), *Choice and perceived control.* Hillsdale, NJ: Erlbaum Associates.

Langston, C. A. (1990). The dynamics of daily life: Responses to positive and negative events, life task activity, mood and well-being. Unpublished doctoral dissertation. Ann Arbor: University of Michigan.

Langston, C. A., & Cantor, N. (1989). Social anxiety and social constraint: When "making friends" is hard. *Journal of Personality and Social Psychology, 56*(4), 649–661.

Larsen, R. J. (1989). A process approach to personality psychology: Using time as a facet of data. In D. M. Buss & N. Cantor (Eds.), *Personality psychology: Recent trends and emerging directions* (pp. 177–193). New York: Springer-Verlag.

Leary, T. (1957). *Interpersonal diagnosis of personality*. New York: Ronald.

Markus, H. (1983). Self-knowledge: An expanded view. *Journal of Personality, 51,* 543–565.

Markus, H., & Wurf, E. (1987). The dynamic self-concept: A social psychological perspective. *Annual Review of Psychology, 38,* 299–337.

Markus, H., Cross, S., & Wurf, E. (1990). The role of the self-system in competence. In R. J. Sternberg & J. Kolligian, Jr. (Eds.), *Competence considered* (pp. 205–225). New Haven: Yale University Press.

Murray, H. A. (1938). *Explorations in personality*. New York: Oxford University Press.

Nasby, W., & Kihlstrom, J. F. (1986). Cognitive assessment of personality and psychopathology. In R. E. Ingram (Ed.), *Information-processing approaches to psychopathology and clinical psychology* (pp. 217–239). New York: Academic Press.

Niedenthal, P. M., Setterlund, M. B., & Wherry, M. B. (1992). Possible self-complexity and affective reactions to goal-relevant evaluation. *Journal of Personality and Social Psychology, 63*(1), 5–16.

Nolen-Hoeksema, S. (1987). Sex differences in unipolar depression: Evidence and theory. *Psychological Bulletin, 101*(2), 259–282.

Norem, J. K., & Cantor, N. (1986a). Defensive pessimism: "Harnessing" anxiety as motivation. *Journal of Personality and Social Psychology, 51,* 1208–1217.

Norem, J. K., & Cantor, N. (1986b). Anticipatory and post hoc cushioning strategies: Optimism and defensive pessimism in "risky" situations. *Cognitive Therapy and Research, 10*(3), 347–362.

Norem, J. K., & Cantor, N. (1990). Cognitive strategies, coping and perceptions of competence. In R. J. Sternberg & J. Kolligian, Jr. (Eds.), *Competence considered* (pp. 190–204). New Haven: Yale University Press.

Norem, J. K., & Illingworth, K. S. S. (1993). Strategy-dependent effects of reflecting on self and tasks: Some implications of optimism and defensive pessimism. *Journal of Personality and Social Psychology, 65,* 822–835.

Pelham, B. W. (1991). On confidence and consequence: The certainty and importance of self-knowledge. *Journal of Personality and Social Psychology, 60,* 518–520.

Price, V. (1982). *The Type A behavior pattern: A model for research and practice.* New York: Academic Press.

Rosenberg (1976). *Conceiving the self.* New York: Basic Books.

Rotter, J. B., Chance, J. E., & Phares, E. J. (1972). *Applications of a social learning theory of personality.* New York: Holt, Rinehart & Winston.

Ryan, R. M., Koestner, R., & Deci, E. L. (1991). Ego-involved persistence: When free-choice behavior is not intrinsically motivated. *Motivation and Emotion, 15,* 185–206.

Sarason, I. G. (1975). Anxiety and self-preoccupation. In I. G. Sarason & C. D. Spielberger (Eds.), *Stress and anxiety,* Vol. 2 (pp. 27–44). Washington, DC: Hemisphere.

Schunk, D. H. (1981). Modeling and attributional effects on children's achievement: A self-efficacy analysis. *Journal of Educational Psychology, 73,* 93–105.

Showers, C. (1988). The effects of how and why thinking on perceptions of future negative events. *Cognitive Therapy and Research, 12*(3), 225–240.

Snyder, M., Tanke, E. D., & Berscheid, E. (1977). Social perception and interpersonal behavior: On the self-fulfilling nature of social stereotypes. *Journal of Personality and Social Psychology, 35,* 656–666.

Strube, M. J. (1987). A self-appraisal model of the Type A behavior pattern. In R. Hogan & W. H. Jones (Eds.), *Perspectives in personality,* Vol. 2 (pp. 201–250). Greenwich, CT: JAI Press.

Swann, W. B., Jr. (1987). Identity negotiation: Where two roads meet. *Journal of Personality and Social Psychology, 53,* 1038–1051.

Thoits, P. A. (1986). Social support as coping assistance. *Journal of Consulting and Clinical Psychology, 54,* 416–423.

Trope, Y., & Ben-Yair, E. (1982). Task construction and persistence as means for self-assessment of abilities. *Journal of Personality and Social Psychology, 42,* 637–645.

Word, C. O., Zanna, M. P., & Cooper, J. (1974). The nonverbal mediation of self-fulfilling prophecies in interracial interaction. *Journal of Experimental Social Psychology, 10,* 109–120.

Wright, J. C., & Mischel, W. (1987). A conditional approach to dispositional constructs: The local predictability of social behavior. *Journal of Personality and Social Psychology, 53,* 1159–1177.

CHAPTER 9

IMPLICIT THEORIES OF INTELLIGENCE

RECONSIDERING THE ROLE OF CONFIDENCE IN ACHIEVEMENT MOTIVATION

YING-YI HONG, CHI-YUE CHIU, AND CAROL S. DWECK

INTRODUCTION

Self-confidence and its related constructs are among the most widely researched variables in the literature on achievement. However, findings on the link between self-confidence and achievement are not consistent. While some researchers have found significant correlations between self-confidence about one's intellectual ability and achievement outcomes (e.g., Brookover & Passalacqua, 1981; J. G. Jones & Grieneeks, 1970; Marsh, 1984; Shavelson & Bolus, 1982; Shell, Murphy, & Bruning, 1989; for a review, see Hattie, 1992), others find only weak associations between the two variables (for a meta-analysis, see Hansford & Hattie, 1982).

YING-YI HONG • Division of Social Science, Hong Kong University of Science and Technology, Hong Kong.   CHI-YUE CHIU • Department of Psychology, Hong Kong University, Hong Kong.   CAROL S. DWECK • Department of Psychology, Columbia University, New York, New York 10027.

Efficacy, Agency, and Self-Esteem, edited by Michael H. Kernis. Plenum Press, New York, 1995.

In this chapter, we argue, first, that confidence level may make less difference than is often thought in how people respond in achievement situations, especially when they meet with failure. Next, we argue that when confidence in one's intelligence does make a difference, its workings must be understood in the context of how people conceive of intelligence in the first place. More specifically, we will propose that people's conceptions or theories of intelligence often (1) play a more fundamental role than does confidence in predicting reactions to achievement setbacks and (2) predict when confidence will or will not make a difference for achievement processes. We also discuss how people's theories of intelligence can affect the maintenance of their self-esteem.

Implicit theories of intelligence are beliefs about the fundamental nature of intelligence, specifically whether intelligence is a fixed entity that cannot be changed (an *entity* theory) or a malleable quality that can be increased through one's efforts (an *incremental* theory). Before beginning, we will discuss more about implicit theories of intelligence and their measurement.

IMPLICIT THEORIES AND THEIR ASSESSMENT

Lay people, like scientists (e.g., Jensen, 1979; Piaget, 1972), may have theories about intelligence. Unlike scientists, however, lay people may not typically articulate their beliefs about intelligence. Thus, their beliefs may take the form of background assumptions or implicit theories. Our research has shown two implicit theories of intelligence to be widely held among lay people, with some believing that intelligence is a fixed permanent entity ("entity theorists"), and others believing that intelligence is malleable and can be increased ("incremental theorists"). We have proposed that these implicit theories of intelligence set up cognitive frameworks within which people interpret and react to relevant information (Dweck, 1991; Dweck & Leggett, 1988; see also Heider, 1958; Kelly, 1963; Murphy & Medin, 1985; Ross, 1989).

How do we assess people's implicit theories of intelligence? We do so by means of a questionnaire developed by Henderson, Dweck, and Chiu (1992). This questionnaire consists of three items, each depicting intelligence as a fixed entity.[1] The items are: (1) "You have a certain amount of

---

[1]Items depicting an incremental theory are not included in this measure because several studies (Boyum, 1988; Leggett, 1985) have shown that even respondents who endorse items depicting entity theories have a strong tendency to endorse opposite items depicting the incremental theory, as well as a tendency to drift toward incremental choices over times.

intelligence and you really can't do much to change it." (2) "Your intelligence is something about you that you can't change very much." (3) "You can learn new things, but you can't really change your basic intelligence." Participants are asked to show their degree of agreement with each item on a 6-point Likert scale, from 1 ("Strongly agree") to 6 ("Strongly disagree"). Thus, the higher the score, the less one believes that intelligence is a fixed entity.

Because, in the current format, endorsement of an entity theory entails agreement with the items, it was important to demonstrate that agreement with these statements did not just represent an acquiescence set. Chiu and Dweck (1994) examined individuals' implicit theory of intelligence together with their implicit theories in other domains (such as people's morality). Their findings revealed that even though implicit theory measures for different domains have the same format, they form clearly independent factors in a factor analysis, suggesting that responses to the implicit theories of intelligence measure are not due to an acquiescence set.

Another issue requiring attention is the issue of whether disagreement with the entity-theory statements can be taken to represent agreement with the incremental theory. In two studies with college students (Chiu, Hong, & Dweck, 1992), participants were given the implicit theories of intelligence measure and asked to explain their responses. Those who disagreed with the entity statements gave clear incremental-theory justifications for their responses. This finding shows that disagreement with the entity-theory statements can be taken to represent agreement with the incremental theory.

Finally, only three items are included because the items are intended to have the same meaning, and continued repetition of the same idea becomes somewhat purposeless and tedious to the respondents. The high internal reliability of the measure ($\alpha = 0.96$, $N = 50$) suggests that this small number of items has not been a problem. Test–retest reliability has also been found to be high ($r = 0.82$, $N = 50$).

On the basis of their responses to the three items, students are classified as entity theorists or incremental theorists. Those with an average score of 3 or lower (suggesting consistent agreement with the statements) are classified as entity theorists, typically about 40% of the respondents. Those with an average score of 4 or higher (suggesting consistent disagreement) are classified as incremental theorists, typically about 50% of the respondents. Those with an average score between 3 and 4 (typically

---

This indicates to us that the incremental items are highly compelling and, perhaps, more socially desirable as well.

about 10% of the respondents) are assumed to have indeterminate or mixed theories and are eliminated from the sample.

ASSESSMENT OF SELF-CONFIDENCE IN INTELLIGENCE

In the studies described below, students' confidence in their own intelligence was assessed by a three-item questionnaire developed by Henderson et al. (1992). For each of the three items, a statement depicting high confidence is pitted against a statement depicting low confidence. The items are: (1) "I usually think I'm intelligent" vs. "I wonder if I'm intelligent." (2) "When I get new material, I'm usually sure I will be able to learn it" vs. "When I get new material, I often think I may not be able to learn it." (3) "I feel pretty confident about my intellectual ability" vs. "I'm not very confident about my intellectual ability." Respondents are asked to choose the one statement that is more true for them and then to indicate how true it is for them on a scale from 1 ("Very true") to 3 ("Sort of true"). Responses to this measure are recorded into a 6-point scale, ranging from low to high confidence. Previous findings have shown high internal reliability for the measure ($\alpha = 0.81$, $N = 69$), and test-retest reliability over a 1-week period has also been found to be high ($r = 0.83$, $N = 50$).

This confidence measure has also been compared to other established measures of self-confidence and self-esteem. For example, it has been found to correlate highly ($r = 0.77$, $N = 33$) with the perceived intellectual competence subscale of the Self-perception Profile for College Students (Neemann & Harter, 1986). It is also moderately correlated with the Rosenberg (1965) Self-Esteem Scale ($r = 0.43$, $N = 55$), which is theoretically less similar to our confidence measure than the Neemann and Harter measure but provides an interesting comparison. In short, these findings indicate that our confidence measure is a reliable and valid measure of individuals' confidence in their intellectual abilities.

Respondents with average scores below the mean for the sample are classified as having low confidence; those with average scores above the mean are classified as having high confidence. Those at the mean are eliminated from the sample.

In most of the studies described below, students filled out both the implicit theories of intelligence questionnaire and the confidence in intelligence questionnaire at the same time in small groups of 6–8. On the basis of their scores on both questionnaires, students were categorized into four groups: low confidence entity theorists, high confidence entity theorists, low confidence incremental theorists, and high confidence incremental theorists. It is also noteworthy that nonsignificant correlations were found between scores on the implicit theories and confidence measures [e.g., $r = 0.02$, $p = 0.89$ (Hong & Dweck, 1994, Experiment 1); $r = 0.13$, $p = 0.30$ (Hong & Dweck, 1994, Experiment 2)]. This finding indicates that the two measures are more or less independent, and this allows us to dichotomize the implicit theories and the confidence scores without significantly increasing the probability of committing Type I errors in our data analyses (cf. Maxwell & Delaney, 1993).

THE ROLE OF IMPLICIT THEORY IN NEGATIVE SELF-INFERENCES ABOUT INTELLIGENCE

Much research on achievement motivation has focused on how people respond to negative events, that is, failures or setbacks. Previous studies have found that drawing negative inferences about one's ability from failure is a critical mediating factor leading to debilitation in the face of negative events (e.g., Dweck, 1975; see also Abramson, Seligman, & Teasdale, 1978; Beck, 1967; Weiner, 1985).

One would think that having low self-confidence would make negative ability inferences more likely than having high self-confidence—that those who are more certain of their high ability would be less inclined to doubt their ability when they encounter failure than those who are less certain. Yet research in our laboratory has shown that individuals' self-confidence in intelligence often plays a less important role than their entity vs. incremental conception of intelligence in predicting negative ability inferences from failure (Hong & Dweck, 1994; MacGyvers & Dweck, 1994). Why might that be?

Entity theorists, who by definition believe that their intelligence is a fixed trait, are particularly concerned with documenting their level of intellectual ability (Bandura & Dweck, 1985; Dweck & Leggett, 1988). As a result, when a negative outcome occurs, they may view it as indicative of their intellectual inadequacy (Henderson & Dweck, 1991; Zhao & Dweck, 1994). In contrast, incremental theorists, who by definition believe that intelligence is malleable and can be developed, are less concerned with diagnosing their ability (vs. developing it) and therefore should be less likely to make global ability inferences from negative outcomes (Dweck & Leggett, 1988; Henderson & Dweck, 1991; Zhao & Dweck, 1994; cf. Epstein, 1992; Kernis, Brockner, & Frankel, 1989).

In a recently completed study [Hong and Dweck, 1994 (Experiment 1)], we found that entity theorists (regardless of their confidence level) were more likely than incremental theorists (regardless of their confidence level) to make negative ability inferences from failure. In this study, college students' implicit theories of intelligence and confidence in their ability were assessed some time before they participated individually in the main study. In the main study, students reacted to ability words following a failure experience, and their reaction times served as an index of their ability inferences from failure. We reasoned that negative ability inferences following failure would engender a heightened emotional reactivity to ability words (such as "smart" and "dumb") and thus would result in longer response latencies to ability adjectives. Thus, we predicted that relative to incremental theorists, entity theorists would take longer to respond to ability adjectives after negative performance feedback.

To test this prediction, half the participants (those in the experimental condition) were given a logical reasoning test to work on and were then given negative performance feedback.[2] The other half (those in the control condition) were not given the test or the negative feedback. Following this manipulation, all participants were given an adjective decision task. On this task, they were presented with an adjective on each trial and asked to decide as quickly as possible whether the adjective could normally be used to describe a person. Included were six ability words: *smart, capable, intelligent, dumb, stupid,* and *inept.*

The findings supported our hypotheses. As expected, participants' implicit theories of intelligence, but not their confidence level, predicted their response latencies. Specifically, entity theorists took significantly longer to respond to ability adjectives than incremental theorists after receiving negative feedback. However, no such differences were found in the control condition, in which no performance test and feedback were given. This pattern of findings suggests that entity theorists show altered reaction times to ability adjectives following failure, but do not have a chronic reactivity to ability adjectives in the absence of an evaluative intelligence task and negative feedback.

Also as expected, no significant reaction time differences were found between entity theorists and incremental theorists in the experimental and control conditions when the participants responded to adjectives that described personality but not ability. Thus, the longer reaction times exhibited by entity theorists were not simply due to generalized debilitation.

In all the conditions, confidence level did not significantly predict any

---

[2]We have taken great care in debriefing participants in studies that involve false performance feedback. Specifically, participants are told that the negative feedback shown to them was preprogrammed and did not reveal their actual performance on the task. We then explain the purpose of the research in detail and invite them to express their opinions and feelings about the study. Older participants are also given references to pertinent literature if they wish to learn more about the research area. All participants are again reassured about their performance and their ability before they leave the experiment.

reaction time differences, suggesting that confidence level did not play a role in predicting reactions to failure.

These results provide support, albeit indirect support, for the view that negative performance feedback raised concerns among entity theorists about their ability, possibly eliciting negative ability inferences. Although our data do not allow us to pinpoint the precise underlying processes involved, we believe that the negative performance feedback did not merely make the ability dimension more salient or more cognitively accessible to entity theorists (cf. Higgins, Rholes, & Jones, 1977) or change their working self-concepts (Markus & Kunda, 1986). If only these processes were involved, we would expect to find a shorter average reaction time, rather than a longer one, in entity theorists in comparison to incremental theorists. The fact that we found a significantly longer average reaction time in entity theorists suggests that the underlying processes involved reactions, such as emotions or ruminations, that distracted them from the adjective identification task at hand. This speculation is consistent with past findings that words that are consonant with an individual's contemporary concern may cause emotional arousal and that individuals usually need longer to process words that elicit emotional reactions (Bock & Klinger, 1986). Similarly, individuals need a longer time to generate word associations when the cue presented is consonant with their psychological complex or concern (Jung & Riklin, 1904/1973). In short, our predictions are more consistent with the idea that the failure feedback heightened concerns and emotional reactivity in entity theorists than with the idea that the failure feedback merely increased the salience of the ability dimension for entity theorists.

To summarize, our finding that entity theorists on average took longer than did incremental theorists to identify ability adjectives after receiving negative feedback provides indirect support for the notion that entity theorists are more likely than incremental theorists to make negative ability inferences following failure.

More direct evidence showing that entity theorists (regardless of their confidence level) are more likely than incremental theorists (regardless of their confidence level) to draw negative ability inferences is provided by our next study.

Hong and Dweck (1994 [Experiment 2]) asked college students to perform an intellectual task and then provided them with negative feedback. Later, when the students were asked to explain their failure, entity theorists, compared to incremental theorists, were more likely to attribute their failure to lack of ability than to lack of effort. Again, the students' level of self-confidence did not predict their failure attributions. Similar findings were obtained by MacGyvers and Dweck (1994) in a study of junior high school students. In this study, the students were asked to respond to a hypothetical situation in which they received poor grades in school. Again, implicit theory was a much stronger predictor of students' attributions than was confidence. Entity theorists were more prone to make ability attributions than incremental theorists, who in turn were more likely to attribute the failure to lack of effort.

It is important to note that the greater tendency among entity theorists to make negative self-inferences in the face of negative feedback is not warranted by the reality. For example, as in previous studies, Hong and Dweck (1994) found that prior to negative feedback, entity theorists as a group displayed levels of performance that equaled those of the incremental theorists. Thus, it is not the case that entity theorists simply have lower ability and are quick to recognize this when setbacks occur. Instead, our findings suggest that it may be the fixed view of intelligence that creates a greater propensity to infer a lack of ability from a negative performance outcome.

MASTERY-ORIENTED VS. HELPLESS COPING

In addition to making negative self-inferences more likely, will holding an entity theory of intelligence make other aspects of maladaptive or helpless responses to failure more likely?

Two response patterns to academic challenges, namely, the mastery-oriented and helpless response patterns, were first described in detail by Diener and Dweck (1978, 1980). Diener and Dweck (1978) observed that when children were presented with challenging intellectual tasks, some children, despite their excellent performance on similar but easier tasks moments before, displayed helpless responses. These responses were characterized by negative self-inferences, performance decrements, and negative affect. In contrast, when facing the same intellectual challenges, some children displayed the mastery-oriented response pattern. They focused on effort and strategy, rather than self-blame, experimented with new problem-solving strategies, and displayed positive affect in the face of setbacks.

In a study of students' achievement patterns over the transition to junior high school, MacGyvers and Dweck (1994) found that entity theorists were more likely than incremental theorists to display cognitive, affective, and behavioral aspects of helpless responses in the face of academic challenges. In contrast, holding an incremental theory increased the likelihood of mastery-oriented responses to academic challenges. Again, in this study, students' level of self-confidence in their intellectual ability played no role in predicting mastery-oriented vs. helpless responses to academic challenges.

Specifically, the study conducted by MacGyvers and Dweck (1994) was designed to determine whether an entity vs. incremental theory of intelligence would predict helpless vs. mastery-oriented patterns in the face of real-life academic challenges. Compared to grade school, in junior high school, schoolwork becomes relatively challenging, is usually presented in a less personalized manner, and is accompanied by relatively stringent grading criteria (Brophy & Evertson, 1976; Eccles & Midgley, 1989; Eccles, Midgley, & Adler, 1984; Midgley & Feldlaufer, 1987). Thus, MacGyvers and Dweck reasoned that the transition from grade school to junior high school may create the conditions under which helpless reactions would occur and theories of intelligence would predict academic achievement more strongly. To test this idea, MacGyvers and Dweck (1994) assessed 7th-graders' theories of intelligence at the beginning of the school year. They also obtained information about the students' academic performance in the 6th grade and their subsequent performance in the 7th grade. In addition, information pertaining to the students' affective experiences related to their schoolwork was assessed (as well as their attributions for failures, as reported earlier).

The results were consistent with the predictions. First, in terms of actual academic performance, entity theorists earned lower grades than did incremental theorists in junior high school even when their academic achievement in grade school was controlled for. For entity theorists, those who had received low grades in the 6th grade tended to receive low grades in the 7th grade, and many of those who had earned high grades before showed substantially lower achievement levels in the 7th grade. For incremental theorists, in contrast, those who had received high grades in the 6th grade tended to remain high achievers in the 7th grade, and many of those who had gotten low grades before earned relatively high grades in the 7th grade. In addition, entity theorists on average reported feeling more apprehensive about their schoolwork than did incremental theorists. Again, the students' level of self-confidence in intellectual ability did not predict junior high school grades over and above what the students' prior achievement predicted, and it did not predict the students' affective responses to the relatively challenging schoolwork in junior high school.

To summarize thus far, our findings indicate that it is the students' implicit theory of intelligence more than their level of self-confidence that predicts important cognitive and affective reactions, as well as achievement outcomes, when students are faced with challenging intellectual tasks.

DOES CONFIDENCE HELP?

Given that having high self-confidence does not seem to prevent negative ability inferences and performance decrements, one may ask whether self-confidence plays any role in mitigating maladaptive responses to failure and, if it does, what that role might be. Specifically, does having high confidence alleviate the severity and certainty of the negative ability inferences made among entity theorists and does having low confidence intensify them? To answer this question, we [Hong and Dweck, 1994 (Experiment 2)] asked students to perform an intellectual task and then provided them with negative feedback. Following the feedback, we assessed students' perceptions of their performance level and their perceptions of the validity of the task as an index of intelligence.

The results revealed that compared to incremental theorists, entity theorists with low confidence (1) more frequently estimated their performance as being below average among their peers than did the incremental theorists and (2) perceived the test as more valid in reflecting their (low) conceptual ability. As predicted, entity theorists who were confident in their ability were somewhat less self-derogating on these measures than their low confidence counterparts. Specifically, entity–high confidence students' estimates of their performance were as high as those of the incremental theorists, while their perceptions of test validity lay between the perceptions of high test validity of the entity–low confidence subjects and the perceptions of lower test validity of incremental theorists. Confidence did not make a difference within the incremental framework. (If anything, the low confidence incremental theorists looked least self-derogating among the four groups.) In short, having low confidence in the entity framework seems to intensify the tendency toward self-derogation. Having high confidence does not prevent low ability attributions in the face of failure but does seem to affect how low that ability is perceived to be and how certain one is of that low ability.

Taken together, our findings suggest that confidence does not have as strong an impact when students confront failure as it is often believed to have. In the studies we have reported, it did not prevent ability blaming and helpless reactions among entity theorists, and it made little difference among incremental theorists, who were mastery-oriented regardless of confidence level. Confidence simply predicted higher performance perceptions and lower test validity estimates among entity theorists.

Given these findings, how would we explain the positive relation between self-confidence and academic achievement frequently found in past studies (e.g., Brookover & Passalacqua, 1981; J. G. Jones & Grieneeks, 1970; Marsh, 1984; see also Hansford & Hattie, 1982; Skaalvik & Hagtvet,

1990)? In our view, we need to distinguish two roles confidence may play (cf. Scheirer & Kraut, 1979). First, confidence may serve as an index of past or present performance outcomes. Second, it may motivate achievement strivings vis-à-vis future performance.

How does confidence play these two roles? Because self-confidence about one's ability may be influenced by the performance outcomes one has been experiencing, a strong relation is likely to be found between self-confidence and recent performance. Moreover, as long as the learning environment remains stable and contains a minimum of failures and set-backs, self-confidence may continue to predict achievement. However, confidence may not be a good predictor of future achievement when the achievement environment becomes more challenging, as in the transition from grade school to junior high school, or in situations in which students are likely to face setbacks.

This view is consistent with the findings from MacGyvers and Dweck (1994) described above. First, consistent with the idea that self-confidence reflects current achievement level, in this study, students' confidence levels measured at the beginning of the 7th grade correlated highly with their grade point averages in the 6th grade. However, consistent with the view that confidence does not predict future achievement when the learning environment changes to become relatively challenging, MacGyvers and Dweck (1994) found that confidence level did not predict students' gains and losses in achievement (grades) from the 6th to the 7th grade or their absolute achievement levels (grades) in junior high school. In short, although a high correlation between self-confidence and recent performance can be expected when the learning environment is stable and the tasks remain relatively familiar and unchallenging, with changes in the learning environment toward higher levels of intellectual challenge, this correlation between self-confidence and performance may become greatly attenuated.

Our findings have implications for interventions designed solely to bolster students' confidence in the belief that this will make them become mastery-oriented (e.g., Flowers, 1991; Purkey, 1970; cf. Scheirer & Kraut, 1979). The findings lead us to believe that such interventions may not be as effective as their designers might think. Results of a study by Dweck (1975) were consonant with this view and showed that an intervention designed to bolster confidence was less successful in altering maladaptive responses to failure than an intervention that addressed negative self-inferences. Perhaps guiding students to change their beliefs about intelligence from a fixed view to a malleable one may help to alleviate maladaptive inferences and thus may help students cope better with the obstacles that are inevitable in a challenging intellectual environment.

IMPLICIT THEORIES AND THE MAINTENANCE OF SELF-CONFIDENCE

In the last section, we argued that self-confidence confers some benefits only with an entity theory but not with an incremental theory. In this section, we further argue that within an entity theory framework, self-confidence is fragile and difficult to maintain.

Why may self-confidence within an entity framework be difficult to maintain? First, as our research has indicated, entity theorists, regardless of their level of self-confidence in their ability, have a significantly greater tendency to infer low ability from failures or setbacks than do incremental theorists. Thus, for entity theorists, more than for incremental theorists, self-confidence may be put to test on every challenging intellectual task. Under these circumstances, many entity theorists may eventually feel undermined.

Research in our laboratory has identified other factors that may make self-confidence more vulnerable within an entity theory framework. This research has shown that in comparison to incremental theorists, entity theorists have higher and more stringent performance standards (Hong & Dweck, 1993). Thus, entity theorists are not only more likely than incremental theorists to make ability inferences from failure, given these high standards for success, but also may be more likely to experience "failure" in the course of learning. Finally, we will review evidence showing that the goals entity theorists pursue in an achievement setting may discourage them from taking the risks necessary to attain success and maintain confidence.

STANDARDS

The concept of standards is a key construct in understanding human functioning because of the important role of standards in guiding actions (e.g., Higgins, 1990). In our research, we were interested in whether entity and incremental theorists might set different minimum standards for success. The fact that among entity theorists a single setback is often sufficient to call their ability into question suggests that entity theorists may set different standards for themselves than incremental theorists. For example, they may define success as being able to solve almost all problems, regardless of how hard the problems are.

In a study designed to examine this question, Hong and Dweck (1993) showed 160 college students sample items from several aptitude tests that measured different kinds of ability and knowledge (i.e., vocabulary, general knowledge, logical reasoning, aptitude in visual art, and abstract reasoning). The sample items selected for each test varied in difficulty, causing the tests to range from moderately difficult to extremely difficult. In this study, the students were not asked to take the tests. Instead, they were asked to study the sample items carefully, and then to (1) rate the difficulty of each test, from 1 ("Not at all") to 9 ("Extremely difficult"), and (2) state the percentage of correct answers they would have to get on the test to feel satisfied.

Results showed that entity theorists on the whole set significantly higher standards than did incremental theorists; that is, they required a higher percentage correct to feel satisfied. Moreover, entity theorists perceived the tests to be as difficult as did incremental theorists, suggesting that entity theorists did not set higher standards simply because they perceived the tests to be less difficult than did incremental theorists.

In addition, entity theorists set a *much* higher standard than incremental theorists on tests that both theory groups perceived to be extremely difficult. The reason they did so is that entity theorists, who had set a very high standard for moderately difficult tests to begin with, did not lower their standards for tests that they perceived to be more difficult. In contrast, when test difficulty increased, incremental theorists set a significantly lower standard for themselves. In short, entity theorists may not adjust their standards in a way that allows much leeway for positive self-evaluations.

These findings suggest that an entity theory may set up a framework in which proving one's intelligence to be adequate requires the consistent attainment of high standards of performance. If so, then entity theorists' confidence in their ability may more often be challenged and potentially undermined.

ACHIEVEMENT GOALS

Another factor that may make it difficult for entity theorists to maintain their self-confidence in the long run relates to the goals they tend to pursue in achievement situations. As we suggested above, students may often base their self-confidence on their performance. Thus, to maintain self-confidence in the long run, it may be necessary for students to master progressively advanced skills and to acquire progressively abstract knowledge. In our research, we have found that when entity theorists enter an achievement situation, they tend to perceive the situation as one in which they must document their ability (Bandura & Dweck, 1985; Dweck & Leggett, 1988). This goal of "looking smart" will often lead them to avoid valuable learning opportunities through which they may acquire the new skills and knowledge that are important for future success.

In contrast, incremental theorists, not believing in fixed intelligence, are not as concerned about documenting their intelligence as entity theorists are. Instead, relative to entity theorists, they are more concerned with developing their skills and knowledge in achievement situations, and they select novel and challenging tasks that will provide opportunities for them to do so (Bandura & Dweck, 1985; Dweck & Leggett, 1988). Thus, with an incremental theory, these learning goals may carry individuals through temporary setbacks to the mastery that is important for long-term achievement.

In short, the tendency for entity theorists to adopt the goal of documenting their ability may lead them to avoid challenging learning situations. As a result, they may deprive themselves of opportunities to build the skills that bring success, which may in turn jeopardize building and maintenance of self-confidence.

VULNERABILITY OF THE SELF SYSTEM AND A POSSIBLE ALTERNATIVE INTERVENTION

Thus far, we have reviewed findings suggesting that implicit theories of intelligence serve as the background assumptions that guide how individuals interpret and understand achievement situations. When students believe that intelligence is fixed, they are more concerned about how intelligent they are and perceive the achievement situation as one that tests their ability. Thus, negative performance outcomes are likely to be interpreted as indicators of ineptitude. Moreover, given their somewhat more stringent standards, entity theorists may be more likely than incremental theorists to perceive an outcome as a failure.

In contrast, when individuals believe that intelligence is malleable, they are oriented toward learning new skills and developing their intelligence. They are relatively willing to take on new and challenging tasks even when frustrations with these tasks are likely. Moreover, with an incremental theory, feedback information is less likely to be interpreted as an indication of their fixed level of intelligence.

An implicit theory of intelligence with its allied pattern of achievement motivation (cognitive, affective, and behavioral components) may be seen as forming a self-system in the achievement domain. That is, each theory about one's self-attribute appears to create a motivational system that is qualitatively different from the other system in the criteria it uses to evaluate performance information, in how the information is interpreted, and in how the interpretations guide actions.[3] Furthermore, as we have seen, the different self-systems are differentially vulnerable to the impact of setbacks in the course of learning.

Indeed, the vulnerability of the entity self-system may go beyond the academic self. To the extent that entity theorists base their self-esteem on the evaluation of their own intelligence, they may find it difficult to maintain their self-esteem as well. Indeed, Hong and Dweck [1994 (Experiment 1)] found that after entity theorists received negative performance feedback on an intellectual task, they displayed heightened reactivity to a group of words containing words that conveyed global self-evaluation (e.g., "inadequate," "worthless"). This finding suggests that entity theorists may find their global self-esteem at risk when they receive negative performance feedback (cf. Tesser, 1988). In other words, it is possible that entity theorists' self-esteem, like their self-confidence in ability, is fragile and difficult to maintain (cf. Rosenberg, 1986). This further suggests that individuals' implicit theories may be able to predict the stability of their self-esteem (cf. Kernis, Grannemann, & Barclay, 1989; see also Kernis, Grannemann, & Mathis, 1991; Markus & Kunda, 1986; Rosenberg, 1986).

Interestingly, entity theorists do not appear on average to have lower global self-esteem than incremental theorists. Indeed, we found a nonsignificant correlation between scores on the implicit theories of intelligence measure and the Rosenberg (1965) Self-Esteem Scale ($r = 0.001$, $p = 0.99$ in a sample of 55 students; $r = 0.142$, $p = 0.12$ in another sample of 121 students). This finding suggests that implicit theories and level of global self-esteem are not related. However, as noted, because entity theorists tend to draw negative self-inferences when they meet with failure, we predict that their self-esteem may fluctuate more than that of incremental theorists. A longitudinal study that examines the self-esteem of students through an academic year as a function of academic feedback would be able to test this hypothesis. We predict that students who believe in an entity view of intelligence may have more self-esteem fluctuations, given fluctuations in academic performance feedback, than those who believe in an incremental view of intelligence.

Given the vulnerability of the self-system associated with an entity theory, educators interested in fostering adaptive coping with adversity among students should consider working directly with students' implicit theories of intelligence. Indeed, this possibility is suggested by a series of

---

[3]Another interesting aspect of the two self-systems is how they might foster intrinsic vs. extrinsic motivation. This issue is somewhat beyond the scope of this chapter, but interested readers can refer to Dweck and Leggett (1988) and Heyman and Dweck (1992) for a detailed discussion of how the two systems may relate to intrinsic vs. extrinsic motivation.

recent studies in which researchers have been able to experimentally manipulate students' entity vs. incremental theories of intelligence [Bergen, 1991; Dweck, Tenney, & Dinces, 1982 (as cited in Dweck & Leggett, 1988); E. E. Jones & Cutler, 1993]. Their success in experimentally manipulating students' theories not only opens up numerous possibilities for interventions, but also implies that students' theories of intelligence are not fixed dispositions that cannot be altered. In these studies, students' implicit theories were typically manipulated by providing students with reading materials that compellingly presented either the entity or the incremental theory. Following this manipulation, the students' level of persistence, or goal choice, or performance attributions were assessed. Relative to the students who read the incremental article, students who read the entity article showed less persistence in the face of failure (Bergen, 1991), were less likely to adopt learning goals (Dweck et al., 1982), and made stronger ability attributions (E. E. Jones & Cutler, 1993). Although the efficacy of educational interventions that modify theories remains to be systematically studied, these findings suggest that our approach presents a promising alternative to bolstering self-confidence alone.

CONCLUDING REMARKS

Contrary to common beliefs about self-confidence, our research has shown that self-confidence often plays less of a role than students' implicit theories in predicting individuals' responses to failures. Specifically, confidence level per se was not a good predictor of negative ability inferences or adaptive coping in the face of adversity, although having high confidence within an entity theory framework seemed to mitigate somewhat the severity and certainty of negative ability inferences. Moreover, we have argued that confidence within an entity theory framework may be fragile and difficult to maintain.

To conclude, in psychology, the self is an extremely complex system to study, partly because of the ample information individuals have about themselves (Markus, 1977) and partly because of the emotional involvement in matters related to the self (e.g., Greenwald, 1980; Kunda, 1987; Pelham & Swann, 1989; see also Swann, Pelham, & Krull, 1989; Tesser, Pilkington, & McIntosh, 1989). In this chapter, we have reviewed evidence that individuals' subjective experiences and their responses in achievement situations may be organized around their implicit theories of intelligence. In line with the growing emphasis on the importance of implicit theories in guiding thoughts and actions (e.g., Murphy & Medin, 1985; Ross, 1989; Wittenbrink, Gist, & Hilton, 1993), our research has documented a systematic link between holding an entity vs. incremental view of intelligence and the vulnerability of the self-system in failure situations. As such, implicit theories of intelligence may potentially be an important construct in understanding the self.

REFERENCES

Abramson, L. Y., Seligman, M. E. P., & Teasdale, J. D. (1978). Learned helplessness in humans: Critique and reformulation. *Journal of Abnormal Psychology, 87*, 49–74.

Bandura, M. M., & Dweck, C. S. (1985). The relationship of conceptions of intelligence and achievement goals to achievement-related cognition, affect and behavior. Unpublished manuscript. Cambridge: Harvard University.

Beck, A. T. (1967). *Depression: Clinical, experimental, and theoretical aspects.* New York: Harper & Row.

Bergen, R. S. (1991). Beliefs about intelligence and achievement related behaviors. Unpublished doctoral dissertation. Urbana: University of Illinois.

Bock, M., & Klinger, E. (1986). Interaction of emotion and cognition in word recall. *Psychological Research, 48*, 99–106.

Boyum, L. A. (1988). Students' conceptions of their intelligence: Impact on academic course choice. Unpublished master's thesis. Urbana: University of Illinois.

Brookover, W. B., & Passalacqua, J. (1981). Comparison of aggregate self-concepts for populations with different reference groups. In M. D. Lynch, A. A. Norem-Hebeisen, & K. J. Gergen (Eds.), *Self-concept: Advances in theory and research* (pp. 283–294). Cambridge: Ballinger.

Brophy, J. E., & Evertson, C. M. (1976). *Learning from teaching: A developmental perspective.* Boston: Allyn & Bacon.

Chiu, C., & Dweck, C. S. (1994). A meaning–action system approach to justice and moral beliefs. (submitted).

Chiu, C., Hong, Y., & Dweck, C. S. (1992). Reliability and validity of the implicit theories measures. Unpublished raw data.

Diener, C. I., & Dweck, C. S. (1978). An analysis of learned helplessness: Continuous changes in performance, strategy and achievement cognitions following failure. *Journal of Personality and Social Psychology, 36*, 451–462.

Diener, C. I., & Dweck, C. S. (1980). An analysis of learned helplessness. II. The processing of success. *Journal of Personality and Social Psychology, 39*, 940–952.

Dweck, C. S. (1975). The role of expectations and attributions in the alleviation of learned helplessness. *Journal of Personality and Social Psychology, 31*, 674–685.

Dweck, C. S. (1991). Self-theories and goals: Their role in motivation, personality, and development. In R. Dienstbier (Ed.), *Nebraska symposium on motivation, 1990*, Vol. 38 (pp. 199–235). Lincoln: University of Nebraska Press.

Dweck, S. C., & Leggett, E. L. (1988). A social–cognitive approach to motivation and personality. *Psychological Review, 95*, 256–273.

Dweck, C. S., Tenney, Y., & Dinces, N. (1982). [Implicit theories of intelligence as determinants of achievement goal choice.] Unpublished raw data.

Eccles, J. S., & Midgley, C. (1989). Stage/environment fit: Developmentally appropriate classrooms for early adolescents. In R. Ames & C. Ames (Eds.), *Research on motivation in education*, Vol. 3 (pp. 139–186). San Diego: Academic Press.

Eccles, J. S., Midgley, C., & Adler, T. (1984). Grade-related changes in the school environment: Effects on achievement motivation. In J. G. Nicholls (Ed.), *The development of achievement motivation* (pp. 283–331). Greenwich, CT: JAI Press.

Epstein, S. (1992). Coping ability, negative self-evaluation, and overgeneralization: Experiment and theory. *Journal of Personality and Social Psychology, 62,* 826–836.

Flowers, J. V. (1991). A behavioral method of increasing self-confidence in elementary school children: Treatment and modeling results. *British Journal of Educational Psychology, 61,* 13–18.

Greenwald, A. G. (1980). The totalitarian ego: Fabrication and revision of personal history. *American Psychologist, 35,* 603–618.

Hansford, B. C., & Hattie, J. A. (1982). The relationship between self and achievement/performance measures. *Review of Educational Research, 52,* 123–142.

Hattie, J. (1992). *Self-concept.* Hillsdale, NJ: Erlbaum Associates.

Heider, F. (1958). *The psychology of interpersonal relations.* New York: John Wiley.

Henderson, V., & Dweck, C. S. (1991). Motivation and achievement. In S. Feldman & G. Elliott (Eds.), *At the threshold: Adolescent development.* Cambridge: Harvard University Press.

Henderson, V., Dweck, C. S., & Chiu, C. (1992). A measure of implicit theories of intelligence. Unpublished manuscript. New York: Columbia University.

Heyman, G. D., & Dweck, C. S. (1992). Achievement goals and intrinsic motivation: Their relation and their role in adaptive motivation. *Motivation and Emotion, 16,* 231–247.

Higgins, E. T. (1990). Personality, social psychology, and person–situation relations: Standards and knowledge activation as a common language. In L. A. Pervin (Ed.), *Handbook of personality: Theory and research* (pp. 301–338). New York: Guilford Press.

Higgins, E. T., Rholes, W. S., & Jones, C. R. (1977). Category accessibility and impression formation. *Journal of Experimental Social Psychology, 13,* 141–154.

Hong, Y., & Dweck, C. S. (1993). Implicit theories of intelligence as predictors of achievement standards. Unpublished raw data.

Hong, Y., & Dweck, C. S. (1994). A test of implicit theory and self-confidence as predictors of self-inferences after failure. (submitted).

Jensen, A. R. (1979). g: Outmoded theory or unconquered frontier? *Creative Science and Technology, 2,* 16–29.

Jones, E. E., & Cutler, A. D. (1993). Theories of intelligence and ability attribution. Unpublished manuscript. Princeton, NJ: Princeton University.

Jones, J. G., & Grieneeks, L. (1970). Measures of self perceptions as predictors of scholastic achievement. *Journal of Educational Research, 63,* 201–203.

Jung, C. G., & Riklin, F. (1904/1973). The associations of normal subjects (L. Stein & D. Riviere, translators). In H. Read, M. Fordham, G. Adler, & W. McGuire (Eds.), *Experimental researches—The collected works of C. G. Jung,* Vol. 2 (pp. 3–196). Princeton, NJ: Princeton University Press.

Kelly, G. A. (1963). *A theory of personality: The psychology of personal constructs.* New York: Norton.

Kernis, M. H., Brockner, J., & Frankel, B. S. (1989). Self-esteem and reactions to failure: The mediating roles of overgeneralization. *Journal of Personality and Social Psychology, 57,* 707–714.

Kernis, M. H., Grannemann, B. D., & Barclay, L. C. (1989). Stability and level of self-esteem as predictors of anger arousal and hostility. *Journal of Personality and Social Psychology, 56,* 1013–1022.

Kernis, M. H., Grannemann, B. D., & Mathis, L. C. (1991). Stability of self-esteem as a moderator of the relation between level of self-esteem and depression. *Journal of Personality and Social Psychology, 61,* 80–84.

Kunda, Z. (1987). Motivated inference: Self-serving generation and evaluation of causal theories. *Journal of Personality and Social Psychology, 53,* 636–647.

Leggett, E. L. (1985). Children's entity and incremental theories of intelligence: Relationships to achievement behavior. Paper presented at the annual meeting of the Eastern Psychological Association, Boston, March 1985.

MacGyvers, V. L., & Dweck, C. S. (1994). Responses to the early adolescent transition: A test of a theoretical model of motivation. (submitted).

Markus, H. (1977). Self-schemata and processing information about the self. *Journal of Personality and Social Psychology, 35,* 63–78.

Markus, H., & Kunda, Z. (1986). Stability and malleability of the self-concept. *Journal of Personality and Social Psychology, 51,* 858–866.

Marsh, H. W. (1984). Self-concept: The application of a frame of reference model to explain paradoxical results. *Australian Journal of Education, 28,* 165–181.

Maxwell, S. E., & Delaney, H. D. (1993). Bivariate median splits and spurious statistical significance. *Psychological Bulletin, 113,* 181–190.

Midgley, C., & Feldlaufer, H. (1987). Students' and teachers' decision making fit before and after the transition to junior high school. *Journal of Early Adolescence, 7,* 225–241.

Murphy, G. L., & Medin, D. L. (1985). The role of theories in conceptual coherence. *Psychological Review, 92,* 289–316.

Neemann, J., & Harter, S. (1986). Manual for the self-perception profile for college students. Unpublished manuscript. Denver: University of Denver.

Pelham, B. W., & Swann, W. B. (1989). From self-conceptions to self-worth: On the sources and structure of global self-esteem. *Journal of Personality and Social Psychology, 57,* 672–680.

Piaget, J. (1972). *The psychology of intelligence.* Totowa, NJ: Littlefield Adams.

Purkey, W. W. (1970). *Self-concept and school achievement.* Englewood Cliffs, NJ: Prentice-Hall.

Rosenberg, M. (1965). *Society and the adolescent self-image.* Princeton, NJ: Princeton University Press.

Rosenberg, M. (1986). Self-concept from middle childhood through adolescence. In J. Suls & A. G. Greenwald (Eds.), *Psychological perspectives on the self,* Vol. 3 (pp. 107–136). Hillsdale, NJ: Erlbaum Associates.

Ross, M. (1989). Relation of implicit theories to the construction of personal histories. *Psychological Review, 96,* 341–357.

Scheirer, M. A., & Kraut, R. E. (1979). Increasing educational achievement via self concept change. *Review of Educational Research, 49,* 131–150.

Shavelson, R. J., & Bolus, R. (1982). Self-concept: The interplay of theory and methods. *Journal of Educational Psychology, 74,* 3–17.

Shell, D. F., Murphy, C. C., & Bruning, R. H. (1989). Self-efficacy and outcome expectancy mechanisms in reading and writing achievement. *Journal of Educational Psychology, 81,* 91–100.

Skaalvik, E. M., & Hagtvet, K. A. (1990). Academic achievement and self-concept: An analysis of causal predominance in a developmental perspective. *Journal of Personality and Social Psychology, 58,* 292–307.

Swann, W. B., Pelham, B. W., & Krull, D. S. (1989). Agreeable fancy or disagreeable truth? Reconciling self-enhancement and self-verification. *Journal of Personality and Social Psychology, 57,* 782–791.

Tesser, A. (1988). Toward a self-evaluation maintenance model of social behavior. In L. Berkowitz (Ed.), *Advances in experimental social psychology,* Vol. 21 (pp. 181–227). San Diego: Academic Press.

Tesser, A., Pilkington, C. J., & McIntosh, W. D. (1989). Self-evaluation maintenance and the mediational role of emotion: The perception of friends and strangers. *Journal of Personality and Social Psychology, 57,* 442–456.

Weiner, B. (1985). *Human motivation.* New York: Springer-Verlag.

Wittenbrink, B., Gist, P. L., & Hilton, J. L. (1993). The perceiver as alchemist: Conceptualization stereotypes as theories. Paper presented at the Fifth Annual Convention of the American Psychological Society, Chicago, June 1993.

Zhao, W., & Dweck, C. S. (1994). Implicit theories and vulnerability to depression-like responses. (submitted).

CHAPTER 10

NEED FOR CONTROL AND SELF-ESTEEM

TWO ROUTES TO A HIGH DESIRE FOR CONTROL

JERRY M. BURGER

INTRODUCTION

Personal control has been among the most ubiquitous topics in social and personality psychology for many years now. I recently thumbed through the tables of contents of several social psychology textbooks and could not find one chapter topic that researchers had not in some way tied to how much control people believe they have over events or the extent to which people are motivated to exercise personal control. Conformity, aggression, attitude change, gender roles, attributions, group dynamics, person perception, and the like all have been examined as a function of perceived control or motivation for control. Perhaps this ubiquity should come as no surprise. In any given situation, whether I believe I can control events or whether I want to control events intuitively is linked to the kind of action I decide to take.

One aspect of the research on personal control that I have been par-

JERRY M. BURGER • Department of Psychology, Santa Clara University, Santa Clara, California 95053.

Efficacy, Agency, and Self-Esteem, edited by Michael H. Kernis. Plenum Press, New York, 1995.

ticularly involved in concerns individual differences in what I call *desire for control*. As part of this work, I developed the Desirability of Control Scale to measure the extent to which people generally prefer to feel in control of important events in their lives (Burger & Cooper, 1979). People who score high on the scale like to make their own decisions, often seek out leadership roles, like to control their interactions with others, and typically are uncomfortable when confronted with important events they cannot influence. On the other end of this personality dimension are those low in desire for control. These people are more willing to relinquish responsibility to others, are not inclined toward leadership roles, are content to let others make decisions for them, and are better able than most people to tolerate uncontrollable and unpredictable events.

A few years ago, I reviewed all the research I could find that I and others had conducted with the Desirability of Control Scale (Burger, 1992). I found more than 100 studies tying individual differences in desire for control to a wide range of behaviors and personality variables. Scores on the scale were found to predict conformity behavior, reactions to crowding, health habits, achievement behavior, attributional activity, and gambling behavior, among others. I argued from these findings that the scale measures a very general, widely applicable need for control. A person high in desire for control is likely to express this need at the office, in relationships, on the tennis court, and when visiting his or her physician.

This chapter examines the relationship between desire for control and self-esteem. For now, I will limit my review and speculation to what is generally referred to as *global* self-esteem. Two questions will be addressed in this chapter. First, what is the relationship between desire for control and self-esteem? This question is relevant to a larger question concerning desire for control and well-being. Past studies suggest that the relationship is not a simple one. Although people with a high desire for control score lower on measures of anxiety than people with a low desire for control (Burger, 1992), on occasion they are *more* likely to respond to stressful events with increased arousal and temporarily high levels of anxiety (Braith, McCullough, & Bush, 1988; Hatton, Gilden, Edwards, Cutler, Kron, & McAnulty, 1989; Lawler, Schmied, Armstead, & Lacy, 1990). Whereas people with a high desire for control tend to use more effective coping strategies than lows (Burger, 1992), they also may be more susceptible to depression when confronted with uncontrollable events (Burger, 1984; Burger & Arkin, 1980). Thus, understanding the relationship between desire for control and self-esteem can provide a piece of the desire for control–well-being puzzle.

The second question concerns the developmental antecedents of desire for control, particularly as they relate to self-esteem. Until recently, very few data were available on the development of high and low desire for control, and there were no longitudinal studies examining changes in desire for control over time. I'll look at a few recent studies that address this issue. However, the data from these investigations already suggest that again no simple explanation is likely to be found when searching for the causes of a high desire for control.

DESIRE FOR CONTROL AND SELF-ESTEEM

There are several reasons to expect desire for control to be related to self-esteem (Burger, 1992). At first glance, descriptions of people with a high desire for control sound similar to descriptions of people with high self-esteem. Like those with high self-esteem, people with a high desire for control typically feel that they are capable, efficacious individuals. They are eager to demonstrate their mastery over challenging events and typically succeed in these efforts. They also are more likely than lows to be optimistic and intrinsically motivated. They believe they have the ability to handle themselves in most situations and to make the most of opportunities handed to them. In short, like people with high self-esteem, people with a high desire for control think well of themselves, at least in relation to control-relevant issues.

Although a case can be made for drawing the causal arrow between self-esteem and desire for control in either direction, for now suffice it to say that the two concepts most likely are intertwined. High self-esteem probably contributes to a high need for control, and a high need for control may contribute to high self-esteem.

The most obvious way to examine the relationship between desire for control and self-esteem is to look at correlations between individual difference measures. Enough studies have been conducted with the Desirability of Control Scale to provide two sets of relevant correlations for this analysis. First, several researchers have measured both desire for control and global self-esteem in the same population and report correlations between the two scores. Second, correlational data are available comparing desire for control scores with individual difference measures that are related to or are a component of self-esteem.

Correlations with Measures of Self-Esteem

I am aware of 13 studies that report correlations between scores on the Desirability of Control Scale and a measure of self-esteem. The data from these studies are shown in Table 1. As can be seen in the table, 10 of the

TABLE 1. Correlations between Desire for Control and Self-Esteem[a]

r	p	Subjects	Source
0.40	0.001	Undergraduates	Burger (unpublished)
0.27	0.01	Undergraduates	Daubman (1990)
0.45	0.01	Male teachers	Schonbach (1990)
0.54	0.01	Female teachers	Schonbach (1990)
0.21	0.10	Male college students	Schonbach (1990)
0.38	0.01	Female college students	Schonbach (1990)
0.26	0.01	Male high school students	Schonbach (1990)
0.50	0.01	Female high school students	Schonbach (1990)
0.20	0.05	Male college students	Schonbach (1990)
0.33	0.01	Female college students	Schonbach (1990)
0.38	0.01	Male adults	Schonbach (1990)
0.19	0.10	Female adults	Schonbach (1990)
0.49	0.001	Undergraduates	E. P. Thompson (1990)

[a]Because a high score on the scale used by Schonbach indicates low self-esteem, the direction of the correlations has been reversed here.

studies come from the work of Peter Schonbach using a German version of the scale. However, the most striking feature of the data is the consistency of the results. In every case, a positive correlation between desire for control and self-esteem is reported. Although most of the studies examined undergraduate college students, Schonbach finds the same relationship when examining a variety of populations.

To obtain a better idea of this relationship, I combined the results of the 13 studies reported in table 1 in a meta-analysis. First, a simple unweighted average of the 13 correlations produced an average correlation of 0.35. Next, a weighted combination of the 13 correlations produced an overall correlation of 0.34 with a combined sample size of 1022. Although there is always the danger that unreported correlations could reduce this effect—the "file drawer" problem (Rosenthal, 1979)—the size and the consistency of the findings argue strongly that scores on the Desirability of Control Scale reliably predict scores on self-esteem measures. People with a high desire for control tend to be high in self-esteem.

CORRELATIONS WITH MEASURES RELATED TO SELF-ESTEEM

Correlational data between desire for control and other individual difference measures also paint the picture we would expect if a high desire for control is related to high self-esteem. For example, Snyder and his colleagues have examined desire for control in their work on *hope* (Snyder, 1989; Snyder et al., 1989; Snyder et al., 1991). Snyder divides the hope concept into two components he calls *agency* and *planning*. The first component refers to a person's sense that he or she has met and will continue to meet important goals. The latter component refers to the sense that one has the opportunity and means to succeed in meeting these goals.

According to Snyder, hope represents an important process through which we develop and maintain a positive view of our self. Thus, hope is highly related to global self-esteem. In the same way that self-esteem is described, Snyder describes hope in terms of relatively stable individual differences and has developed two versions of a Hope Scale to measure this concept. When scores from these scales are compared with scores on the Desirability of Control Scale, the same pattern found with the self-esteem correlations is uncovered. Snyder (Snyder, 1989; Snyder et al., 1989, 1991) reports correlations between hope and desire for control that range from 0.45 to 0.54 for the overall hope score. Similarly, desire for control scores are highly correlated with the Agency ($r = 0.43$) and Pathways ($r = 0.49$) subscale scores (Snyder et al., 1989). These data argue that people with a high desire for control have a strong belief in their ability to know what they want and to go out and get it. They believe that they can set important goals and that they have the ability to reach those goals.

People with a high desire for control show a similar high self-esteem pattern on other individual difference measures. For example, a high desire for control is related to high levels of achievement motivation (Burger, 1992) and low levels of loneliness (Solano, 1987). People with a high desire for control tend to score high on the Deci and Ryan (1985) measure of self-determination (Burger, 1992). That is, these people tend to seek out opportunities to demonstrate their mastery over the environment. Similarly, people with a high desire for control consistently score lower on measures of trait anxiety. I am aware of ten reports of correlations between desire for control scores and scores on various anxiety scales (Burger, 1992). In each case, a high desire for control was indicative of low anxiety. In another study, I compared desire for control scores with scores on the Bradburn (1969) Affect Scales (Burger, 1992). The affect scales simply ask subjects how often they have experienced five positive emotions (e.g., proud of an accomplishment) and five negative emotions (e.g., loneliness) during the past few weeks. I found a strong positive relationship between desire for control and positive affect, $r = 0.40$, $p < 0.001$. However, there was no relationship between desire for control and negative affect, $r = -0.03$. People with a high desire for control tend to experience positive affect more often than lows, but neither group is more likely to experience negative affect.

In short, an examination of available correlational data indicates that a high desire for control is associated with high self-esteem. Researchers find that high scores on the Desirability of Control Scale not only consistently predict high scores on self-esteem measures, but also predict scores on other relevant measures consistent with the description of a high self-esteem individual.

TWO ROUTES TO A HIGH DESIRE FOR CONTROL

Many theorists have argued for the existence of an innate need to exercise control over significant events in one's life (cf. deCharms, 1968; White, 1959). Indeed, Rothbaum and Weisz (1989) have argued that this need for control takes many forms and presents many opportunities for growth as well as problems as children develop through childhood and adolescence. Nonetheless, research on desire for control makes it clear that there are individual differences in this need. Some people are highly motivated to exercise control over all aspects of their worlds, while other resign themselves to lives characteristic of helplessness and passivity. Where do these individual differences come from? While I do not deny that a biological component might be playing a role, I will argue that certain types of experiences go a long way in determining whether a person will have a high or low desire for control.

I propose that there are at least two developmental routes to a high desire for control. One of these routes, by far the more common, is associated with high self-esteem. As the preceding review suggests, there seems to be a consistent positive relationship between self-esteem and desire for control. Of course, these correlational data cannot tell us whether high self-esteem leads to a high desire for control or vice versa. However, the data certainly suggest that if the two concepts are causally related, typically it is *high* self-esteem that is associated with a high desire for control.

Nonetheless, I will argue that this simple relationship is only part of the picture. There may be another, more intriguing route to a high desire for control that comes by way of *low* self-esteem. Admittedly, data in support of this two-route model are skimpy at this point, and much of what follows is speculative. But some interesting findings from a few recent investigations hint strongly that there may be more than one way to alter a person's desire for control level.

THE HIGH SELF-ESTEEM ROUTE

Perhaps the most obvious explanation for the development of individual differences in desire for control maintains that a high desire for control reflects high self-esteem. According to this view, people with a high desire for control have had the opportunity to exercise control over significant events in their lives, probably during crucial periods in their development. A large experimental literature demonstrates that exercising control is desirable and rewarding in most cases (Burger, 1989). People who feel in control of events obtain a sense of mastery, a feeling that they are capable, responsible individuals. Along with control often comes the power to obtain what we want in a given situation. Consequently, people who feel in control can be optimistic that things are likely to turn out in the future as they wish them to. Successful experiences with the exercise of control lead to an appreciation of the benefits that come from exercising control and consequently to a higher desire to be in control of the important events in one's life. These efficacious feelings about oneself, of course, go hand in hand with high self-esteem.

From this high self-esteem perspective, what kind of environment might an individual with a high desire for control have experienced when growing up? We can imagine a home in which the child is allowed to express his or her needs for autonomy and control in an encouraging and reinforcing environment. At appropriate ages, parents allow the child to make decisions and to see the benefits that come from exercising responsibilities. Although too much responsibility can be anxiety-provoking and overwhelming at early ages, there are probably appropriate avenues for children to express their innate desire to manipulate the environment at all ages (Eccles, Buchanan, Flanagan, Fuligni, Midgley, & Yee, 1991; Rothbaum & Weisz, 1989).

Is one's level of desire for control set during childhood years? On the basis of some data presented later, I will argue that positive experiences with exercising control may alter the level of desire for control even in adulthood. Although the kinds of opportunities to express a need for control change with life circumstances, effective exercise of control may lead to a higher desire for control at any age.

What evidence is there to support this description? Naturally, the strongest indication that a high desire for control is related to high self-esteem comes from the correlational data presented earlier. However, data from a few additional investigations provide more direct evidence of the link between control-enhancing experiences and desire for control.

A recent set of findings by Eccles et al. (1991) supports the notion that encouragement from parents and practice at effective mastery of one's environment at an early age can lead to a high desire for control. These researchers examined early adolescents' desire for control over their educational experiences. They found an increase in desire for control as students moved from the 6th to the 7th grade. However, whether this translated into intrinsic motivation for schoolwork and higher self-esteem depended on how much autonomy the adolescents were given by their families. Eccles and her colleagues found that adolescents given an opportunity to participate in family decision making at home developed a higher level of interest in schoolwork and liked school more than those not given this opportunity by their parents. Moreover, the students who were allowed to participate in decision making showed an increase in self-esteem over the course of the study, whereas those who were denied this participation showed a decrease in self-esteem.

In short, the researchers found that allowing adolescents at this critical age to experience some control over their home environment appears to result in an increase in intrinsic motivation and higher self-esteem. I have argued elsewhere (Burger, 1992) that intrinsic motivation for schoolwork reflects a desire to exercise control over an important part of the person's life. Thus, the data of Eccles et al. (1991) argue strongly that early experiences with control seem to contribute to higher levels of desire for control and higher self-esteem.

This conclusion is further supported by two studies I have conducted directly measuring levels of desire for control in adults. The first of these is an exploratory study I conducted with Randall Husbands (Burger, 1992). We generated a list of 58 childhood experiences that we reasoned might be related to adult desire-for-control level. Some of these items were written to examine the role of parental encouragement and experiences with independence and decision making. Other items were written to examine the control-deprivation explanation of desire for control described later. Undergraduate subjects were asked to indicate on 9-point scales the extent to which each item described their experiences when they were between 6 and 12 years old. Because this was an exploratory study, we simply used a $p < 0.05$ confidence level and compared the items that the high and low desire-for-control subjects differed on.

Although a great deal of caution needs to be exercised in drawing conclusions from this kind of retrospective investigation, a relatively clear pattern of results emerged. Compared to the lows, subjects with a high desire for control were more likely to report that their parents encouraged them, took them places, and praised them for their extracurricular activities. The subjects with a high desire for control were also more likely to recall that they were accepted by and interacted with other children than did lows. On the other hand, the subjects with a low desire for control were more likely to report that their parents structured their day for them. These low desire-for-control subjects indicated that they often turned to their parents for help when working on projects (such as when working on puzzles or homework), rather than completing the projects on their own.

In short, the high and low desire-for-control students in this study seemed to describe different childhood experiences. The students with a high desire for control remembered parents who were encouraging, but who allowed them some degree of independence. The students with a low desire for control recalled a more dependent relationship with their parents, one in which the parents tended to make decisions for the child.

The second relevant set of findings comes from a recent longitudinal study I conducted with Cecilia Solano examining gender differences in desire for control (Burger & Solano, in press). Subjects in this investigation were students in an introductory psychology course attending a Southwestern liberal arts university in the fall of 1980. All subjects completed the Desirability of Control Scale. Consistent with other research at the time, we found that males had significantly higher desire-for-control scores than females. We contacted the subjects again 10 years later, in the fall of 1990. We were able to locate most of the subjects in the original sample through the university's alumni office, and 61.1% of those contacted completed and returned our questionnaire. Naturally, the questionnaire contained the Desirability of Control Scale. Thus, we were able to compare subjects' desire-for-control levels in 1990 with their scores from a decade earlier.

We found a great deal of consistency in desire for control for the male subjects. These subjects' 1980 scores correlated significantly with their 1990 scores, $r = 0.63$. Moreover, the average desire-for-control score for the males did not change significantly over the 10-year period. However, a completely different pattern was found for the females. The 1980 desire-for-control scores for these subjects were poor predictors of their 1990 scores, $r = 0.11$. Most important, the females' desire-for-control scores increased from an average of 97.57 in 1980 to 104.27 a decade later. By 1990, the males and females did not differ significantly on desire for control.

The findings from this study are particularly intriguing because they provide the only clear evidence to date of changes in desire for control over time. Why did the women in this sample increase in desire for control so dramatically during the decade of the 1980s? Of course, the nature of longitudinal research necessarily limits our ability to disentangle two possible sources for the effect. That is, one possibility is that the increase in desire for control reflects changes in women's roles during the decade of the 1980s. Gender roles changed, and women were encouraged to become more assertive and less dependent during these years. On the other hand, the increase in desire for control for the females in our sample may have been the result of experiences these women went through between the approximate ages of 20 and 30. Perhaps the experience of leaving home, going away to college, and beginning one's career contributed to the women's increased need to be independent and exercise control over important events in their lives.

We have argued that both changes in society and the challenging experiences of school and the workplace may have contributed to the increase in desire for control for the women in our study. But in either case, the data can be interpreted in support of the high self-esteem route to a high desire for control. That is, as the women encountered situations that required or encouraged them to exercise control, they responded to these demands and discovered the value in exercising control over the important events in their lives. Virtually every woman in our sample was career-bound. The women who approached the challenges inherent in most careers with a low desire for control probably ran into a number of difficulties. Dependence and nonassertiveness likely lead to ineffective management and job performance in many of the work environments the women encountered. Consistent with the earlier description, it is possible that many of these women learned to exercise control and discovered the advantages that come from exercising control over such situations. Certainly this is the message that many of these women received from various sources during this decade. Although we did not examine this in our study, I would speculate that the women who increased their level of desire for control during these years also experienced an increase in their self-esteem.

In sum, although relatively few studies have addressed the question of developmental antecedents and changes in desire for control, some of the available data are consistent with the notion that experience with effective exercise of control leads to an increase in one's desire for control and self-esteem.

THE LOW SELF-ESTEEM ROUTE

Although correlational data argue that most people with a high desire for control are also high in self-esteem, there may be a subgroup of people with a high desire for control who do not share this characteristic. This alternative interpretation has its roots in the writings of Alfred Adler. Adler described a central motivational construct in his theory of personality that he called *striving for superiority* (Adler, 1930; Ansbacher & Ansbacher, 1956). Although there are differences in the two descriptions, in general Adler's notion of striving for superiority is similar to the concept of motivation for control I have been working with. According to Adler, people are motivated to demonstrate their mastery over life's challenges. We constantly strive for the next level of achievement "by the attainment of which we shall feel strong, superior, and complete" [Adler (quoted in Ansbacher & Ansbacher, 1956, p. 104)].

Where does this striving for superiority come from? Adler's answer seems to contradict the link between desire for control and self-esteem established earlier, for according to Adler, people strive for superiority to avoid feelings of inferiority and helplessness rooted in childhood. The greater the inferiority experience, the stronger the need to demonstrate mastery and superiority. In other words, a high need for control does not reflect a pattern of reinforced exercise of control and a sense of well-being. Rather, a high need for control is born out of a sense of inferiority to those around us. According to this perspective, exercising control and setting and meeting high standards of achievement are efforts to fend off feelings of helplessness and uncontrollability.

If we apply Adler's thinking more directly to the desire-for-control construct, a case could be made that people with a high desire for control should be *low* in self-esteem. Of course, we know the data generally do not support this conclusion. Nonetheless, it is possible that *some* people with a high desire for control, probably a small percentage of those who score high on the scale, do fit the Adlerian description.

Who might these people be? Some possibilities are suggested from the observations of clinical psychologists working with special populations. For example, many psychologists have observed a high need for control among adult children of alcoholics (Brown, 1988; West & Prinz, 1987). In contrast with the encouraging and reinforcing environment described earlier, children growing up in alcoholic homes experience a great deal of chaos and unpredictability. The children may learn that they have little ability to influence events at home, particularly those associated with the parents' drinking. The children attempt to cope with the uncontrollability of events at home by exercising as much control over other aspects of their lives and other people in their lives as possible. Similar to the Adlerian analysis, clinicians argue that the high need for control that children develop from such experiences helps them deal with their feelings of vulnerability (Brown, 1988). Not surprisingly, researchers also find that children from such homes often suffer from low self-esteem (West & Prinz, 1987).

The high need for control among adult children of alcoholics often surfaces in their personal and romantic relationships. Clinicians report that these individuals typically try to control the behavior of their romantic partners. They may make all the important decisions in the relationship and may attempt to control how their partner dresses, acts, and so on (Brown, 1988). Needless to say, these efforts to exercise control often lead to relationship problems and an inability to sustain a romantic partnership.

Is there any evidence that a lack of control can result in an increase in a person's need for control? Although researchers often find that a perceived lack of personal control results in helplessness and passivity, reactions to a loss of personal control vary considerably as a function of a large number of personal and situational variables (cf. Burger, 1989; S. C. Thompson, Cheek, & Graham, 1987; Wortman & Brehm, 1975). At least in controlled laboratory experiments, subjects sometimes show an increase in their need for control when exposed to uncontrollable events.

However, evidence of changes in relatively stable levels of desire for control as a function of long-term and early experiences is not easy to find. Although clinicians often describe a high need for control in adult children of alcoholics, until recently few strong data were available to support these observations. Consequently, I examined the relationship between growing up in an alcoholic home and desire for control in a recent investigation (Burger, McCormack & Pinckert, 1994). We surveyed 181 undergraduates in this study. Past research indicates that a large percentage of college students come from homes in which one or more parent experienced a significant alcohol problem. Using several self-report criteria, we identified 34 students who seemed to fit the diagnosis of adult children of alcoholics. Students who clearly reported no alcohol problems in their homes as they were growing up served as the comparison group.

We compared students in both groups on their scores on the Desirability of Control Scale. Students from the homes with no alcohol problems had an average desire-for-control score very similar to that found in other college student samples. However, the adult children of alcoholics had significantly higher desire-for-control scores than the comparison group.

Although this finding is subject to a large number of interpretations and potential confounding variables, it is consistent with clinicians' observations about adult children of alcoholics and our description of the low self-esteem route to a high desire for control. This small but significant percentage of the population (18% of our sample) would appear to represent an important exception to the rule. The adult children of alcoholics probably did not develop a high desire for control because of opportunities to exercise control when they were growing up. Rather, it may have been the very lack of such experiences that led to their need for control.

Of course, not all children from alcoholic homes respond with a high desire for control. Some may react to these experiences with an increased sense of helplessness. This notion is also consistent with Adler's theorizing. According to Adler, some people respond to the threat of inferiority with increased efforts to demonstrate competence, while others fall into the classic inferiority complex. Certainly, identifying the variables responsible for this difference represents an important step in understanding the link between experiences with uncontrollability and desire for control.

The possibility that some people develop a high desire for control as a type of defensive reaction against experiences with uncontrollability and unpredictability leads to yet another speculation. It's possible that these individuals with a high desire for control express their need for control differently than those who come from the high self-esteem route. For example, people with a high desire for control from the high self-esteem route might express more confidence and trust when interacting with others than do people with a high desire for control from alcoholic homes. Past studies find that people with a high desire for control are sometimes assertive and even dominant when interacting with others, but are sometimes hesitant and cautious (Burger, 1990). Which of these interaction styles the person with a high desire for control typically relies on may be a function of which developmental route he or she experienced.

Although admittedly highly speculative, one recent study hints that there may be something to this notion. Addison (1992) looked at individual differences in desire for control among victims of child abuse. Like adult children of alcoholics, victims of child abuse grow up in homes that are chaotic and unpredictable. These victims also typically suffer from low self-esteem (Kendall-Tackett, Williams, & Finkelhor, 1993). We might expect, therefore, that many of these children would develop a high desire for control. However, unlike our data with adult children of alcoholics, Addison (1992) found no differences in desire-for-control levels when comparing victims and nonvictims. Thus, some of the victims developed a high desire for control (relative to nonvictims), but just as many did not.

However, an interesting pattern of results emerged when Addison examined correlations between desire for control and scores on the Rotter (1967) Interpersonal Trust Scale. There was a significant positive correlation between the two scales among the nonvictims ($r = 0.25$), indicating that a high desire for control was associated with high interpersonal trust. However, the opposite relationship was found among the victims ($r = -0.21$). That is, adults with a high desire for control who had not gone through the traumatic experiences the victims had experienced tended to hold a high degree of trust toward others. But the adults with a high desire for control who had experienced child abuse earlier in their lives tended to not trust others.

Although much more work needs to be done on this question before we can have confidence in drawing any strong conclusions, the findings of Addison (1992) are intriguing. Essentially, he has identified two kinds of people with a high desire for control. People with a high desire for control from nonvictim backgrounds are different from those who experienced victimization as children, at least in terms of interpersonal trust. Finally, although the number of people with a high desire for control who suffered from child abuse may not be large, one recent finding suggests that the untrusting person with a high desire for control may not be so uncommon. Fenigstein and Vanable (1992) found a positive correlation between desire for control and paranoia ($r = 0.29$). The high desire-for-control college students in this study were more likely than lows to engage in self-centered thought, suspiciousness, assumptions of ill will from others, and even conspiratorial intent.

Like the adult children of alcoholics data, Addison's findings with the victims of child abuse are subject to a large number of interpretations. Nonetheless, they are consistent with our speculation about the two routes to a high desire for control. This leads to a final bit of speculation. Perhaps future research can identify two distinctively different styles of expressing one's high desire for control, each reflecting a different developmental history. That is, it is possible that people with a high desire for control from the high self-esteem route satisfy their need for control through personal achievements, accepting leadership positions in groups, and taking responsibility for their own actions. In contrast, the lack of trust that may characterize people with a high desire for control from the low self-esteem route might lead to very different expressions of control. These people may inappropriately dominate their partner in relationships or maintain a sense of control through concealment and manipulation. In short, there are many ways to obtain a sense of control over the events in one's life. The way a person satisfies his or her need for control may very well reflect the reasons behind that need.

CONCLUSIONS

I addressed two questions in this chapter. First, what is the relationship between desire for control and self-esteem? From a simple correlational analysis, it seems clear that people high in desire for control typically are high in self-esteem. This finding addresses part of the larger question about desire for control and well-being. Combining the self-esteem data with the results of other investigations, it appears that a high desire for control in most cases is part of a good sense of well-being. Although on occasion they may experience more frustrations and anxieties than lows, people with a high desire for control in general are happier, healthier, and more achieving than the average person. Most people with a high desire for control feel good about themselves, and their desire to express control probably stems in part from this high self-esteem.

However, there may be some important exceptions to this pattern. This cautious note is reflected in the answer to the second question I addressed in this chapter concerning the causes of individual differences in desire for control. Although definitive studies assessing desire for control and self-esteem over time have yet to be conducted, there is some evidence that two people with a high desire for control can come from two very different developmental histories. Sometimes a high desire for control indicates a belief in oneself, a sense of mastery, and a desire to express one's sense of personal efficacy. This desire for control comes through what I am calling the high self-esteem route. But sometimes a high desire for control tells another developmental story. Sometimes a high need for control may be an effort to cope with a fear of uncontrollability. This desire for control reflects a lack of confidence in oneself and perhaps a poor sense of personal efficacy. This is the low self-esteem route to a high desire for control. A better understanding of the low self-esteem route may be especially relevant for clinicians working with specific populations, such as adult children of alcoholics and victims of child abuse.

REFERENCES

Addison, J. R. (1992). Perceptions of control and responsibility as factors in the revictimization of adult survivors of childhood sexual abuse. Unpublished doctoral dissertation. London: Oxford University.

Adler, A. (1930). Individual psychology. In C. Murchison (Ed.), *Psychologies of 1930* (pp. 138–165). Worcester, MA: Clark University Press.

Ansbacher, H. L., & Ansbacher, R. R. (Eds.) (1956). *The individual psychology of Alfred Adler*. New York: Basic Books.

Bradburn, N. (1969). *The structure of psychological well-being*. Chicago: Aldine.

Braith, J. A., McCullough, J. P., & Bush, J. P. (1988). Relaxation-induced anxiety in a subclinical sample of chronically anxious subjects. *Journal of Behavior Therapy and Experimental Psychiatry, 19*, 193–198.

Brown, S. (1988). *Treating adult children of alcoholics: A developmental perspective*. New York: John Wiley.

Burger, J. M. (1984). Desire for control, locus of control and proneness to depression. *Journal of Personality, 52*, 71–89.

Burger, J. M. (1989). Negative reactions to increases in perceived personal control. *Journal of Personality and Social Psychology, 56*, 246–256.

Burger, J. M. (1990). Desire for control and interpersonal interaction style. *Journal of Research in Personality, 24*, 32–44.

Burger, J. M. (1992). *Desire for control: Personality, social and clinical perspectives*. New York: Plenum Press.

Burger, J. M., & Arkin, R. M. (1980). Prediction, control and learned helplessness. *Journal of Personality and Social Psychology, 38*, 482–491.

Burger, J. M., & Cooper, H. M. (1979). The desirability of control. *Motivation and Emotion, 3*, 381–393.

Burger, J. M., McCormack, W. A., & Pinckert, S. (1984, April). Desire for control and adult children of alcoholics. Paper presented at the annual meeting of the Western Psychological Association, Kona, HI.

Burger, J. M., & Solano, C. H. (in press). Gender differences in desire for control: A ten-year longitudinal study. *Sex Roles*.

Daubman, K. A. (1990). The self-threat of receiving help: A comparison of the threat-to-self-esteem model and the threat-to-interpersonal-power model. Unpublished manuscript. Gettysburg, PA: Gettysburg College.

deCharms, R. (1968). *Personal causation: The internal affective determinants of behavior*. New York: Academic Press.

Deci, E. L., & Ryan, R. M. (1985). The general causality orientation scale: Self determination in personality. *Journal of Research in Personality, 19*, 109–134.

Eccles, J. S., Buchanan, C. M., Flanagan, C., Fuligni, A., Midgley, C., & Yee, D. (1991). Control versus autonomy during early adolescence. *Journal of Social Issues, 47*, 53–68.

Fenigstein, A., & Vanable, P. A. (1992). Paranoia and self-consciousness. *Journal of Personality and Social Psychology, 62*, 129–138.

Hatton, D. C., Gilden, E. R., Edwards, J., Cutler, J., Kron, J., & McAnulty, J. H. (1989). Psychophysiological factors in ventricular arrhythmias and sudden cardiac death. *Journal of Psychosomatic Research, 33*, 621–631.

Kendall-Tackett, K. A., Williams, L. M., & Finkelhor, D. (1993). Impact of sexual abuse on children: A review and synthesis of recent empirical studies. *Psychological Bulletin, 113*, 164–180.

Lawler, K. A., Schmeid, L. A., Armstead, C. A., & Lacy, J. E. (1990). Type A behavior, desire for control, and cardiovascular reactivity in young adult women. *Journal of Social Behavior and Personality, 5*, 135–158.

Rosenthal, R. (1979). The "file drawer problem" and tolerance for null results. *Psychological Bulletin, 86*, 638–641.

Rothbaum, F., & Weisz, J. R. (1989). *Child psychopathology and the quest for control*. Newbury Park, CA: Sage.

Rotter, J. B. (1967). A new scale for the measurement of interpersonal trust. *Journal of Personality, 35*, 651–665.

Schonbach, P. (1990). *Account episodes: The management of escalation of conflict*. Cambridge, U.K.: Cambridge University Press.

Snyder, C. R. (1989). Reality negotiation: From excuses to hope and beyond. *Journal of Social and Clinical Psychology, 8*, 130–157.

Snyder, C. R., Harris, C., Anderson, J. R., Gibb, J., Yoshinobu, L., Langelle, C., Harney, P., Holleran, S., & Irving, L. M. (1989). The development and validation of an individual difference measure of hope. Paper presented at the annual meeting of the American Psychological Association, New Orleans.

Snyder, C. R., Harris, C., Anderson, J. R., Holleran, S. A., Irving, L. M., Sigmon, S. T., Yoshinobu, L., Gibb, J., Langelle, C., & Harney, P. (1991). The will and the ways: Development and validation of an individual-differences measure of hope. *Journal of Personality and Social Psychology, 60*, 570–585.

Solano, C. H. (1987). Loneliness and perceptions of control: General traits versus specific attributions. *Journal of Social Behavior and Personality, 2*, 201–214.

Thompson, E. P. (1990). Individual difference moderators of extrinsic reward effects: A person × situation approach to the study of intrinsic motivation processes. Unpublished master's thesis. New York: New York University.

Thompson, S. C., Cheek, P. R., & Graham, M. A. (1987). The other side of perceived control:

Disadvantages and negative effects. In S. Spacapan & S. Oskamp (Eds.), *The social psychology of health* (pp. 69–93). Newbury Park, CA: Sage.

West, M. O., & Prinz, R. J. (1987). Parental alcoholism and childhood psychopathology. *Psychological Bulletin, 102,* 204–218.

White, R. (1959). Motivation reconsidered: The concept of competence. *Psychological review, 66,* 297–330.

Wortman, C. B., & Brehm, J. W. (1975). Responses to uncontrollable outcomes: An integration of reactance theory and the learned helplessness model. In L. Berkowitz (Ed.), *Advances in experimental social psychology,* Vol. 8 (pp. 277–336). New York: Academic Press.

PART III

CONCLUSION

CHAPTER 11

EFFICACY, AGENCY, AND SELF-ESTEEM

EMERGING THEMES AND FUTURE DIRECTIONS

MICHAEL H. KERNIS

INTRODUCTION

A perusal of the self-esteem literature will reveal an abundance of research that focuses on the differences between low and high self-esteem individuals with respect to their perceptions of and reactions to positive and negative events. Questions that have received considerable attention over the years include these: Do high self-esteem persons self-enhance in response to positive events and self-protect in response to threatening events more than do low self-esteem persons? Are there self-esteem differences in the tendency to seek out positive vs. negative self-relevant information or to embrace positive or negative self-aspects? Such questions are important and deserving of the attention that they have received. Unfortunately, however, the emphasis on them has left some gaps in our understanding of self-esteem processes. It is hoped that the diversity of issues addressed in this volume will foster an expansion of the types of questions focused

MICHAEL H. KERNIS • Department of Psychology and Institute for Behavioral Research, University of Georgia, Athens, Georgia 30602.

Efficacy, Agency, and Self-Esteem, edited by Michael H. Kernis. Plenum Press, New York, 1995.

on by people who are interested in self-esteem. Though time will tell how successful this endeavor has been, my experience editing this book has convinced me more than ever that such expansion is both necessary and viable.

In this chapter, I will briefly discuss some of the major issues pertaining to self-esteem that were raised by the contributors to this volume, examine commonalities and differences in how these issues were dealt with, and suggest some agendas for future research. It is not my intention to provide an exhaustive or definitive summary of the contents of this volume. Rather, I want to point out some interesting and provocative issues that I hope will stimulate further thought and research.

EMBEDDING THE CONSTRUCT OF SELF-ESTEEM WITHIN BROAD THEORETICAL FRAMEWORKS

Self-esteem research and theory often seem to develop in isolation from other important psychological characteristics. As noted explicitly by Epstein and Morling in Chapter 1, much can be gained from integrating the role of self-esteem into broad theoretical perspectives on personality and motivation. Fortunately, several contributors to this volume do so. In this section, I will briefly summarize these perspectives and their relevance to self-esteem related issues.

To quote Epstein and Morling in their discussion of the role of self-esteem from the perspective of Cognitive–Experiential Self-Theory (CEST). "According to CEST, people's personalities are best understood in terms of their implicit theories of reality, which consist of self-theories, world-theories, and connecting schemata." These theories are grounded in four basic human needs, accompanied by networks of four basic, implicit beliefs: (1) to maximize pleasure and minimize pain; (2) to develop and maintain a positive self-view; (3) to achieve a coherent, stable conceptual system; and (4) to establish meaningful relationships with others. According to CEST, none of these needs takes precedence over any other, and in fact, behavior (and reactions in general) are viewed as reflecting compromises among them. Optimal psychological functioning is achieved through the synergistic fulfillment of all these needs. If one need predominates over others, fulfillment of it is likely to be at the expense of fulfillment of the others.

These assertions have very important implications for our understanding of self-esteem processes. That is, behaviors and responses are often examined with regard to how they fulfill people's self-esteem needs (or needs for a coherent self-system) without regard to how they may affect other needs, particularly the need for relatedness. As noted by Tennen and Affleck (1993), some responses attributed to high self-esteem individuals (e.g., derogation of others following threat, self-enhancing and self-protective attributional styles) can undermine the integrity of one's relationships with others. Is it so important for high self-esteem individuals to feel good about themselves that they will sacrifice their relations with others in the process? Research reported by Epstein and Morling suggests that the answer to this question is no. Moreover, the chapters by Beach and Tesser and by Leary and Downs (which I discuss later) focus on the interdependencies of self-esteem and relatedness needs. These are all exciting developments. One can hope that they will stimulate sustained efforts to examine the boundary conditions that surround people's satisfaction of their self-esteem needs, as well as how people negotiate the complexity of fulfilling multiple needs (for examples pertaining to the interplay of self-enhancement and self-verification needs, see Swann, 1990; Swann, Hixon, Stein-Seroussi, & Gilbert, 1990).

Another important aspect of CEST is the delineation of two qualitatively different conceptual systems for processing information: a logical, rational system that operates in a deliberative manner and an experiential, affectively based system that operates more automatically. Self-esteem is a component of each system, which Epstein and Morling refer to as *explicit* and *implicit* self-esteem, respectively. Explicit self-esteem is directly accessible through self-reports, whereas implicit self-esteem can only be inferred through behaviors and emotional reactions. Though these two forms of self-esteem may converge, the more interesting cases involve instances in which they do not. As Epstein and Morling put it: "We are all aware of people who profess a positive self-evaluation and attempt to impress others with their superiority, yet demonstrate in their behavior and emotional reactions that they are defensive, insecure, and lacking in confidence, all hallmarks of low implicit self-esteem." I return to this issue of the multifaceted nature of self-esteem shortly.

In Chapter 2, Deci and Ryan also take a need-based approach to self-esteem, though in their framework, self-esteem is not given the status of a need in its own right. Rather, from their organismic perspective, self-esteem derives from the extent to which one "acts agentically within a context that allows satisfaction of the three fundamental psychological needs for autonomy, competence, and relatedness . . . ." Central to their perspective is the concept of self, which, through the "organismic integration process," is constantly elaborated and refined: "Behavior that emanates from one's integrated sense of self is said to be autonomous or self-determined . . . . As one behaves autonomously . . . the behavior promotes further development of self and a stronger sense of true self-worth."

Also critical to their theory is an exposition of various motivational and self-regulatory processes, some of which are associated with self-determination and the integrated self and others of which are not. Specifically, Deci and Ryan argue that self-regulatory processes vary along a continuum reflecting the extent to which they are autonomous (and reflective of the self) or controlled by some force emanating from outside the self (although perhaps intrapsychically). Intrinsically motivated activities constitute the prototype of autonomously regulated actions. Extrinsically motivated activities can be completely controlled through external contingencies, regulated through the operation of introjects (i.e., powerful controls that are intrapersonal, but external to one's sense of self), identified with and accepted as personally important, or successfully integrated into one's coherent sense of self. According to Deci and Ryan, self-esteem that is based on autonomous (i.e., intrinsically motivated) or integrated self-regulation will be associated with true self-esteem that is stable, secure, and does not need constant validation. In contrast, self-esteem that is based on introjected self-regulation will have a more tenuous and pressured quality, as the person will seek continual validation either by matching standards of excellence or by living up to his or her own or others' expectations. True high self-esteem will be associated with positive mental health, whereas contingent high self-esteem may not be, and in fact may be related to negative psychological outcomes. Deci and Ryan make it clear that our understanding of self-esteem can be substantially enhanced by linking it to motivational and self-regulatory processes that themselves are related to psychological health and well-being.

An important counterpoint to Deci and Ryan's theorizing is that of Greenberg, Pyszczynski, and Solomon in Chapter 4. Rather than grounding self-esteem in "growth-oriented motivation," Greenberg and colleagues explicate the defensive-oriented nature of self-esteem from the perspective of their Terror Management Theory. Briefly, Terror Management Theory holds that as a consequence of possessing considerable intelligence and the capacity to anticipate the future, humans are acutely aware of their own fragility and mortality. This awareness, if left unmanaged, would create such intense anxiety that people would be essentially paralyzed. Through the development of cultural worldviews that provide the opportunity for actual or symbolic immortality, people can minimize their potential for experiencing such debilitating terror. For anxiety to be successfully minimized, however, people must believe that they are valuable contributors to their accepted worldview. From the perspective of Terror Management Theory, the extent to which people believe that they are valuable contributors to their worldview provides the basis for self-esteem. Self-esteem is defensive, then, in the sense that it ultimately derives from existential anxiety. Importantly, Greenberg and colleagues assert that it is the *appearance* of being competent (to self and others) and thus a valuable contributor, rather than competence itself, that is more critical within this system. As they suggest, such concerns with appearing competent and valuable give rise to a variety of self-deceptive and self-protective distortions, as well as self-presentational strategies.

In their current formulation described in Chapter 4, they allow for the operation of growth-oriented motivation akin to Deci and Ryan's notion of intrinsic motivation. Guided by the writings of Otto Rank, Greenberg and colleagues theorize that human behavior can be accounted for by the complex interplay of these dual motives—one that is defensive, symbolic, and geared toward preservation of the me (the self as known) and another that is expansive, direct, and geared toward the enrichment of the I (self as knower). What accounts for the relative prepotency of these two motives? Importantly, Greenberg and colleagues suggest that the defensive motive system is generally prepotent. Thus, if people are having difficulty maintaining their faith in a meaningful cultural worldview or their sense of value within it, much of their behavior will be geared toward restoring these things, rather than toward satisfaction of their enrichment or growth-oriented strivings. However, life-styles that provide ample opportunities for enrichment concerns to be satisfied may, at least temporarily, reduce the influence of defensive, anxiety-reducing concerns. Greenberg and colleagues suggest that, somewhat ironically, this relief from terror is tenuous and that it may merely reflect a defensive form of distraction, rather than true growth-oriented concerns. Thus, they argue that the notion of an individual wholly concerned with expansive concerns, completely free of fears and anxieties, is impossible, and perhaps not even desirable.

In this new dual-motive conceptualization, self-esteem may take on qualities not previously recognized within the terror management perspective. In the words of Greenberg and colleagues: "Whereas self-esteem concerns serve the minimization of negative affect and anxiety, enrichment motives serve a sense of mastery and positive affect." [Enrichment concerns can] ". . . lead to behaviors and accomplishments that, as a by-product, ultimately enhance self-esteem. Indeed, by encouraging the acquisition of skills and creative achievement, such activities may, ironically, provide a more durable basis of self-esteem—more stable high self-esteem in Kernis et al.'s (1992) terms—than activities specifically guided by self-esteem needs."

These three perspectives obviously differ from one another in many respects. What they have in common, though, is that each shows the value of linking self-esteem to other motivational and personality processes. Together, they provide a wealth of empirical and conceptual issues worthy of further consideration—for example, the interplay of self-esteem with other basic needs, the need to consider both conscious and unconscious feelings of self-worth, how self-esteem relates to self-regulatory processes that in turn are associated with psychological well-being, and defensive vs. proactive processes that are associated with self-esteem. Interestingly, in raising these issues, each set of authors concluded that the construct of self-esteem itself may be multifaceted. It is to this issue that I now turn.

SELF-ESTEEM IS MULTIFACETED

A number of chapters in this volume focus on the notion that self-esteem is not necessarily a unitary construct. As noted already, Epstein and Morling distinguish between explicit and implicit self-esteem, Deci and Ryan distinguish between true and contingent self-esteem, and Greenberg and colleagues distinguish between self-esteem that is based entirely in defensive concerns and self-esteem that emerges as a by-product of "growth-oriented" concerns. In addition, Greenier, Kernis, and Waschull (Chapter 3) distinguish between self-esteem that is stable or unstable, and Leary and Downs (Chapter 6) distinguish between state and trait forms of self-esteem. Two related themes can be discerned from these various discussions. The first theme is that how people respond to traditional trait measures of self-esteem may not give us the full picture of the role of self-esteem in psychological functioning and well-being. The second theme is that to achieve a full understanding of self-esteem processes, we must consider factors other than the positivity of one's chronic and conscious self-feelings. Note that these themes are not without historical precedent in the clinical as well as the personality/social psychology literatures. Horney (1950), for example, differentiated between true and defensive high self-esteem. More recently, Rosenberg (1986) differentiated between baseline self-esteem (relatively stable, chronic self-feelings) and barometric self-esteem (short-term, contextually based fluctuations) (for a summary of other related work, see Tennen and Affleck, 1993).

At best, people's responses to standard trait measures of self-esteem inform us about the self-feelings that they are consciously aware of. At worst, they tell us nothing more than the self-feelings that respondents want other people to know about. In either case, Epstein and Morling assert that these deliberate, explicit self-feelings may be less informative about people than are their more automatic, implicit self-feelings. In addition, Epstein and Morling suggest that defensiveness may be especially intense when explicit self-feelings are favorable, but implicit self-feelings are negative. This point of view bears some similarity to earlier conceptualizations of defensive high self-esteem. Where it differs in important ways is how to assess "defensiveness." Traditionally, defensiveness is assessed through responses to a measure of socially desirable responding. The rationale for this is that people with defensive high self-esteem possess deep-seated negative self-feelings, but because of strong approval motives, they are unwilling to report them on a self-esteem scale. However, according to Epstein and Morling, implicit self-esteem is not implicit because people are unwilling to report on it, but because they essentially are unable to do so. Thus, use of a measure of socially desirable responding that taps approval motives is generally unlikely to be successful in tapping implicit self-esteem. Recently, however, Paulhus (e.g., Paulhus, 1991) has distinguished between two types of socially desirable responding: impression management and self-deceptive positivity. The former reflects attempts to foster a favorable impression in others, whereas the latter refers to honest, but overly positive, responses (see Linden, Paulhus, & Dobson, 1986; Paulhus and Reid, 1992). These overly positive responses may reflect attempts on the part of the cognitive system to deal with the potential spillover of implicit negative self-feelings. Though measurement of self-deceptive positivity is cognitively based, it may be useful in delineating the interplay of explicit and implicit self-esteem, especially if used along with other techniques suggested by Epstein and Morling to measure implicit self-esteem.

Epstein and Morling's notion of high explicit/low implicit self-esteem differs from both Deci and Ryan's description of contingent high self-esteem and Greenier and colleagues' description of unstable high self-esteem. Contingent and unstable high self-esteem each imply fragility in one's feelings of self-worth, not negativity per se. That is, as long as expectations or standards of performance are met successfully, favorable feedback is received, or positive self-relevant information is activated, self-feelings will be positive. Yet even in these circumstances, these feelings will have a tenuous if not pressured quality, as they need constant nourishment. As with high explicit/low implicit self-esteem, threats will not be taken lightly, and when they are encountered, defensiveness and other self-protective or self-deceptive processes will be instantiated. Note that in all three perspectives, it is not high self-esteem per se that promotes defensiveness or self-aggrandizement. Instead, it is some weakness in the basic foundation of high self-esteem (Deci and Ryan, Greenier and colleagues) or accompanying nonconscious negative self-feelings (Epstein and Morling) that is critical.

Although contingent and unstable high self-esteem presumably share some features (i.e., heightened ego-involvement), direct empirical verification that they are tapping into the same motivational processes is lacking at this point in time. Interestingly, Greenier and colleagues suggest in

Chapter 3 that there may be additional factors that promote unstable self-esteem, perhaps especially among individuals with low self-esteem. Specifically, unstable (perhaps especially low) self-esteem may be linked to such self-concept qualities as lack of clarity (Campbell, 1990) or certainty (Baumgardner, 1990).

Contingent high self-esteem appears to bear some similarity to the Type A coronary-prone behavior pattern, in that both may be associated with being driven to constantly achieve high standards of excellence. Perhaps one reason that people with contingent high self-esteem are so driven is that they are acutely aware that their self-feelings ebb and flow with every success and failure. Interestingly, research by Kernis, Grannemann, and Barclay (1992) suggests that people may not be aware of how stable or unstable their self-esteem is. Rather, people with unstable self-esteem may be confused or lack clarity with regard to their self-feelings or self-concepts, which (apart from, or in combination with, heightened ego-involvement) results in contextually based fluctuations. If unstable self-esteem is associated with such confusion, there may be instances (i.e., extremely unstable self-esteem) in which it is associated with psychological disorders such as borderline personality. Furthermore, Kernis (1993) reported that self-esteem instability is correlated with higher scores on the Affect Intensity Measure [$r = 0.29$ (Larsen, 1984)]. People who score high on this measure tend to experience both positive and negative emotions more intensely than do people who score low. Thus, it may also be fruitful to examine the extent to which unstable self-esteem is related to affective disorders, in particular manic–depression. More generally, the extent to which contingent, unstable, and implicit self-esteem are related to clinically relevant phenomena (as well as to each other) is a highly fertile area for theoretical and empirical development.

SELF-ESTEEM IN CONTEXT: SELF-EVALUATION MAINTENANCE AND STATE SELF-ESTEEM

Another broad theme that emerged is that a full understanding of self-esteem processes will necessitate greater consideration of factors that are reciprocally related to the ebb and flow of both contextually based (i.e., state) and trait self-esteem. More specifically, several contributors addressed how achievement and relationship maintenance concerns can directly and indirectly affect both state and trait self-esteem.

Leary and Downs, for example, provide in Chapter 6 considerable evidence for the intriguing assertion that state self-esteem functions as a sociometer that is sensitive to cues of social exclusion. For example, events that people think will raise or lower their feelings of self-worth the most are precisely those events that are most likely to lead to their rejection by other people. Moreover, actual exclusion or rejection by a group or an individual reduced state self-esteem. Leary and Downs emphasize that the function of the sociometer is primarily aimed at avoiding exclusion rather than enhancing inclusion. In other words, they suggest that state self-esteem is more sensitive to instances of social rejection than it is to instances of social acceptance. As an aside, this assertion may provide a basis for integrating Leary and Down's perspective with that of Greenberg and colleagues, discussed earlier. That is, behaviors that are most likely to lead to social rejection may also be those that violate people's cultural world-views (as represented in consensually validated behaviors). In some cultures (if not at present, at least in our evolutionary past), the most severe forms of social exclusion result in the rejectee's demise. An interesting question, then, is the extent to which social exclusion increases the salience of one's mortality. [For more comprehensive statements pertaining to the (in)compatibility of the social exclusion and terror management perspectives, see Baumeister & Tice (1990) and Greenberg, Pyszczynski, & Solomon (1990).]

Leary and Downs also focus on cases in which the sociometer "malfunctions." Sociometers may be calibrated at too high a level (so that the person is not sensitive enough to social-exclusion cues) or too low a level (so that the person is hypersensitive to such cues), or they may be unreliable (and produce changes in self-esteem "that are only loosely contingent on changes in the social environment"). An important direction for future work is to examine directly how the quality of peoples' "sociometers" relates to individual differences in contextually based fluctuations in global self-esteem (i.e., stable or contingent self-esteem). Also, attachment and object relations perspectives should serve as sources for additional insights into the functioning of the sociometer.

In Chapter 8, Harlow and Cantor also argue for the importance of examining state fluctuations in self-esteem, particularly as they relate to people's negotiations of various life tasks. However, from their vantage point, people's judgments of task-relevant competence or self-doubt are even more important. They show that people who are uncertain (but not negative) about their academic competence, but for whom successful academic performance is important, are likely to bring achievement concerns into otherwise social situations. The portrait of these "outcome-focused" individuals is one of ego-involved individuals whose social lives are tainted by academically related reassurance-seeking behaviors in social settings. Are they also individuals who possess unstable or contingent self-esteem? My guess would be that they are, but this is a question that awaits additional research.

In any event, life tasks are typically interdependent, and self-doubts in one domain can have substantial implications for satisfaction in another domain. To discover these repercussions, with regard to both task satisfaction and overall well-being, Harlow and Cantor note that "it is essential to understand the full profile of an individual's self-perceived competence, over time and across life-task pursuits." These same challenges face self-esteem researchers. That is, to fully understand the role of self-esteem in psychological well-being, we must better understand the ongoing reciprocal relations among life-task pursuits, self-perceived competence related to these life tasks, and global self-esteem. More generally, contextual factors that relate to variations in self-esteem deserve considerably more attention than they have received to date. Isolated efforts in this regard do exist, however. For example, Wells (1988) studied the self-esteem of mothers in various contexts, with and without their children present. She reported that overall, mothers had higher self-esteem in contexts that did not include their children. In future research, it would be interesting to examine whether life-task appraisals (of the task "raising children"), or the strategies employed to negotiate this task, would predict how much women's self-esteem diminished when in the presence of their children.

In Chapter 7, on self-evaluation maintenance (SEM) processes in close relationships, Beach and Tesser treat self-esteem as a set of processes rather than as an individual difference variable. In fact, Beach and Tesser suggest that high and low self-esteem individuals may not differ in their tendencies to employ SEM processes. Rather, they emphasize how SEM processes within the context of close relationships can either directly or indirectly affect one's global self-esteem. Beach and Tesser note that competence in domains of high importance to the self is an important building block of global self-esteem and that SEM processes serve, in part, to protect the perception of competence in domains of high importance. From the perspective of the individual (and the original SEM model), displaying competence (and maintaining favorable self-evaluations) need not be tempered by interpersonal considerations. However, as described in the extended SEM model, people in close relationships respond not only to their own performances, but also to their partners' performances. A number of important implications follow from this insight. For example, Beach and Tesser suggest that within close relationships, SEM processes invoke considerable pressures for each partner to develop unique areas of competence and expertise. In so doing, one or both partners may need to change the domains in which they claimed competence prior to the development of the relationship. If both partners enter the relationship as expert gardeners, for example, pressures from SEM processes may compel the couple to jointly define one partner as the "gardener," to create sub-areas of gardening within which each can claim competence, or to share gardening so thoroughly that comparisons are impossible. Alternatively, one partner may continually allow a partner to outperform him or her in an important domain, especially if the domain is also important to the partner. Over time, such strategic failures (cf. Baumgardner & Brownlee, 1987) may undermine one's global self-esteem. On the more positive side, partners may convince one another to develop new areas of expertise, resulting in the taking on of additional self-definitions. To the extent that one is competent in these new self-definitional roles, the building blocks of global self-esteem may be fortified. To summarize their view on these matters, Beach and Tesser state that "... close relationships should provide a context in which the self-definition can be either enriched or impoverished. The pressure to change self-definition, change relative performance, or adopt new self-definitions should not be directly related to global self-esteem in the short term, but these processes might well shape the constituent elements of global self-esteem, and so become related to global self-esteem over the longer term or in interaction with other factors." In short, understanding the ebb and flow of self-esteem will require consideration of people's performances (and the importance accorded to them) within the context of their close relationships.

One question that can be raised is whether "outcome-focused" individuals (Chapter 8) are attuned to SEM processes in their choice of people from whom they seek reassurance. From an SEM perspective, such individuals may be viewed as having the comparison process chronically activated in academically relevant contexts. Do they then seek reassurance from people whom they outperform or who do not view the life-task domain as being as important as they do? While this question cannot be answered definitively, Harlow and Cantor do report that outcome-focused people are more likely to seek out non-outcome-focused people for reassurance. In so doing, outcome-focused individuals can avoid the potential conflicts that could arise from having to take into consideration their (similarly "stressed out") partner's perspective. That is, if the people from whom they seek reassurance are also insecure and ego-involved in achievement settings, they would have to deal not only with their own insecurities, but also with their partner's. Thus, it seems plausible that outcome-focused individuals may be especially sensitive to the type of SEM processes (in particular, the comparison process) described by Beach and Tesser.

There are numerous differences among the frameworks presented by Leary and Downs, Harlow and Cantor, and Beach and Tesser. These differences should not be overlooked, for they illuminate unique aspects of the relations between global self-esteem, competence and self-doubts, and relationship dynamics. Nonetheless, they do share a common and important focus on contextual and interpersonal factors that warrant substantial attention in the years to come.

COGNITIVE FACTORS

Both Showers (Chapter 5) and Hong, Chiu, and Dweck (Chapter 9) discuss cognitive factors that have implications for self-esteem processes. Showers argues that above and beyond the content of one's self-beliefs, how these beliefs are organized has important implications for one's reactions to evaluative events and for one's global feelings of self-worth. Positive-compartmentalized self-knowledge (PC) refers to possessing sets of self-beliefs that are all or mostly positive, important, and frequently activated. PC is thought to relate to especially favorable reactions to positive events, as well as to more positive global self-esteem. Conversely, negative-compartmentalized self-knowledge (NC) refers to possessing sets of self-beliefs that are all or mostly negative, important, and frequently activated. NC is hypothesized to relate to especially adverse reactions to negative events and to lower global self-esteem. Evaluatively integrated self-knowledge (EI) involves sets of self-beliefs that contain a mixture of positive and negative information. This type of organization is proposed to minimize the impact of both positive and negative self-relevant events.

Interestingly, evaluative organization may have implications for the influence of self-evaluation maintenance processes on global self-esteem. For example, being continually outperformed by one's partner on an important dimension may have less dire consequences for individuals with either PC or EI organization than for individuals with NC organization. Furthermore, the partner's evaluative organization of self-knowledge may either accentuate or diminish the extent to which the partner's point of view (with regard to relative performance and relevance) is taken into account. For example, one may acquiesce much more readily to being outperformed by one's partner on a mutually important dimension if the partner is known (or thought) to be NC rather than PC. Such knowledge may be fairly common (though perhaps more implicit than explicit) among people in close relationships because of the mutual sharing of reactions to evaluative events that is likely to take place. If this type of acquiescence continues over a long time period, one's own self-esteem may suffer through some of the processes described by Beach and Tesser.

Evaluative organization of self-knowledge also may be involved in the relation between self-doubt and life-task negotiation (as described by Harlow and Cantor). Life tasks that are associated with NC may be those in which people avoid or use ineffective strategies, those associated with PC may be associated with optimal functioning, and those with EI may be associated with various compensatory strategies like reassurance-seeking or defensive pessimism. In addition, perhaps the comparability of evaluative organization *across* life tasks is one factor that determines whether a strategy used in one domain is also used in another domain. Recall that reassurance-seeking occurs among people with self-doubts in the achievement domain but not in the social domain (Harlow and Cantor), raising the possibility that the evaluative organization of self-knowledge in these two domains may be different. In short, evaluative organization of self-knowledge within and across life-task domains may have important, but as yet unexplored, implications for the types of strategies that people use.

Likewise, people's implicit theories (of intelligence and other domains) may also have implications for SEM processes and life-task negotiation. In Chapter 9, Hong, Chiu, and Dweck distinguish between an entity theory and an incremental theory of intelligence. An entity theory involves the general belief that intelligence is a fixed entity that is not subject to change, whereas an incremental theory involves the belief that intelligence is malleable and increasable through effort. Compared to people who hold an incremental theory, people who hold an entity theory are more emotionally reactive to failure, more likely to attribute failure to lack of ability, and more likely to perform poorly in challenging academic situations. Furthermore, among entity theorists (but not incremental theorists), self-confidence is highly fragile and difficult to sustain. Consequently, entity theorists may feel particularly challenged when they are outperformed by a close other. In addition, if their confidence is high with respect to performance in a particular domain, they may be especially resistant to taking into account a close other's perspective. Incremental theorists, in comparison to entity theorists, may be less likely to engage in SEM processes in general (see Chapter 7 for further discussion of possible individual differences). Note also that entity theorists may be overrepresented among the "outcome-focused" individuals discussed by Harlow and Cantor and among people with contingent or unstable self-esteem.

CONTROL, SELF-DETERMINATION, AND SELF-ESTEEM

As already discussed, Deci and Ryan suggest in Chapter 2 that self-determination (acting autonomously from the self) underlies the development of true self-esteem. From a different vantage point, Harlow and

Cantor suggest in Chapter 8 that the strategies people use to overcome self-doubt reveal their "capacities for creating agency in their daily lives, because such strategies represent individuals' efforts to *take control* of a task where we might otherwise expect self-defeat." To the extent that these strategies are successful, they may also contribute to the development and maintenance of high self-esteem. Likewise, in Chapter 10, Burger presents data indicating that high scores on his measure of desire for control are associated with high self-esteem. People high in desire for control ". . . typically feel that they are capable, efficacious individuals . . . are eager to demonstrate their mastery over challenging events and typically succeed in these efforts . . . are more likely than lows to be optimistic and intrinsically motivated. They believe they have the ability to handle themselves in most situations and to make the most of opportunities handed to them." However, when confronted with uncontrollable events, they may also be more susceptible to depression than people low in desire for control (Burger, 1984; Burger & Arkin, 1980).

One might reasonably ask whether these concepts of self-determination (Deci and Ryan), agency and taking control (Harlow & Cantor), and high desire for control (Burger) are the same. On the surface, they seem to share many similarities. However, a closer analysis reveals that they may differ in important ways. According to Deci and Ryan, self-determination involves either intrinsically motivated behaviors or behaviors that stem from integrated regulation. Harlow and Cantor's "outcome-focused" individuals, while certainly taking control and exhibiting "agency" in some sense, appear to be doing so more out of introjected self-regulation (to use Deci and Ryan's terminology). Thus, we might expect their reassurance-seeking to have a pressured quality. Burger's discussion of people high in desire for control suggests the possibility that desire for control reflects self-determination for some people, but not for others. Specifically, his description of the low self-esteem route to high desire for control suggests that some people are "driven" to want control over important events in their lives because their experiences with uncontrollability have been so aversive. Within the high self-esteem route, it would seem that high desire for control is often accompanied by self-determination. Yet, as we have seen, some high self-esteem people do not appear to be fully self-determining. That is, people with contingent or unstable high self-esteem may manifest their desire for control in different ways than do people with true or stable high self-esteem. One potential way to approach this question is to examine reactions to uncontrollable situations. Those whose desire for control is accompanied by a strong sense of self-determination should have less adverse reactions to uncontrollability than individuals who are "driven" to be in control (Deci, 1980). In fact, consideration of the linkages between desire for control and self-determination, true and contingent self-esteem, and stable and unstable self-esteem may show that there are even more forms of high desire for control than those described so astutely by Burger. Given the pervasiveness of control-related issues in psychological well-being (and the substantial insights that Burger and others have provided over the years), such an endeavor is certainly worthwhile.

EVOLUTIONARY CONSIDERATIONS

Several contributors commented on how evolutionary concerns may shape global self-esteem, as well as more specific self-evaluations. One view, espoused by Beach and Tesser and by Leary and Downs, emphasizes the social significance of self-esteem-related processes. In this view, global self-esteem and self-evaluation maintenance processes facilitate individuals' functioning in small group environments, which predominated over much of human evolutionary history (Barkow, 1980). Specifically, global self-esteem may guide the selection of interpersonal strategies that limit the potential for individuals to be excluded from the important social groups that are essential to their survival. On the other hand, SEM processes may guide people in their quest to be valuable contributors to these small social groups, by stimulating them to develop unique areas of expertise as well as to be appreciative of other group members' unique talents. These two systems, as discussed by Beach and Tesser, may interact in ways that promote the survival and efficiency of primary social groups.

A different view can be found in Terror Management Theory (presented in Chapter 4 by Greenberg and colleagues), which holds that self-esteem is part of "a motivational system directed toward self-preservation in an organism intelligent enough to be aware of its own vulnerabilities and ultimate mortality." In this view, believing that one is a person of worth (i.e., a valuable contributor to a meaningful worldview) protects one from being paralyzed with terror, which would quickly result in one's destruction (see also Becker, 1973). Yet a third view is grounded in the assertion that self-esteem derives from the satisfaction of growth-oriented motives (Deci and Ryan and Greenberg and colleagues). Growth-oriented motives underlie the acquisition of new skills to deal with an ever-changing environment (both social and nonsocial in nature), thereby fostering survival of the individual as well as the transmission of one's genes. At this point in time, evidence can be marshaled in support of each of these views, and frankly, choosing one view over another may serve only to stifle further conceptual and empirical advances. Such an occurrence would be most unfortunate, because continued theorizing on the evolutionary significance of self-esteem-related processes is likely to generate numerous hypotheses worthy of investigation.

SUMMARY

In this chapter, I have attempted to highlight some of the common themes that appeared in the contributions to this volume. Admittedly, there are others that could be addressed. Nonetheless, several important agendas pertaining to self-esteem research and theory were identified. First, it is evident that self-esteem should not be considered in isolation from other motivational and personality constructs. Much can be gained from embedding the construct of self-esteem within broad theoretical perspectives. Second, it is important that we move beyond conceptualizing self-esteem as reflecting only the positivity of one's chronic self-feelings. The implicit or explicit nature of self-esteem, whether it is true or contingent, stable or unstable—all are important components of self-esteem that are likely to bear heavily on the quality of individuals' psychological well-being. Third, there are a variety of contextual and interpersonal factors that are reciprocally related to self-esteem and that deserve considerable attention in the future. Fourth, the role of self-esteem in people's ongoing attempts to deal with the challenges and opportunities of everyday life has yet to be fully explored. In this regard, life-task appraisals, personal desire for control, implicit theories of intelligence, and the evaluative organization of self-knowledge are all important foci worthy of additional attention. Finally, continued attention directed toward the evolutionary significance of self-esteem and related processes will undoubtedly yield important dividends.

Editing this volume has been an extremely thought-provoking and enjoyable experience for me. Each and every chapter increased my appreciation of the importance of continuing our efforts to understand the role of self-esteem in psychological well-being. I hope and trust that readers will share in these reactions.

REFERENCES

Barkow, J. (1980). Prestige and self-esteem: A biosocial interpretation. In D. R. Omark, F. F. Stayer, & D. G. Freedman (Eds.), *Dominance relations* (pp. 319–332). New York: Garland.

Baumeister, R. F., & Tice, D. M. (1990). Anxiety and social exclusion. *Journal of Social and Clinical Psychology, 9,* 165–195.

Baumgardner, A. H. (1990). To know oneself is to like oneself: Self-certainty and self-affect. *Journal of Personality and Social Psychology, 58,* 1062–1072.

Baumgardner, A. H., & Brownlee, E. A. (1987). Strategic failure in social interaction: Evidence for expectancy disconfirmation processes. *Journal of Personality and Social Psychology, 52,* 525–535.

Becker, E. (1973). *The denial of death.* New York: Free Press.

Burger, J. M. (1984). Desire for control, locus of control and proneness to depression. *Journal of Personality, 52,* 71–89.

Burger, J. M., & Arkin, R. M. (1980). Prediction, control and learned helplessness. *Journal of Personality and Social Psychology, 38,* 482–491.

Campbell, J. D. (1990). Self-esteem and clarity of the self-concept. *Journal of Personality and Social Psychology, 59,* 281–294.

Deci, E. L. (1980). *The psychology of self-determination.* Lexington, MA: Lexington Books.

Greenberg, J., Pyszczynski, T., & Solomon, S. (1990). Anxiety concerning social exclusion: Innate response or one consequence of the need for terror management? *Journal of Social and Clinical Psychology, 9,* 202–213.

Horney, K. (1950). *Neurosis and human growth: The struggle toward self-realization.* New York: W. W. Norton.

Kernis, M. H. (1993). The roles of stability and level of self-esteem in psychological functioning. In R. Baumeister (Ed.), *Self-esteem: The puzzle of low self-regard* (pp. 167–182). New York: Plenum Press.

Kernis, M. H., Grannemann, B. D., & Barclay, L. C. (1992). Stability of self-esteem: Assessment, correlates, and excuse making. *Journal of Personality, 60,* 621–644.

Larsen, R. J. (1984). Theory and measurement of affect intensity as an individual difference characteristic. *Dissertation Abstracts International, 85,* 2297B (University Microfilms No. 84-22112).

Linden, W., Paulhus, D. L., & Dobson, K. S. (1986). Effects of response styles on the report of psychological and somatic distress. *Journal of Consulting and Clinical Psychology, 54,* 309–313.

Paulhus, D. L. (1991). Measurement and control of response bias. In J. P. Robinson, P. R. Shaver, & L. S. Wrightsman (Eds.), *Measurement of personality and social psychological attitudes,* Vol. 1 (pp. 17–60). San Diego: Academic Press.

Paulhus, D. L., & Reid, D. B. (1992). Attribution and denial in socially desirable responding. *Journal of Personality and Social Psychology.*

Rosenberg, M. (1986). Self-concept from middle childhood through adolescence. In J. Suls & A. G. Greenwald (Eds.), *Psychological perspectives on the self,* Vol. 3 (pp. 107–135). Hillsdale, NJ: Erlbaum Associates.

Swann, W. B. (1990). To be adored or to be known? The interplay of self-enhancement and self-verification. In E. T. Higgins & R. M. Sorrentino (Eds.), *Handbook of motivation and cognition, Vol. 2, Foundations of social behavior* (pp. 408–448). New York: Guilford Press.

Swann, W. B., Hixon, J. G., Stein-Seroussi, A., & Gilbert, D. T. (1990). The fleeting gleam of praise: Cognitive processes underlying behavioral reactions to self-relevant feedback. *Journal of Personality and Social Psychology, 59,* 17–26.

Tennen, H., & Affleck, G. (1993). The puzzles of self-esteem: A clinical perspective. In R. Baumeister (Ed.), *Self-esteem: The puzzle of low self-regard.* New York: Plenum Press.

Wells, A. J. (1988). Variations in mothers' self-esteem in daily life. *Journal of Personality and Social Psychology, 55,* 661–668.

INDEX

Achievement motivation. *See* Goal-directed behavior

Affect, in sociometer/self-esteem system, 134–135

Amotivated behavior, 36

Anxiety
  and existential terror, 75–76
  and mortality salience manipulations, 130
  self-esteem as buffer against, 78–80, 126

Beach, Steven R. H., 145
Burger, Jerry M., 217

Cantor, Nancy, 171
Chi-Yue Chiu, 197
Cognitive-experiential self-theory (CEST), 9–26, 238–239
  adaptive and maladaptive behavior in, 21–25
  compromise formation in, 16–18
  and four basic needs, 12–13, 22–23
  maintenance of negative self-views in, 23–25
  and psychodynamics, 13–14
  rational vs. experiential system in, 10–13, 18, 19–21
  and self-enhancing illusions, 23

Deci, Edward L., 31
Defensiveness, and stability of self-esteem, 80–81
Desire for control, 217–231
  and Desirability of Control Scale, 218
  and high self-esteem, 222–226
  and low self-esteem, 226–230

Downs, Deborah L., 123
Dweck, Carol S., 197

Epstein, Seymour, 9
Evaluatively integrated self-knowledge (EI), 104, 105–108, 248–249
Extrinsic motivation, 37–45
  regulatory processes in, 38–40
  and social context, 42–45

Feedback
  controlling and noncontingent, 43, 57
  effect on high- vs. low-esteem people, 135

Goal-directed behavior, 197–213
  and confidence level, 204–207
  intrinsic vs. extrinsic, 41–42
  and life transitions, 187–189
  life-task strategies in, 172–191
  and maintenance of self-confidence, 208–210
  mastery-oriented vs. helpless coping in, 204–205
  negative self-inferences from failure in, 201–204
  reassurance-seeking as, 176–187
  task appraisals in, 175–176
  and vulnerability of self system, 210–212
Greenberg, Jeff, 73
Greenier, Keegan D., 51
Growth-oriented enrichment motives, 82–84, 251
  and defensive terror management motives, 73–74, 86–93

Growth-oriented enrichment motives
    (*Cont.*)
    integration with defensive motives, 73–
        74, 84–94, 241–242

Harlow, Robert E., 171
High self-esteem
    and defensiveness, 80–81
    and self-esteem motives, 135–136
    and self-protective strategies, 61–64
    and self-enhancement strategies, 60–61
    and unstable self-esteem, 58–64
Human agency
    autonomous vs. controlled activity in, 37,
        42
    defined, 35
    and self-efficacy theory, 37

Implicit theories of intelligence, 197–213
    assessment of, 198–201
    entity theorists vs. incremental theorists
        in, 198–207
    maintenance of self-confidence in, 208–
        210
    mastery-oriented vs. helpless coping in,
        204–205
    negative self-inferences from failure in,
        201–204
    self-confidence and failure correlation in,
        206–207
    vulnerability of self system in, 210–212
Information processing systems
    automatic nature of, 14
    rational versus experiential, 10–12, 13,
        19–21
Intrinsic motivation, 37–38, 40–45
    and self-determination, 43–44
    and social context, 42–45

Leary, Mark R., 123
Life transitions, and self-concept revision,
    187–189
Low self-esteem
    and self-esteem motives, 132, 135–136
    and unstable self-esteem, 64–67

Morling, B., 9
Mortality salience effects, 76–79, 130
Motivation. *See* Goal-directed behavior; Ex-
    trinsic motivation; Intrinsic motivation

Negative-compartmentalized self-
    knowledge (NC), 105, 248

Positive feedback, and intrinsic motivation,
    43
Positive-compartmentalized self-
    knowledge (PC), 105, 248
Pyszczynski, Tom, 73

Reassurance-seeking behavior, 176–187
Romantic attraction, and compromise for-
    mation, 16–18
Ryan, Richard M., 31

Self-concept revision, and life transitions,
    187–89
Self-determination
    and desire for control, 250–251
    extrinsic regulation in, 38–40
    motivated behaviors in, 36–38
    and positive feedback, 43
    and self-concept, 33–36
    and social context, 42–45
Self-doubt, in achievement domain, 171–
    191, 245–246
    and defensive pessimism, 173, 177, 184
    and reassurance-seeking strategies, 176–
        187
    and self-at-task images, 175–176
    and task appraisals, 175–176
Self-efficacy
    and autonomous vs. controlled activity,
        37
    and intrinsic motivation, 43–44
Self-enhancement vs. self-verfication, 14–18
Self-esteem
    domains of, 137–138
    explicit and implicit, measurement of,
        19–21
    and motivation, intrinsic and extrinsic,
        37–45
    measurement scales, 102
    as multifacted construct, 242–244
    stable, 51–52, 113–114
    and support vs. control, 42–45
Self-esteem, global
    evolutionary considerations, 127–128,
        165–167, 251–252
    and self-evaluation maintenance pro-
        cesses, 146–147, 158–161, 164–167

Self-esteem, state, 125, 131–132
Self-esteem, trait, 124–125
Self-esteem, true
   vs. contingent, 32–33
   and human agency, 37
Self-esteem instability, 52–58
   assessment of, 53–54
   defined, 52–54
   and early childhood experiences, 57–58
   and ego involvement, 54–56
   and high self-esteem, 58–64
   and impoverished self-concepts, 56–57
   and low self-esteem, 64–67
   and noncontingent and/or controlling
      feedback, 57–58
   and self-enhancement strategies, 60–61
   and self-protection, 61–64
Self-esteem motive, 123–140
   and dominance, 127–128
   and goal achievement, 126–127
   of high- vs. low-self esteem people, 135–
      136
   and inclusion facilitation, 133–134
   and positive affect, 125–126
   and social exclusion, 128–135
   and state self-esteem, 125
   threats and esteem-deflating events, 132–
      133
Self-evaluation maintenance (SEM) model,
      in dyadic relationships, 145–168, 246–
      247
   affective outcroppings in, 151–154
   competency and performance issues,
      159–160
   and distribution of power, 155–156
   and help-giving, 163–164
   and jealousy and envy, 157–158
   original model, reflection and compa-
      rison in, 147–148

Self-evaluation maintenance (SEM) model
      (Cont.)
   and problem-solving, 156–157
   and relationship dissolution, 162–164
   and self-definition, 158–159, 160–161
   and shared activities, 154–155
Self-knowledge, evaluative organization of,
      101–118
   and affective states, 115
   cognitive categorization in, 115
   evaluative compartmentalization in, 104–
      105, 108–110
   evaluative integration in, 104, 105–108
   motivational perspective in, 116–117
   and self-esteem stability, 113–114
Self-verification vs. self-enhancement, 14–
      18
Social exclusion, and self-esteem motiva-
      tion, 128–134
Sociometer model of self-esteem, 129–139,
      244–245
Solomon, Sheldon, 73

Terror management theory, 73–82, 240–
      241
   cultural anxiety buffer in, 76–80, 91–92
   and cultural worldviews, 74–79
   defensive orientation in, 76–82
   dual-motive conceptualization in, 73–74,
      84–94, 241–242
   and growth-oriented enrichment motive,
      82–84
   mortality salience effect in, 76–79, 251
Tesser, Abraham, 145
Thematic Apperception Tests (TATs), 20

Waschull, Stefanie B., 51

Ying-Yi Hong, 197